Anonymous

The Army Reunion

with reports of the meetings of the societies of the Army of the Cumberland - the

Army of the Tennessee - the Army of the Ohio - and the Army of Georgia

Anonymous

The Army Reunion
with reports of the meetings of the societies of the Army of the Cumberland - the Army of the Tennessee - the Army of the Ohio - and the Army of Georgia

ISBN/EAN: 9783337734466

Printed in Europe, USA, Canada, Australia, Japan

Cover: Foto ©Andreas Hilbeck / pixelio.de

More available books at **www.hansebooks.com**

THE

ARMY REUNION:

WITH

REPORTS OF THE MEETINGS

OF THE SOCIETIES OF

THE ARMY OF THE CUMBERLAND;

THE ARMY OF THE TENNESSEE; THE ARMY OF THE OHIO:

AND

THE ARMY OF GEORGIA.

———

Chicago, December 15 and 16, 1868.

Publishing Committee :

F. T. SHERMAN,   R. W. SMITH,
WM. E. STRONG,   A. C. McCLURG.

CHICAGO:
S. C. GRIGGS AND COMPANY.

1869.

THE CHICAGO EXECUTIVE COMMITTEE, to whom was entrusted the local preparation for the Army Reunion in this city in December of last year, have the pleasure of presenting this memorial volume to the members of the various societies represented in that Reunion. It was intended that it should be issued much earlier in the year, but the labor of collecting the material from the various secretaries, and from the many speakers at the Opera House Meeting and the Banquet, and the necessity of submitting the proof, for correction, to various persons interested, have rendered delay unavoidable. While it is hoped that this delay has been favorable to its completeness and correctness, it would be presumption to hope that a volume of this kind, hastily prepared, and by so many hands, could entirely escape errors.

The sub-committee, to whom its publication was intrusted, are indebted to the Rev. Edward C. Towne, for valuable assistance; and to his taste and judgment must be credited whatever of merit there may be in the introductions and general editorial arrangement of the material.

It is proper to add, that a small portion of the expense of the publication is borne by the treasuries of the different societies.

INTRODUCTION.

———

THE proposal of a Grand Reunion of all the Western Armies originated with General W. T. Sherman, whose position as the common commander of all suggested an equal interest in all, and excited a desire to gather, on one grand occasion, representatives of the whole host, undivided and indivisible in spirit and labors, which had been employed in the West in prosecuting the struggle of the Nation against rebellion. Four separate organizations, composed of these Armies respectively, the Army of the Tennessee, the Army of the Cumberland, the Army of the Ohio, and the Army of Georgia, had been formed, or were contemplated, with a common view to perpetuate the memories and help to preserve the record of camp, and march, and battle; and two of these were about being called to meet for the annual celebration of 1868. The Society of the Army of the Tennessee was expected to convene in Chicago in September, and that of the Army of the Cumberland was anticipating a reunion, also in Chicago, on the 15th of December. So early as March (1868), General Sherman had given a good deal of thought to a scheme of reunion of all the soldiers of the Western Armies, and had written to distinguished officers in regard to it. From Generals Thomas, Schofield, and Slocum, representing the Cumberland, Ohio, and Georgia Armies, he had received highly satisfactory assurances of cordial concurrence with his proposal for a Grand Reunion; and on the 24th of March he wrote from the headquarters of the Military Division of the Mississippi, at St. Louis, to the President of the Society of the Army of the Tennessee, General John A. Rawlins, to propose the postponement of their meeting from the autumn to the winter, and their acceptance of the plan of reunion. The prompt and hearty concurrence of General Rawlins and his comrades at once removed every obstacle to the consummation of General Sherman's desires, and enabled the distinguished commander, who so often had summoned the armies of the West to the labors and dangers of battle, to send out his call to all to meet, once at least, amid the securities of established peace, for a common celebration of the deathless memories of the war. Accepting the day which a brother commander—a soldier always to be named in history with the great captains under whom he was ever modestly content to serve, General George H. Thomas—had fixed for the assembling of the Society of the Army of the Cumberland, General Sherman designated the 15th and 16th of December, "the days that we gained Savannah and Thomas fought at Nashville," for a common meeting of all the Western Armies, in the city of Chicago. None who know how thoughtfully and cordially General Sherman has invariably promoted good feeling in those attached to the service with him, and how generously and zealously he has cared for the good name of those who have earned the highest distinction under his command, will fail to reflect that he must have named with extreme satisfaction, for the grandest occasion of military reunion yet known to American history, the day already selected, by the man who "fought at Nashville," for the assembling of the gallant and famous Army of the Cumberland.

The scheme of the celebration itself, as well as the conception and proposal of it, was matured and brought forward by General Sherman. In his letter to General Rawlins of the 24th of March, he proposed that while the several Army Societies should meet separately during the days of the 15th and 16th, the evenings should be devoted, in grand reunion, the first to commemorative orations from representatives of the respective armies, and the second to a reunion banquet, which should be as complete a festival of social communion as the wisdom of a joint local committee could devise.

The necessity for early action in the matter of orators from the respective Army Societies was met at once by the selection, on the part of these Societies, of the following distinguished gentlemen;—General W. W. Belknap, of the Army of the Tennessee; General Charles Cruft, of the Army of the Cumberland; General J. D. Cox, of the Army of the Ohio; and General William Cogswell, of the Army of Georgia. And for the further execution of the plans thus matured, General Sherman issued the following notice and invitation:

WASHINGTON, D. C., *April* 20, 1868.

Notice is hereby given, that the Societies representing the Armies of the Tennessee, Cumberland, Ohio, and Georgia, will meet on the 15th and 16th days of December, 1868, at Chicago, Illinois. The object is purely social, and designed to preserve the memories of the war, and to cherish the friendships formed during that period of our national history. All are cheerfully invited to be present and participate.

An orator has been appointed for each Army, and addresses will be delivered on the night of the 15th of December, and a grand banquet will be held on the night of the 16th.

Letters of inquiry may be addressed to General William E. Strong, Chicago, Illinois, who will attend to all preliminary business, until a joint committee of arrangements has been appointed to carry into effect the above plan.

W. T. SHERMAN,
Lieutenant-General U. S. A.

The joint committee alluded to in General Sherman's call, to which was committed the work of preparing for the Grand Reunion, was composed of the following committees, named by

the several Army Societies:—ARMY OF THE TENNESSEE;—
General John McArthur, Chairman; General John M. Corse;
General Joseph Stockton; General William E. Strong; Colonel
John Mason Loomis; Major D. H. Gile. ARMY OF THE CUM-
BERLAND;—General F. T. Sherman, Chairman; General A. C.
McClurg; Major A. H. Boyden. ARMY OF THE OHIO;—
General R. W. Smith, Chairman; General W. Scott Stewart;
General Julius White; General Thomas J. Henderson; Colonel
W. W. Wheeler. ARMY OF GEORGIA;—General A. C.
McClurg, Chairman; General E. S. Salomon; General J. D.
Morgan; General William Coggswell; General H. A. Barnum;
Major H. W. Buck.

These committees, representing the several Army Societies,
were organized as the Executive Committee of the Reunion, at
a joint meeting held in Chicago, October 24. The following
were chosen officers of the Committee;—General F. T. Sherman,
Chairman; General William E. Strong, Secretary. For a short
time after the organization of the Committee, the engrossing
engagements of the Presidential campaign required the postponement of active preparations for the Reunion, but immediately
upon coming together, on the 8th of November, when the political
contest had been settled by the election of General Grant, the
Executive Committee called to its aid a large number of brother
officers resident in Chicago and the vicinity, and designated the
following sub-committees:*—*Finance*, Colonel John Mason
Loomis, Chairman; *Banquet*, General William E. Strong,
Chairman; *Railroads and Transportation*, General I. N. Stiles,
Chairman; *Invitations*, General John McArthur, Chairman;
Reception, General J. D. Webster, Chairman; *Halls*, General
A. C. McClurg, Chairman; *Decorations and Flags*, Major W.
L. B. Jenney, Chairman; *Printing and Badges*, Major S. S.
Hart, Chairman; *Music*, Captain L. B. Church, Chairman.

* A full list of the members of these committees is given at p. 202.

The labors of these committees were entered upon as soon as the Presidential election was over, and preparations pressed forward as vigorously as possible. The Secretary of the General Committee, General William E. Strong, was instructed to send a dispatch through the Associated Press, requesting officers throughout the country to at once advise the Committee if they intended being present at the Reunion, in order that timely notice might be had of the number for whom provision should be made. An early invitation was extended to General Sherman to deliver an Address of Welcome on the evening of the 15th, and his acceptance secured; the Committee feeling that such words would come most properly from the common commander who had suggested and summoned the gathering, and around whom, with the President elect, and their honored comrades, the other great captains of the war, the soldiers of the Western Armies would most cordially rally.

Another important feature of the preparation undertaken by the joint Executive Committee was the obtaining of colors and battle-flags, which had been carried by troops sent by different States into the Armies of the West, and had finally been laid away, at the capitals of these States, as sacred memorials of the march and the battle, and almost holy emblems of patriotic devotion to country. Urgent and repeated applications were made, in the hope of obtaining a complete collection of these endeared and venerated relics, and with a highly gratifying result. The natural hesitation of those in charge of these priceless memorials prevailed in some instances, but the Committee had every occasion to return most cordial thanks to those who cheerfully assisted them to reproduce the most hallowed and powerful associations of the old war days.

Special invitations, amounting to considerably more than one hundred, were issued by the Committee, requesting the presence, as honored guests, of the President and Heads of Departments at

Washington; the General, Lieutenant-General, Major-Generals and Brigadier-Generals of the regular army; Corps Commanders of Armies in the war not included in the Reunion; Governors of States which furnished troops for any of the Western Armies, and ex-Governors of these States, who were in office during the war.

The more strictly local arrangements for the grand festival were also prosecuted with gratifying success. By the generosity of citizens of Chicago, who had given honorable distinction to the metropolis of the North-west in the dark days of the war, when labors, sacrifices and suffering were more in order than festive celebrations, ample means were placed in the hands of the Finance Committee for all the necessary expenses of the Reunion. The Opera House was secured for the evening of the 15th, and for the banquet of the 16th the commodious Chamber of Commerce was freely tendered by the Chicago Board of Trade, and was thankfully accepted. The decoration of these places of assembling, and every other feature of the preparations required for the proposed nights of high festival, engaged the careful attention of the Committee. The feast was generously spread; music and song were enlisted; banners, battle-flags and colors, and other accessories of a tasteful and brilliant display, were arranged; and nothing left undone to prepare a scene worthy, as near as might be, of the noble company to be convened. Facilities for coming from all parts of the country, at a moderate expense, were solicited, and obtained, from the railroads; headquarters for the various Army Societies were designated; the ample resources of private hospitality were put in requisition; and the entire community was stirred with patriotic ardor to give a fitting welcome to the representatives of those armies whose deeds had been our redemption, and whose fame had become a household word in every corner of our land.

In placing on record the proceedings of the Army Reunion for which these preparations had been made, we are obliged to

remember that the grand occasion embraced at once distinct
meetings of separate Army Societies, held during the days of the
15th and 16th, and Reunion meetings, for which the evenings
were set apart.

The Society of the Army of the Tennessee was organized at
Raleigh, North Carolina, in the spring of the last year of the
war, before its members had turned their backs on the scenes of
their last campaign—the brilliant march of Sherman through
the heart of the Confederacy. It met for the first time, after the
coming of peace in the land, in Chicago, in the fall of 1865. A
second meeting was held the following year in Cincinnati, and a
third in St. Louis in 1867. The meeting of December 15th and
16th, in Chicago, in connection with the great festival of Reunion,
was the fourth in order from the founding of the Society. Originally appointed to be held in September, it was considerately
postponed to the date of the Grand Reunion, a generous concession
from the oldest of the Army Societies, in order that the common
meeting might take place after the engagements and excitements
of the presidential campaign should be over. The official report
of the proceedings of this meeting shows that the Society of the
Army of the Tennessee emphatically and decisively determined
to continue its separate organization. The committee appointed
by it to consider propositions for the consolidation of the several
Army Societies, were strictly instructed not to accept any such
proposition.

The Society of the Army of the Cumberland was organized in
February, 1868, at a general meeting of the Army in Cincinnati.
The meeting reported in this volume is thus the second which the
Society has held. The third reunion was appointed, it will be
noticed, to be held at Indianapolis, in the present year, and the
idea of a united society of all the Western Armies was only so far
entertained, that a committee was appointed for the purpose of
conferring with such committees as might be appointed by the

other Societies in reference to a joint meeting at the same time and place.

The members of the Army of the Ohio, who came with their comrades of other armies to attend the general reunion summoned by the common commander, improved the occasion to organize a Society, for purposes similar to those which had called into existence the older Army Societies. Similar action was taken by the members of the Army of Georgia, which had met the preceding year with the Army of the Cumberland, to which a large proportion of them had belonged until the organization of the Army of Georgia, at Atlanta, in the last year of the war. Henceforth, therefore, the Society of the Army of the Ohio, and the Society of the Army of Georgia, will do their part, with sister societies of soldiers who served in Western Armies, to preserve the memories, and perfect the records, of that portion of the great conflict which was waged by forces mainly organized, or employed, in some part of the western half of the country.

But the portion of this reunion record which takes precedence, by common consent, is the report of the two general meetings, the imposing assemblage of gallant soldiers in the Opera House, on the evening of the 15th, to listen to commemorative orations from representatives of the several Army Societies, after fit words of noble welcome from the almost incomparable Captain of the March to the Sea, and while the stoutest and stanchest of patriot Generals sat in the chair of peaceful command; and again, the festival throng of the following evening, in the great hall of the Board of Trade, when a feast of good things, with song and speech, and numberless varied demonstrations of fellowship, brought back to brave men the recollection of camp and battle days, and melted a thousand hearts with one glowing and ennobling sense of the joy and honor it had been to have part in the grand undoing of wicked rebellion. The simplest record of these scenes will amply preserve, for those who took part in them, the memory of a great occasion.

None of the great soldiers of the war had aroused in the Armies of the West a more worshipful enthusiasm than he who sat first among the leaders assembled on the ample platform of the Opera House, on the evening of the 15th—General George H. Thomas. The events of his career, and the qualities of his character, had equally wrought in all observers the conviction that history rarely shows the world a man more compact of all the abilities and manners of a great soldier, and rarely affords to greatness a finer opportunity than was his on the memorable field of Chicka-mauga, and when the last desperate advance of the Rebellion was crushed before Nashville. An incident of this evening of com-memoration, the unexampled burst of irrepressible emotion which greeted a reference to General Thomas in the oration of General Belknap, strikingly confirmed the judgment of those who selected this modest hero and admirable soldier to sit between Grant and Sherman at the head of the great Reunion assemblage. With gallant courtesy the orator of the Army of the Tennessee had spoken of " the determined soldier" and "beloved commander" of the Army of the Cumberland, " Thomas, the rock of Chicka-mauga," when with instant accord every heart in the vast assembly, soldiers of every army and all ranks, leaped beyond all bounds of usual excitement, into such a storm of applause as hardly once in a century falls upon human ears. It was a fit recognition of one who is justly thought to have shown himself, by the side of his great equals, an ideal soldier.

The Presidential election of November 7th had set the seal of accomplished history to the nation's appreciation of our most eminent commander, when the Reunion of the Western Armies was held. Fitly, on every ground, therefore, the guest of the hour, in the seat of honor on the right of General Thomas, was the General of the Army of the United States, the President elect of the nation. Inflexibly silent, a doer of deeds and not a man of speech, his part played always in the simplest and most practical fashion, the quiet presence of General Grant, first in honor as in rank, sufficiently indicated the exceptional dignity of the occasion.

At the left hand of the president of the evening every eye in the vast assemblage marked the third of these equal masters of war, a soldier who uses his pen as happily as he handles 'he sword, and to whom had been assigned the task of speaking the welcome of the leaders to all who had met them in reunion. The form which had moved so often through the ranks of battle, like victory's own standard, bent as gently as a woman's for the courtesies of the hour, and eyes which had flashed the great rage of war were kindly as a mother's looking into the devotion of that sea of martial faces. No soldier there needed to be told that General Sherman keeps the aspect of severity for the uses of war, and that as man to man he bears always a countenance of kindliest courtesy.

We have mentioned only the first names of the long list of leaders of the Armies of the West who had gathered to the grand Reunion. Grant, and Sherman, and Thomas, were the centre of a company such as no previous American occasion, of war or of peace, had gathered. So many distinguished military men had never before, in all the history of the country, been brought into a single scene. Besides distinguished guests from other armies, here were a large proportion of the army, corps, and division commanders who had led into battle the Armies of the West. To even call the roll of their honored names, and make the briefest fit mention of each, would far exceed the limits we are bound to keep.

And it is all the more necessary not to enter upon particular mention of the large number who sat rank behind rank around Grant and Sherman and Thomas, because in front of them, densely crowding the great audience-space of the Opera House, were hundreds upon hundreds who had won, in their places, a

name in the war, and who brought now the dignity of heroism
and the honor of noble deeds to enhance the significance of this
splendid occasion. And with these, in such parts of the house as
could be set apart for them, sat others, not less than they soldiers
of the great conflict and heroes of the great battles, those true and
tried women of mercy and sisters of compassion, those wives and
daughters and sisters who had buckled on courage, and carried
the tenderness of love and the sweetness of home wherever the
soldier's path had led, under the cloud and through the sea, until
the days of wandering and suffering, of painful toil and painful
endurance, were all ended. No hearts of all that great reunion
company throbbed in quicker, finer, holier sympathy with the
sacred commemoration of the hour.

When General Thomas rose before this assemblage, and called
for the *reveille* by the drum corps, an outbreak of enthusiasm
from reunited comrades followed, which, for the moment, made
all other demonstration insignificant. The call which the drums
gave was that which had, through all the war, roused the soldier
from his hurried rest, to preparation for his long days of labor
and peril. Its notes were familiar as the ticking of the home
clock over the domestic hearth, while their associations were of
scenes and events, incidents and deeds, at the remembrance of
which the coolest blood became on fire, and the least ardent souls
were kindled with inspiration. It had not been expected that
this *reveille* would be sounded, and when the martial tones of
the drums were heard, a passion of ardor swept through the
throng of soldiers, and a storm of great emotions rose and broke,
rose and broke again, as if a hundred score of gallant men had
said, Let our country but call again, and we are still ready. So,
nobly, as heroes should, did those who participated in the grand
reunion, listen to the orations to which it is now time to turn.

THE ORATIONS.

THE assemblage of the evening of December 15th, to listen to Orations from representatives of the several Army Societies, was called to order by General George H. Thomas, who said ;—

COMRADES OF THE ARMIES OF THE TENNESSEE, CUMBERLAND, OHIO, AND GEORGIA: Having been selected to preside over this interesting meeting, I take this occasion to express to you my most heartfelt thanks for the honor conferred upon me. As a good deal of time has already been spent in arranging your seats, we will now proceed to the business before the meeting in its regular order. The first thing will be the *reveille* by the drum corps.

After the outbreak of enthusiasm which greeted the *reveille* ordered by General Thomas, the following address of welcome was made by Lieutenant-General Sherman :

GENERAL SHERMAN'S ADDRESS.

FELLOW-SOLDIERS : It is made my pleasant duty to address to you this evening words of welcome to the feast that is to be spread before you. From the city and the country, from the town and village, you have come together, the representatives of four of those grand volunteer armies, which responded to our country's call in her hour of danger, fought her battles — sometimes, side by side ; sometimes far apart ; yet always in unison — and then, at her bidding, returned to your homes as farmers or mechanics, as artizans and citizens.

2

After a short rest you have again assembled to stand, as it were, on a high pinnacle, to look back across that wide valley wherein you struggled so long, to point out to each other the spots of greatest interest, and to live o'er again the hours and days and months of deepest anguish or of joy.

I know that you have laid aside forever the feelings of animosity and anger, then so natural and proper, and that you have dropped into oblivion the little jealousies and rivalries of the hour, and now stand here with hand extended in fraternal friendship to every soldier in the land, whether he belonged to your regiment or in your division, whether in your army or any other, whether upon the land or the sea, provided only he fought for the Union of our fathers, and the flag of our whole country. No mere feeling of self-glorification now animates you, but a just pride in your own actions, and a deep and intense love for the comrade who stood by your side in the day of battle, and shouted with you in the hour of victory. Happily, my friends, you did not belong to that class of our people in whose very youth was planted the pernicious doctrine, that the highest allegiance was due to the place of birth or of residence, and that a citizen should love a part of his country better than the whole. You were reared in a better school, and taught to revere the Constitution of your whole country, and to believe that under its wise and genial influence, man would here attain the largest measure of security and happiness consistent with the general safety. We believed that, by the law of majorities and a frequent resort to the ballot box, we had discovered a panacea for the ills that had from earliest history afflicted the human family, and that we should escape the conflicts and ravages which war had caused in all preceding ages. But we were doomed to realize that we formed no exception to the general rule, that minorities would not always submit to so peaceful a decree, and that we, too, must fight to maintain the privileges of our birthright.

You may search history in vain for a more flagrant violation of faith, a more causeless breach of a national compact than that which resulted in our civil war. Never before was an unwilling people so ruthlessly, so needlessly, dragged into a long and bloody conflict, and never before was a Government so utterly unprepared for it. All attempts to avoid its outbreak were charged to cowardice, and the whole civilized world was made to believe that that "bright particular star," which had for a time shone so clear in the Western firmament, had sunk forever, and that the fair fabric which had been dedicated to liberty, had vanished as a dream before the first storm of passion which had assailed it.

Here at home reason was unseated; the laws were derided and scorned; the public property was seized or appropriated as though it were a waif upon the ocean. Good men every where begged and implored for a little forbearance, offering Rebellion the blank sheet whereon to write its own terms of compromise, and were answered back with insult. The orator wasted his eloquence in vain; the statesman exhausted his last peaceful remedy; and then, and not till then, did war, the last arbiter of kings and peoples, assume absolute dominion over this great land of freedom.

The volunteer soldier stepped upon the arena, and offered his life and his services to defend and maintain the Government against all its enemies and opposers whomsoever. He swore the oath that rebellion and anarchy should not rule this land of ours, but that liberty, justice and law should be restored to their rightful throne. He has kept his oath, and we now behold again the good ship of State, full-rigged, once more on her course, destined toward that future which is hidden from all mortal eyes; and the flag is still there unchanged — "not a star obliterated, not a stripe dimmed"; that same old flag that we have followed so often in the glare of a scorching sun, by the moon's pale beams, and by the light of the lurid, blazing pine-torch. Shall I not, then, claim for you, who represent this volunteer soldier, the higher honor — yea, the highest honor that is conceded to mortal upon earth.

You can easily recall how long the war seemed to us in its progress, and how short now looking back upon it after a period of little more than three years. How inconceivably short, then, will it appear to those who a hundred years hence will grope through the pages of history to learn of the events and causes that led five millions of people to rebel, when no single act of oppression or tyranny was even alleged? We owe it to them, while still in the vigor of life and health, to record the parts we played in this grand drama of life, with the motives and feelings that actuated us through its various stages.

Many a time and oft you have lain upon the bare ground, with no canopy above but that of heaven, with its hosts of glittering stars, and I know you have dreamed of a time to come like this, when, seated together in security and peace, surrounded by admiring friends, you would be crowned with a tiara of light which now hangs over your heads. Accept this, then, as the fruition of your dream, and enjoy the hour!

Four of your comrades, one from each of the armies specially represented here, will address you and tell you of the deeds you have done. Give them a willing and attentive ear, and when you go back to your homes tell them all that these armies, though dispersed in the flesh, yet live in the spirit as strong and enthusiastic as they were four years ago, when in the very death grapple with the enemies of our country and of civilization.

And now, in the name of the committee that has made these preparations, I extend to you all a cordial greeting — to the veteran of '61, to the recruit of '65, yea, to the convert of the very last hour of grace.

In the name of the people of Chicago, who have provided the means, I bid you welcome, and assure you that a seat awaits you

at every fireside. And in the name of every patriot of the land
I give you welcome, and tell you that the lightning's flash is not
swift enough to satisfy the yearning of their hearts to know what
is done here this night.

The presence of the men about me, their high office, and the
duties they have left to be with you here, all attest the interest
and grandeur of the occasion, and in their names, too, comrades
all, I bid you thrice welcome.

The several Army Society Orations were delivered, following
the address of General Sherman, in the following order ;— The
Oration of General W. W. Belknap, on the part of the Society
of the Army of the Tennessee ; the Oration of General Charles
Cruft, of the Society of the Army of the Cumberland ; the Oration of General J. D. Cox, of the Army of the Ohio ; and the
Oration of General William Cogswell, of the Army of Georgia.

General Belknap spoke as follows, after the singing of
" America" by the Glee Club.

GENERAL BELKNAP'S ORATION.

Soldiers of the Armies of the Cumberland, the Ohio, and Georgia; Comrades of the Army of the Tennessee: It all seems like a dream,—the insult to the flag; the President's call for troops; the great uprising of the people; the unfurling to the breeze, from every mast and staff and spire of the North, of the nation's emblem; the enthusiastic meetings of men of all classes to devise means in that solemn hour to strike a blow for union and save the nation; the prompt response of the young men of the land; the muster-in of armed hosts; the waving of handkerchiefs, and the hand-shakings at parting, and the last kisses of the loved; the first battles in the West; the eager demand for news; the victory at Donelson, where began the public life of a new leader of the Nation; the field of Shiloh, with its bloody victory seized from defeat; the gradual opening of the Father of Floods; Vicksburg with its memorable siege; the return home as veterans of those who but a short time before had left as untried youth; the proud consciousness of the youthful soldier, as he told of his deeds afar off in the wars; the return to the field; the flankings and fightings of our great Captain about Atlanta, until it was "ours and fairly won;" the sudden departure, as, turning their backs on home, the men of this Army made their march to the sea; Savannah and its pleasant holidays of rest; the seemingly unceasing swamps of Carolina; the toilsome march to Raleigh; the welcome words of the announcement which told of the surrender of the flower of the Armies of the South; the joy of that happy hour turned to gloom, as the hushed intelligence of the death of the nation's Chief was broken in low

words to the men; the final march to Washington; the grand
review at the nation's Capital; the last order, and the welcome
muster out;— all these memories seem not like memories, but
like the faint glimpses of an imagined picture, as, panorama like,
it passes before the eye, and leaves here and there an impress,
and is gone;—like the half-faded recollection of something that
we have seen, and yet at times can scarce believe that we have
witnessed. And as, day after day, in the quiet walks of civil life,
he who was a soldier pursues those duties which are so different
from the routine of military life, the meeting with a comrade, the
sound of a voice which he has heard on distant fields, reminds
him of the days when, by the camp-fire and with his comrades of
the bivouac, care was banished in anticipation of a future of
victory and peace. And then the vision vanishes, and breaking
upon him the realized truth thrills his heart with the treasured
memory that he was once a volunteer soldier of the Army of the
Tennessee. And yet again, as he turns the pages of his little
journal, and reads the hasty jottings of his army notes, he
can scarce believe that of those scenes his eyes were witnesses,
that of those sounds of artillery his ears were hearers, that on the
march his step gave its part to the universal tramp, and that in
all of which he writes he was an actor. It all seems like a
dream!

As the exile from home and friends, after years of separation,
feels his heart bound with joy, as his eyes once more rest on the
familiar faces of honored friends, and the cherished scenes of
earlier days, so are we, my comrades, conscious that to-night our
glistening eyes tell of the happiness of this meeting, our bounding
hearts beat high in remembrance of the proud deeds achieved by
the Armies of the Union. Our hands are clasped with that
earnestness of soldierly friendship, which only intercourse among
scenes of peril and hardship can insure, and our words tell of
those days when life was more earnest, because we spent its hours

where death was a constant companion, and where his presence
lurked in the gleam of every gun; where the realities of hardship
scarce made an impression, so like a luxury did every favor seem
where a blanket was a sumptuous bed; where the repose of the
soldier at night was made none the less refreshing by the reflec
tion that perhaps by *reveille*, he might "sleep a sleep which
knows no waking" here.

And as we revive these memories, and recall these scenes, there
cluster around us the recollections of those days, then unapprecia-
ted but now dear by the associations which gather around them,
as our armies fought for the national life, and put forth their
energies to preserve its liberties. And as the trials and hardships
endured are recalled, how can we fail to be lost in wonder at the
fortitude and faithful bravery, the energy and unflagging devotion,
the perseverance and untiring zeal, which prompted the movements, and nerved the arms, of that remarkable body of men who
formed the volunteer soldiery of the Armies of the United States?
Doubts had entered the minds of many as to the possibility of
procuring the men in numbers sufficient to form an army of the
power and efficiency desired, even were the means at hand to
equip and arm it, but that doubt dissolved, when from every
hamlet and village and city; from every farm and fireside, flocked
the noble hearts to do their country's bidding. The mechanic
left his bench, the farmer's boy forsook his field, the student threw
aside his books, the briefs of the lawyer were forgotten, the phy-
sician left the bedside of the sick, the merchant closed his
accounts, and the ease of quiet life was abandoned by the man of
leisure. All with one will fell into line at the call of the country.
From all these occupations and pursuits, from all these habits of
thought and practices of life, was to be moulded an army, the
power of which no man had conceived, the mighty influence of
which no man had measured, the combined achievements of
which no prophet had predicted; for it was left for the Armies

of the West to write their own histories, to carve their deeds in letters of life on the unbroken columns of their country's union, and to send down to the future, forever to be unforgotten, the names of those men, who, as the leaders of that mighty host, had made themselves immortal.

As the drums beat they gathered; here one and there another, and there a company of two or three. Beneath the protecting banner of their fathers, as its consecrated folds floated in the breeze, with hearts beating with the earnestness of youthful patriotism, and with hands ready for the task, they fastened in the faith those who had once been doubtful, and the flag of the land, touched by the breath of heaven, seemed now to give token more signally than ever, that, while with its blended colors it was the flag of the union, it was also the flag of the free.

Back to those firesides many of them never marched again. There are times when the hearts of men are more easily touched than at others; when the feelings of our better natures tire of the burdens of active life, and, turning to more quiet duties and more peaceful scenes, yield to the quiet influences of home. Thus it was in the solemn moment of the soldier's departure. Family and friends and fireside were to be left, and thoughts of them coming between him and his duty made the strong man weak. The tear of affection's farewell dropped down the cheeks of those whom he loved so tenderly, but it was not the tear of regret. The arms of woman's love were twined around those manly forms, but they pressed them not to stay. The sincere expression which marked the last benediction of those endeared to the soldier by all the ties of kindred and of family, only assured him of the intensity of that devotion which gave him up that the land might live, and when this was all over and he had gone, his form erect and strong, his step firm and soldierly, but ill concealed the grief which truly attests the sorrow of the parting. Though that fireside may now be desolate and lonely, and that form be always

missed, those whom he left will remember that he fell manfully
where heroes love to die, and though that parting was the last,
with their's the tears of thousands mingle.

On us who daily witnessed their efforts, and under whose eye
their labors came, the uncomplaining patience and the untiring
energy of the Western soldier, are impressed with an effaceable
stamp. Though often guided by ambition, yet often forsaken by
hope; though solicitous for advancement, and desirous of position,
yet in the midst of disappointment he was ever dutiful. In the
weary watches of the night, he did his work on the picket post
faithfully and well. On the tiresome march, on roads soft with
mud for miles, and deep with water, he strode along. Losing
sleep when nature was well-nigh exhausted, after a weary day's
march, he was contented with the meal which a haversack
afforded him, and among all the trials and perplexing mishaps of
his soldier-life, was unforgetful of his duty to his country, though
to him she seemed sometimes thankless and ungrateful. The
winter's cold was to him as nothing, for his frame had become
inured to it under the pitiless storms of his Northern home.
The severe heats of a Southern sun beat upon him, but they
seemed only to renew his fainting energies and to render his step
more firm. Though the army's road lay through woods which
before were pathless, the spirit and will of its leader clove a way,
through which this army marched, and its track through the
South was followed, where the axes of the hardy pioneers of the
corps of Dodge and of Logan and of Blair, blazed the way of
the Army of the Tennessee to victory. Through those dark
swamps where the rank growth of tangled briars and thorns
formed a barrier to his progress, he moved, regardless of their
presence; across large tracts where the treacherous earth yielded
to the moving mass, he wearily labored, as the lengthened trains
of the advancing columns were lifted from the quicksand, and
sent on their way.

What the private soldiers of the Army endured, the world will never know. We recall that skirmish-line advancing from point to point, until the sharp cracking of occasional rifles is lost in the opening crash of the conflict. We remember those rifle-pits, so closely under the fire of the enemy, that the snapping of a twig, or the rustling of a leaf, would be the signal of death; those lines of battle in the face of the foe; those embrasures from which the thundering artillery sent its messengers screaming to the front, and those frequent cannonadings, which, with bursting shell, covered the Divisions; and we seem to hear the shouts and yells of the men, as, in the heat of the action, rallying by the side of the flag, which to the fighting soldier among such scenes shines with renewed lustre, the faint-hearted grew strong and the faltering were nerved amid the havoc of the battle. We recall this at Shiloh, when, on the first day, the national lines wavered before the advancing attacks of that well-appointed army; when, on the second day, under the eye and cool leadership of their first commander, they swept to defeat those who had been defiant victors; and at Corinth, where the brightness of the deeds of valor performed by the enemy was dimmed by the mistaken cause for which they fought; and again at Vicksburg, where in charge after charge the men marched *like* men at the blazing mouths of the guns; and still again at Atlanta, where, again and again, on July 22, 1864, flanked and turned, they fought from either side, and both sides, and all sides of the works, and won the victory in a manner peculiarly Western.

And when the contests were over, when the sounds of strife were stilled, and only the low moans of the wounded, or the breathings of the dying, touched the ear, we remember that among those scenes of suffering our wounded comrades lay with scarce a murmur. Among all our visits to the hospitals we can remember the resigned and patient conduct of those who had been stricken down. The hand of affection was not there to

smooth the soldier's pillow; the tender caresses of the loved ones
at home were missed from the field hospital. The hands that
nursed them, though prompted by kindly hearts, were rough;
but from the lips of the dying heroes came no words of complaint,
and no repining, save at times the manly regret that they could
do no more for the country and its cause. The blood of many of
the best and bravest of the Army of the Tennessee moistened the
soil of the South; the bones of many of our comrades whitened
the battle-fields of the war. On field and hill and plain their
graves were made, by the banks of the Tennessee, beneath the
cliffs of Lookout Mountain, under the frowning heights of Kenesaw, and here and there along the line of march, until, for some,
the sea sounds forth a requiem. Peace to their ashes! Remembered be their lives and deeds, while we willingly pause in our
pleasure to drop a soldier's tear on the honored graves of the
early dead. They lie there in companies, battalions, and divisions, and side by side with the private soldier, the true and tried
leader fell in death.

> " Their swords are rust —
> Their good steeds, dust —
> Their souls are with the saints, we trust."

Wherever man could go, they went; whatever man could do,
they did, and as a body of energetic, enterprising and resistless
men, achieved for themselves and their army a name which will
live as long as the land lasts for whose liberties they fought; for
they commanded the prompt approbation of their leaders, and
challenged the admiration of the people, while the astonished
military leaders of other nations, wrapped up in theories of their
own as to the formation of armies, paused in their perusal of the
history of the rebellion, surprised by the reality. And after it
was announced that the cause of the South was a lost cause, and
the shell of the Confederacy was crushed; after the Army of

Northern Virginia had surrendered to our first Commander, and the Rebel Army of Tennessee to our second; after the head of the Rebellion, followed by the quick eye, and pursued by the Cavalry of the untiring Wilson, had yielded to capture, baffled, discomfited and lost, what a sight it was for the contemplation of the world, as the Armies of the Union, passing in review before their leader, and before the Nation's Executive, filed off to their homes, and calmly, peacefully, and gladly returned to the quiet walks of civil life! In no other land could such a scene be witnessed. Years before, the citizens of the Republic had become her soldiers; her youth had become her men, and the smoke of the marches of military life had hidden from their view the green fields of other days, but, as the cloud lifted, it revealed the men of the Army who had survived the shock of War, dropping the weapons of the conflict, and the button of rank, and effacing all traces of the contest in the industrious avocations of life. As quickly as arms were taken up, as promptly were they laid aside, and almost imperceptibly, with the last roll of the drums of the rebellion, an army of strength and power and numbers, was dissolved without commotion. As they were mustered out, hearts which throbbed heavily with anguish during their absence, bounded with joy at their approach; the faces of the aged, marked by the anxiety of separation, as well as by the touch of time, kindled with the old smile as the hour of reunion came; and, clasped in the close embrace of those around whom the best affections of his heart clustered,—mothers, wives, sisters and lovers,—the soldier of the Army, exultant in his well-earned fame, received the rich reward he had won so worthily. What though his marches had been long and weary, his rations sometimes scant and poor, his battles bloody, and his hardships at times unheeded; not a page would he take from the history of the campaigns in which he bore a part, not a word would he blot from the orders which told the congratulations of his chief, and not a leaf would he pluck from the wreath of renown in which these very struggles and trials were woven. In the hearts of the people his reputation was fadeless, for while to the nation he was the defender of its liberties, the character and conduct of the American volunteer were the wonder of the world. Wherever we go, these men are found now, in all the labors that industry invites, and as they were good soldiers, so now they honor the paths they tread. In the presence of the dissolved army, the public men of other nations stand in astonishment. That hundreds of thousands of men, untaught in war, should so suddenly become a skillful army, and as suddenly return again to the work-shop, and the office, and the farm, surpassed even the expectations of the well-wishers of the land; for the occurrence stood without a parallel. As the young Republic emerged from these trials, her leaders sent to nations far beyond the Atlantic lessons in the art of war.

There was a feature of the Western Armies which has been remarked, and which, though personal to every soldier of the corps and divisions represented here to-night, is yet an honest cause of proud satisfaction to us all; that the unity of their actions, the harmony of their counsels, and their combined efforts to conquer, were not impaired or weakened by internal feuds, nor tarnished by unsoldierly jealousy. In the personal valor, in the soldierly honor and persistent energies of their comrades of the armies of the Cumberland, the Ohio, and of Georgia, the Army of the Tennessee ever had firm reliance. Shoulder to shoulder with them they passed through the perils of the Atlanta Campaign, and with joyful ears listened to the salute of exploding magazines, which told that the Twentieth Corps were entering the city; and on the great march from the " Gate City " of Georgia to the coast, the soldier of the West knew that when trouble came, the soldier of the East, adopted into this Western host, would find no word like fail written in his orders. The leader of one of

these armies has been chosen to represent his constituents in
the National Congress; another, with the ability which has ever
characterized him, presides over the Department of War, and
the other is always faithful to duty, true to his trust wherever
found, whether controlling the management of a complicated
command, or, as when the fate of the Western army quivered in
the balance, coolly stemming the tide of battle, he beat back the
rebel host, crushed and conquered, stamping himself as the
determined soldier, whom the pride of state could not allure;
whose name, soldiers of the Army of the Cumberland, is told to
the youth of the land as the synonym of purest patriotism, your
own beloved commander, Thomas, the Rock of Chickamauga!
And this characteristic was not confined to the armies, as armies,
but between corps, divisions of corps, and brigades of the
divisions, extending to smaller organizations, the feeling existed,
and, attached together on the badge of our Commander, may be
seen the acorn of the Fourteenth, the cartridge-box of the
Fifteenth, the arrow of the Seventeenth, the star of the
Twentieth, and the shield of the Twenty-third Corps, suggestive emblems of the complete organization, united like
the commands they represented. Between the Corps of the
Army of the Tennessee, existed that perfect unity of feeling
which showed them to be self-reliant, and still dependent each on
the other; for each knew that neither would take an advance
which the other would not willingly follow. Between them
generous rivalry promoted military union. Their perfect faith in
the army's chief never wavered, and when, as the enemy was
developed, the commencing skirmish grew into actual battle;
McClernand's and Ord's Thirteenth Corps opened a way
through the enemy in its front; Hurlbut's and Dodge's Sixteenth
was a wall of fire; the arrow of Blair's Seventeenth went
surely to its mark; while the cartridges of Logan's Fifteenth
dealt death with the inevitable forty rounds. It was this

patriotic faith which made the engagements of these armies so prominent among the successes of the war, and gave them a fame as unspotted as it is enduring.

And now, Comrades of the Army of the Tennessee, we willingly weave the cypress with the laurel that enshrines the memories of the thousands of our own command whose valor in action, ever conspicuous, remains remembered, though their last fight has been fought, and their camp is with a command higher than any they ever served with here. We do not number them, nor can we tell of all; but drums will cease to beat and bugles to blow ere their examples be lost. Their military life is written. The records of the Rebellion have closed their pages for them. But while there survives a man of his division, he will recall the form and features of Iowa's Crocker, as in the heat of action, chivalric and inspired by the excitement, he gave his whole soul to the cause. The people of his State protect his memory, and in every house and home upon its prairies his honored name is a household word. The sons of Illinois fail to find at their gatherings the form of their loved Ransom. With a heart as gentle as a woman's, he was yet full of that old Roman fire which, gathering its inspiration from famous martial scenes, kindled in his mild eye unwonted light, and gave to the noble gentleman the mien, and attitude, and aspect of the born soldier, Both of them survived many hard fought fields, to die the death so unwelcome to a soldier, — one surrounded by friends of home; — the other away from its comforts and attentions with his last hours soothed by those who, on his staff, had learned to love him; but to the last, both remembered the companions of their campaigns, and with the final beatings of their hearts, sent to us all, the soldier's last farewell.

Since our last meeting, another has gone, who, but twelve months ago with us, listened to the address of our chief at our Annual Meeting, — an officer of our Society, one of its Vice-

Presidents, who gave its interest attention, and was a prompt attendant at its meetings. His wound received at Shiloh, while apparently yielding to treatment, was yet gradually sapping the foundations of his life, and with the sons of his State, we lament the absence of Wisconsin's Fairchild. And while we can not tell of all, we remember that there is yet another. Near his boyhood's home at Clyde, Ohio, rests all that is mortal of McPherson, our third commander. From the front of the action, in full sight of the foe, booted and spurred, he went into the presence of the God of Battles. Of magnetic influence, of courtly presence, and of extraordinary military ability, he was a knightly soldier. Near him, as he fell in the battle near Atlanta, July 22, 1864, was a wounded private, George D. Reynolds, of Company D, Fifteenth Iowa. Though pressed closely by the enemy, this gallant boy refused to forsake his fallen general. From his own canteen he gave water to those trembling lips; with his shattered arm he supported the dying hero's head; from those eyes, ere they became lustreless forever, he received that glance of thankful recognition, which, beyond all pay or promotion was his full reward; and as that great heart ceased to beat, he felt the last faint, grateful pressure of his commander's hand. For McPherson's death came just as it should, amidst the crash of musketry, and the booming of heavy guns; and his comrades of the Army of the Tennessee loving him in his heroic life, and honoring him in his early death, bound upon his youthful brow a laurel crown, and sent his fame to history. The numbers of the enemy's dead upon that field were silent but sure witnesses that his army, under the command and dashing leadership of Logan, avenged the death of their honored chief. His successor in the command has an empty sleeve as the unimpeachable badge of his heroism, and by the oppressed every where honor is done to that Howard whose well-earned reputation

3

during the war shines as brightly as do his philanthropic
endeavors among scenes of peace.

What must have been the feelings of our second commander,
when, four years ago last month, severing the telegraphic wires
as they sent off his and our last message — "all's well" — he
broke the last bar of iron which bound this Army to their Northern home. The measure of his fame was nearly full. The
admiration of the age had crowned the accomplishment of his
successes at Atlanta with generous praise, and high up, on the
column of the world's great captains, was inscribed the name of
Sherman. Reliant upon the confidence of his Army, and grasping with his genius the future of the rebellion, as it was mapped
out before him, he commenced that march which to all time will
be told as "Sherman's March to the Sea." And, as he turned
his face toward the ocean, a long line of departing locomotives,
as, with their living freight of weak and wounded, they moved
to the North, whistled and shrieked out to him their last
farewell.

> " There tracks of blood
> Even to the forest's depth, and scatter'd arms,
> And lifeless warriors, whose hard lineaments
> Death's self could change not, mark the dreadful path
> Of the out-sallying victors; far behind,
> Black ashes note where their proud city stood."

Marching to the sea, he added to the Nation's Christmas Gifts,
four years ago this month, the city of Savannah; a little later he
captured the capital of Secession, and compelled the surrender of
Johnston's baffled army; every where, and always stamping on
his plans the mark of genius, on their execution the signet of a
determined will, and wherever he may be, finding a welcome
home in the hearts of his command.

Above us we see the name of another, whose boundless reputation the Army of the Tennessee claims as its own, for Grant was its first Commander, and has said that "with that Army he felt himself identified to the end of its service." Overcoming the assaults of his enemies at home by his modest manner, and, conquering his foes in the field by his military ability, he achieved for himself a name which is matchless, and has marked him as the leader of leaders, and the General of the Age.

> "Patient in toil; serene amidst alarms—
> Inflexible in faith; invincible in arms"—

1796611

Proud are we of him, who at Donelson, and Vicksburg, announced "unconditional surrender" as his terms; who at Chattanooga told his army, "no enemy can withstand you, and no defences, however formidable, can check your onward march"; who, with Sheridan, effaced from military lexicons the word "can't," and placed there, instead, the memorable phrase, "go in"; who in his last order told you "your marches, sieges and battles dimmed the lustre of the world's past military achievements, and will be the patriot's precedent, in defence of liberty and right, for all time to come;"and who received from President Lincoln the acknowledgment, "you were right, and I was wrong." From us he needs no laurels, for those he wears will be forever green. The Nation which trusted him in war, confides in him in peace, and has placed the soldier-statesman in the line of Presidents which began with Washington. His, and his army's friend, we miss to-night; that noble soldier who from first to last, in depression and in victory, stood by his honored chief; and from the lips of every one of us, as we find he is not here, comes the earnest expression which tells the sentiment of all the soldier hearts throughout the land—"Long live John A. Rawlins!"

Comrades! we stand at a commanding point in the life of the land, in the progressive march of the people, which places the

Nation foremost among the Governments of the world; we can not be found absent when the assembly sounds. The star of the future is bright with hope. This Union, rendered dearer by the blood spilled to insure its life, must remain unbroken by rebellion, and strong against attack. Throughout the land, from Maine to Florida, and from sea to sea, the American citizen must be free to go, unmolested and at home. The bands of iron binding the Continent from ocean to ocean, can not be stronger than the cords of patriotic affection tying heart to heart. And, while from the lips of the President elect comes that noble sentiment, which finds no readier response than from ourselves, " Let us have Peace," back from the past, and from amidst occurrences which presaged the future, comes that prophetic utterance of our second commander, " We must have peace, not only at Atlanta, but in all America." Made stronger in heart than ever by this reunion, striking hands to-night with a fervor that shows that the memories of the past trials and triumphs of these Armies will live and bear fruit, should the country's call ever again be sounded, you feel that, while with honest pride you sustained the honor of the flag, as citizens you will never tarnish the records of the Nation whose standards were borne to triumph by the Armies of the Union, and whose assembled thousands, as they greeted your grand review, on the avenues of the Capital, and strewed your march with flowers, sent to you the grateful acclaim of the people of America:

HAIL AND FAREWELL!

BADGE OF THE SOCIETY

OF THE

40 ROUNDS

1863

ARMY OF THE TENNESSEE.

ORATION OF GENERAL CRUFT.

COMRADES OF THE ARMY OF THE CUMBERLAND: The Society which you have formed, and the meeting of which has called us together, on this occasion, has among its chief objects " the perpetuation of the memory of the fortunes and achievements of the Army of the Cumberland," and the preservation of "that unanimity of loyal sentiment, and that kind and cordial feeling which has been an eminent characteristic of the army, and the main element of the power and success of its efforts in behalf of the cause of the Union." Other, and equally worthy objects, are also interwoven with those stated, but assume lesser importance in the general plan of organization. In furtherance of the grand purpose of the association you have come up hither, from all parts of our broad land, to reawaken, in memory, the valorous deeds of the old Army, and to kindle anew in your hearts that steadfast loyalty and wondrous cordiality which ever distinguished it. Your reunion to-day is one of the glorious rewards which await the gallant soldier. It is one of those privileges for which he has patiently toiled in camp, endured long and dreary marches, and risked his life ofttimes in battle. It is a great and glorious privilege. God grant you all, my comrades, long years to enjoy the like occasions.

In pronouncing an anniversary discourse to you, on matters connected with your Association, the hasty thoughts which I have been enabled to devote to them, resolve themselves into a consideration of the following topics:

1st. The prominent characteristics of the Rebellion.

2nd. The origin of the "Army of the Cumberland," and its exploits in the great struggle for the life of the Republic.

3rd. Its peculiarities as a distinct army in the field.

4th. The teachings of the war.

Of these in their order:

CHARACTERISTICS OF THE REBELLION.

No elaborate discussion of the origin of the sectional differences which caused the late war of the Rebellion, from a political stand-point, is expected, nor would it be in good taste on the present occasion. It is sufficient now to say that a long chain of causes, stretching back through more than a generation, had estranged the people of the North and South. Differences of climate, soil, productions, character of labor, customs, pursuits, and political teachings, all had to do with this. It was not any single cause which brought about the war, but a combination of many. The most note-worthy of these causes was the persistent effort made by the South, so to shape Federal legislation as to foster and extend the institution of African slavery, and to establish the political dogma known as the doctrine of "State rights." Ambitious and cunning politicians fanned these smouldering embers into the flame of civil war. In 1861 the country became the theatre of an armed rebellion, more wonderful in origin—more surprising in extent—more magnificent in resources and combinations than any of which the history of the world gives account. The Rebellion—stripped of all poetical and other surroundings—was an effort, on the part of eleven States of the Union, by force of arms, to throw off the Federal Government, and establish a confederation which should perpetuate the barbarisms of African slavery, and preserve the political heresy of " State rights." To accomplish these purposes, the rebellious States organized a strong civil government, and appealed to the arbitrament of arms. Abandoning diplomacy, they resorted to the musket and cannon—" *ultima ratio regum.*"

The war, which followed, was marvelous, in many respects, and was wholly unlike any in which the armies of the Republic had ever before engaged. No parallel exists, at any point, between the late Rebellion and the war of the Revolution, that of 1812, or the Mexican war. All these contests were with foreign enemies, and were made by our nation as a unit. It was not so, however, with the Rebellion, which was peculiar in many ways.

It was a fratricidal war—a contest of arms between sections of a common country and government. The hand of brother was arrayed against brother, and father against son. All ties of kindred, marriage, friendship and affection were forgotten. Every citizen was forced to decide between loyalty and rebellion, and, in some form, espouse the cause of his choice. Like all civil wars, the Rebellion evoked more bitterness, hate, destructiveness and passion, than attends warfare between different nations, in the same measure that family quarrels are more intense than others.

The Rebellion was a war of sentiment. The South was fighting for a cherished set of social and political ideas, which had been instilled into the generation of the men who inaugurated the war, from the cradle upwards. The North, originally, was contending for the integrity of the Government, and against the supremacy of the States; but, as the contest deepened, the freedom of the negro and other matters assumed various proportions as war measures. Personal manhood and prowess finally became infused into the strife, and, before the war ended, it became also a question of sentiment with the North, though not especially so at the beginning.

·Viewed from the stand-point of the government, the Rebellion was peculiar in the character of the enemy. The troops of the Republic were hastily summoned to face an enemy of greater intelligence and courage than they had ever before encountered; and, by the same rule, an enemy of greater ability, resources and malignity. So far as the United States were concerned, the Rebellion was, to a great extent, necessarily an invasive war within its own borders, and that into the country of an enemy more creative in warlike expedients, more wary and better skilled in military matters, than any people in the world. The populace at the South had been more or less bred to warlike practices and traditions, and had apparently been long provoking and courting the incursion of their Northern neighbors. They were fighting for their homes and firesides, and to establish, upon sure foundations, their boasted chivalry and individual superiority. The physical conformation of their country was fitted to a prolonged struggle, and guerrilla warfare. It was crossed by craggy ridges and mountains, difficult to be passed by soldiers, and impracticable for effective operations of cavalry and artillery. A few troops knowing the topography of the country, could hold important fastnesses, for a long time, against large bodies of well equipped soldiery advancing upon them by ordinary military approaches. The war was, therefore, mostly offensive, on the part of the Government, and was, of necessity, prosecuted upon a theatre where all the movements of the enemy were aided by an accurate knowledge of the country.

The Government met with no partizan aid in the South. The favor of the citizens was toward the cause of the Rebellion. A few isolated instances of towns, districts and individuals, who were loyal to the Union, were encountered, but these were rare and not to be trusted. The aid of a plausible and ingeniously constructed civil government was constantly given to the rebel cause; and it was powerful enough, by early and systematic proscriptions, to drive all the men capable of bearing arms to the ranks of the insurgents. Not only the men, but the women of the South, strongly engaged in the Rebellion. Of course, they did not take the field, as the Amazons of old are said to have done, but they were a tremendous power in the Southern Confederacy. From the very commencement of the war, they were willing to forego all domestic ties to prosper their side, and so continued until they were forced to admit their "cause was lost," only by witnessing the returning fragments of the armies of the Confederacy after Lee's surrender.

Never was more devotion shown to any cause, from commencement to ending, than was exhibited by the women of the rebellious States toward that in which their fathers, husbands, sons and brothers were engaged. Every officer and soldier of the Armies of the Union saw and felt the power which the rebel women of the South exercised during the war. There was no hardship or suffering which they were not willing to undergo — no deceit or falsehood they would not practice — no desperate venture they would not make for their

" Bonnie blue flag, with but a single star."

History furnishes no example of greater zeal and abandon to the fortunes of their cause; not even the women of ancient Sparta excelled them in their fidelity to their flag and kindred.

While the Government had no party in the South, there was a large element in the North in sympathy with the rebellion. This force was dormant, to all appearances, but it was a strong and powerful undertow, and tended to clog the efforts of the Government in every direction — to break down its financial expedients when " gold, which turneth the wheels of war, was wanting " — to prevent enlistment — to encourage desertion — to spread discontent in the Federal armies — to decry their victories, and rejoice over their reverses. This hidden and unseen opposition was practiced by thousands who had not the manliness to array themselves in arms on the side of the Rebellion—even by those whose roofs were kept over them, and firesides protected by the strong arm of the Government, and who held honors and office by its gift.

Another characteristic of the Rebellion was the singular spectacle of four millions of negro slaves standing passive, and making no effort to wrest their liberty by insurrection. They were left at home, in abject servitude, and still kept laboring on for their mistresses and the children of their masters, while their owners had gone to the field. The producing ability of the slaves, and their faithfulness to their masters, really enabled the Southern people to commence the war, and certainly enabled them to prolong it very materially. It was a power in war which had not before been encountered by our nation, and there was no mode of computing or measuring its strength. It had no parallel any where in military history, and no similitude except a faint one in the conduct of the serfs of Russia during the Crimean war; but even here the resemblance fails, for the serfs were serving their Czar under promise of freedom, while the Southern negro had nothing to look forward to but perpetual slavery.

While the Rebellion was a war without nominal allies on either side, yet the rebels had a strong and powerful moral alliance with England, France, Austria, and other European kingdoms. The monarchs and citizens of these countries were in deep sympathy with the cause of the South. They furnished much of the money, arms and material with which to prosecute the war. Their merchantmen were constantly running the blockade of our Southern seaboard, freighted with rich cargoes contraband of war. The small Confederate navy came from England, and to her may be traced all the disasters to American commerce occasioned by the war. The Emperors of France and

Austria, calculating upon the strength of the Rebellion, and the crippled condition of our Government, attempted to strike at our "Monroe doctrine," and establish an empire in the bordering Republic of Mexico. Thus the Confederate Government, while apparently fighting single-handed, had this quasi-alliance — anomalous in the records of war, and difficult to oppose on account of the professed amity existing between these powers and the United States.

The Rebellion was chiefly a contest between land forces. Owing to this fact, and the necessity of maintaining a close blockade in front of the entire Southern sea-coast, our gallant navy had not the usual opportunity to distinguish itself. Wherever occasion offered, however, it added to its former renown. The grand victories at New Orleans, Fort Fisher, Mobile and elsewhere — the splendid action of the Kearsarge in the English channel, in sight of the French cannon at Cherbourg, and of the monitors along the Atlantic coast, the invaluable service of the gunboat marine in the Western waters, all shed imperishable lustre upon our navy.

Another peculiarity of the war of the Rebellion, compared with any in which the Government had before engaged, is to be found in the vast changes and improvements which had been made, during the last few years, in all arms, and also, to some extent, in strategy, logistics, engineering, grand and minor tactics. The rebels had kept pace with all these improvements, and thereby presented themselves as a more formidable enemy than any previous one. The war was found to be a school, in which not only soldiers, but officers of every grade, were pupils. Many of the military theories of past ages were modified or overturned. Gunnery had to be learned anew, with the constant improvement in rifled cannon, and the whole science of projectiles restudied. The masses of soldiery used were so increased as to require new modes of transportation, supply and manœuvre.

Railroads and telegraphs had been brought into requisition as aids in warfare, and changed all the past ideas and practice connected with it.

These were some of the most striking characteristics of the War of the Rebellion, as compared with any former one in which the Federal Government had before engaged. The novel features were all against the United States, and in favor of the insurgents. They contributed to make the war ten-fold harder, in all respects, than any other before undertaken, and greatly to diminish the chances of conquering a peace. He who went to the war, in the outset, with the belief that victory over the Rebels was an easy thing, soon changed his mind, and found that it was no holiday affair. The preparations of the Government, both in men and material, were, in the commencement, totally inadequate. It required at least two years to educate the Cabinet at Washington up to a conception of the power and proportions of the Rebellion. Thousands of Federal soldiers had been wounded and slain, and millions of treasure had been expended, before even the people of the great North awakened to the magnitude of the war, and realized the sacrifices that yet had to be made to save the life of the nation.

The result of the Presidential election of 1860, demonstrated the fact that a rebellion, on the part of the Cotton States, was imminent; yet neither the people of the North, nor the Government appeared to realize it. The seizure of the forts and arsenals, public property, and materials of war of the United States, speedily followed; then came the formal acts of secession of the various States, and the inauguration of the Confederate government. Then occurred the bombardment and reduction of Sumter. This overt act of war ended the temporizing policy of the Government, and aroused the anger of the nation. The last shot fired from the devoted fort in Charleston Harbor, in defence of the nation's starry flag "quickened the beat of millions of loyal hearts," and fixed in them the firm resolve that the Rebellion should be suppressed by arms. The excitement which followed the capture of Sumter has not been surpassed by any that has hitherto swept over the land. The telegraph had scarcely announced the fact when the shrill tones of the fife and the roll of the drum were heard in every city and hamlet of the North, and citizens, leaving their homes and employments, hastened to form themselves into military organizations and tender their services to the Government. The President called for seventy-five three months regiments, which act, viewed in the light of subsequent events, proved to have been a sad error as to numbers.

The war was now actively commenced. Its history is too deeply engraved and scarred into the hearts of our people ever to be forgotten. The Rebels soon concentrated at Manassas, threatening the national Capital. The first great battle was fought and resulted disastrously to the Union arms. That battle and victory ultimately sealed the fate of the Rebellion. It woke the real martial spirit of the North. It first developed the enormous strength of the Rebellion, and deepened and riveted the purpose, on the part of the Government and people, to put it down. Camp-fires forthwith blazed from every hill-top of the North, like the flaming beacons of the Persian fire-worshipers, and every valley echoed the cry, "*to arms!*" In such a war, out of such times, and to aid in saving the life of the Republic, sprang the " Army of the Cumberland," and the other kindred armies of the United States. They did not leap forth into existence, like Minerva, of Grecian fable, in full strength and panoply, but grew slowly, and from feeble beginnings. At first, all the national armies were small and ineffective. The commanders had but little experimental knowledge of war. The rank and file was composed of new recruits. The staff and commissariat were novices. The artillery was scantily and badly horsed. The quartermaster's department had few baggage and draft animals. There were scarce any ordinance or hospital conveniences. The cavalry were few and poorly mounted. Experience, which goes to insure celerity of movement, and certainty of success in military matters, was wholly wanting.

With this view of the general characteristics of the Rebellion, I pass to the origin of the Army of the Cumberland, and a brief statement of its exploits as an independent army in the field, and a slight tracing of its efforts in behalf of the union of the States.

ORIGIN AND SERVICES OF THE ARMY OF THE CUMBERLAND.

The germ of the Army of the Cumberland consisted of that portion of Federal soldiery first organized, at Louisville, Kentucky, in the summer of 1861, by General Robert Anderson. The bulk of these original troops were Western volunteers, and chiefly from the States of Ohio, Indiana and Kentucky. These men had rushed to arms, at the call of the Government, from the fields, work-shops, stores and offices of the West, in the excitement following the disastrous result of the first great battle of the war, and were willing patriots, but undisciplined and untried soldiers. That faithful officer — the hero of Fort Sumter — organized and placed them in the field, but was soon called to another post of duty. He was succeeded by General William T. Sherman, who, during a brief stay, expanded the embryo army into more commanding proportions, and laid the ground-work for its discipline and instruction. General Sherman wisely desired to make his little force somewhat larger, if it was expected to do much towards conquering the newly-fledged Confederacy. His arithmetical ideas, however, clashed with those of the Government, which had already determined that *seventy-five thousand* men were sufficient for the entire undertaking, and he was relieved of his command. Time has signally vindicated General Sherman's view of "the situation" as then expressed.

General D. C. Buell succeeded our present Lieutenant-General. Being an excellent disciplinarian, he at once commenced perfecting the organization of the troops and the instruction of their officers. He bestowed upon his new command its first distinctive name, the "*Army of the Ohio*"—and by a few months of patient and well-directed labor, developed it to the real proportions of an army in the field. The newly-created army laid in training, for a few weeks, with its right along lower Green River, its centre higher up, near Mumfordsville, and its left upon the upper waters of the Cumberland, thus protecting Louisville and northern Kentucky, and holding at bay the rebel forces under Buckner. The young army was, however, soon called to active service, and a short and sharp campaign was made in eastern Kentucky. Then, in January, 1862, the battle of Mill Springs was fought, in which General George H. Thomas gained a signal victory over the rebel forces under Zollicoffer, and which *was the first decided success in the West!* The year 1861 had closed without any complete victories to the Federal arms in the few conflicts which had then taken place, and the new year brought with it a feeling of great despondency throughout the North. The dashing encounter of the young "Army of the Ohio" with the enemy, at Mill Springs, did much to show the metal of which it was composed, as well as to restore public confidence in the prowess of our volunteer soldiery.

The close of the winter of 1861-2 found the newly-formed army on the march towards Nashville, parallel with the movements of the twin-army of the Tennessee, under General Grant, upon Forts Henry and Donelson. One brigade of the "Army of the Ohio" was spared to the Tennessee column, and bore its part in the glories and losses of that brilliant campaign—participating in both the trying days at Shiloh—before returning to its place. The Confederate forces withdrew from before the steady advance of Buell, and hastened to succor their friends in resisting the

column of Grant. Forts Henry and Donelson fell before the
victorious assaults of the "Army of the Tennessee," and Nashville was occupied by the "Army of the Ohio." Here the latter
rested for a while from marching, but worked on, daily and
hourly, at drill and instruction. No pains were spared by commander, or subordinates, to reach the highest point of discipline
that could be attained. The surviving officers and soldiers of the
Army of the Cumberland will remember the toils and studies of
that period, and the alacrity with which they all addressed themselves to the business of learning the art of war. Their chieftain
was indefatigable and exacting, and every one seemed to catch
his systematic and laborious spirit, and share with him in the
determination that they should be soldiers in fact as well as
name. The older regiments that moved from before Louisville
to Nashville, under General Buell, never forgot the lessons
learned upon that march, and always remembered them with
profit.

In the course of events, General Grant soon moved up the
Tennessee and massed his army at Pittsburg Landing. The
" Army of the Ohio" was on the march to join him when it heard
the opening guns of the battle of Shiloh. The advance was
pushed forward with wonderful rapidity and the whole army made
Herculean efforts to reach the field and mingle in the desperate
fray. The leading division came in time to participate somewhat
in the first day's battle, and the bulk of the army to engage
bravely in the operations of the second day.

It is not my purpose to dwell upon battles, or to attempt minute
details or descriptions of them. It requires great genius in poet,
painter, or historian to depict battle-scenes properly and intel-
ligibly. Few, who attempt such description with pen or colors,
succeed. While every soldier, who has witnessed the preparations for a pitched battle between contending armies, knows how

utterly impossible it is to portray the scene by words or picture, yet he fully realizes the feeling described by the Scottish bard,

> "'Twere worth ten years of peaceful life
> One glance at their array."

The seige of Corinth followed the battle of Shiloh. Here the discomfited enemy placed himself behind strong entrench ments and awaited regular approaches. In all the toils and labors of this period the "Army of the Ohio" nobly bore its part, and, when the enemy refused the wager of battle and retreated, made its full share of pursuit.

Here the services of the "twin armies" divided, and they never again served together until the memorable seige of Chattanooga. The "Army of the Tennessee" turned westward to the Mississippi river, and followed the course of its majestic current southward, carving an undying name in history for its magnificent victories. The "Army of the Ohio" faced toward the east — made the celebrated campaign of Northern Alabama, threatened Chattanooga, and finally concentrated in the eastern side of middle Tennessee. These operations consumed the summer of 1862. In the latter part of August it became apparent that the enemy was passing the left flank of our army, on the eastward of the Cumberland range, and was determined on carrying the war to the Ohio river. The "Army of the Ohio" was now rapidly marched westward to Nashville, and the safety of that city being provided for, it was stripped of baggage and all impediments to light marching, and its course turned northward in haste to reach the Ohio before the enemy could possibly do so. All who participated in that rapid march will remember it as one of the most arduous and trying, as well as one of the best conducted marches of the war. The enemy was beaten to Louisville. Here the army was remodeled, and largely increased in numbers, by the infusion

4

of the new levies made in the West in the fall of 1862. The "Army of Kentucky," just organized by General Nelson, was disbanded, and its regiments scattered throughout the brigades of the "Army of the Ohio," adding largely to its numerical strength.

In the early days of that bright autumn the march towards the enemy was commenced, the bloody battle of Perrysville was fought, and the Confederate army started in full retreat southward through the mountain gaps of Kentucky. Pursuit was vigorously made as far as the waters of the Cumberland.

At this stage of affairs, a new commander was sent to the army, in the person of General William S. Rosecrans. He straightway concentrated the army in the vicinity of Nashville, arriving there about the first of November. A few weeks of camp life here were spent in constant drill and instruction. A complete reorganization and refitment was had, and every thing possible was done to make ready for an active winter campaign. The old name "Army of the Ohio" was dropped by General Rosecrans, and it was thenceforth known as the "Army of the Cumberland." A thorough *corps* organization was adopted, and many reforms and improvements introduced.

On the day after Christmas the army took march to encounter its old enemy, behind his rifle-pits and entrenchments at Murfreesboro. The battle of Stone River was one of the most closely contested of the great engagements of the war. It christened the newly-named "Army of the Cumberland" with a baptism of fire. Few pitched battles have been fought of equal duration and equal destruction. The cedar thickets and clearings of that memorable field were reddened with the blood of the slain. Right nobly did the "Army of the Cumberland" bear itself throughout that terrible and exhausting fight; and although victory was for a while doubtful, it finally settled upon the old flag.

Halting before Murfreesboro until mid-summer, the army again started southward to accept battle at Tullahoma. Wisely enough, however, the enemy withdrew from before its advance, and passed beyond the Tennessee. Pursuit was shortly made, and Chattanooga, the objective point of the campaign, was occupied. This much, however, did not satisfy the impetuous and brave leader of the army. He hurried onward to fight the enemy when and where he could overtake him. After arduous marches and counter-marches, it so fell out that the "Army of the Cumberland" became interlaced with the enemy, in a singular manner, and was assaulted by the reinforced army of the rebels, in the valley of the Chickamauga—"river of death," as its name signifies in the fanciful etymology of the Indian. The furious battle of those two bright September days, fought in the thickets along the Chickamauga, was one of the deadliest and most stubborn of the entire war. It was the last general engagement fought by the "Army of the Cumberland" as an independent army. Although not decisive as a pitched battle, yet it accomplished the purpose of preventing the rebel occupancy of Chattanooga, and forced him to undertake to reduce the place by regular siege.

The toils and sufferings of the faithful army, while beleaguered within the defences at Chattanooga, have become historic. After a time, the "Army of the Tennessee," under General Sherman, and two *corps* of the Army of the Potomac, under General Hooker, came to the relief of the Army of the Cumberland, and to open the communications with its base of supplies.

Now occurred another and final change of commanders. General Rosecrans was relieved, and the command devolved upon General George H. Thomas, who entered upon his duties under the most unfavorable auspices, and found himself, without warning, at the head of the besieged and half-starved garrison. The only cheerful thing which met the new commander was the pluck and determination of the troops to hold the position at all hazards, despite the enemy without, and starvation, disease and death within. This indomitable spirit was subsequently placed in terse and soldierly words by General Thomas in his famous declaration, in behalf of his army, " to hold the place till we starved !"

General Grant, then in command of the Military Division of the Mississippi, removed his field headquarters to Chattanooga, and gave personal supervision to the future operations in that vicinity. In two months the valley of the Tennessee was cleared of the enemy. Lookout was stormed, Mission Ridge was carried by assault, the siege of Knoxville was raised, and the enemy driven southward within the mountains of Georgia. In the achievement of all these glorious successes, the Army of the Cumberland took conspicuous part, and the names of all the battles which produced them are inscribed on its standards.

At the opening of the next spring, the grand campaign of Atlanta was undertaken by General Sherman. The three *corps* comprising the Army of the Cumberland were actively engaged in all the battles and marches of this eventful campaign. They made part of the lines of battle and assaulting columns during all the well-known operations against the renowned "Gate City," and, after its capture, the old army divided, never again to meet. Two of the *corps*, the Fourteenth and Twentieth, subsequently constituting the Army of Georgia, under General H. W. Slocum, marched with Sherman, in his modern anabasis, down to the sea ; the other, the "Old Fourth," retraced its steps to assist, with the Army of the Ohio, under General J. M. Schofield, in fighting Hood at Franklin and Nashville, and to be " in at the death" of the Rebellion in the West. Perhaps no severer tests of manhood and personal bravery were tried during the war, than those at Franklin and Nashville, and surely no cleaner victory was won than at the latter place. It broke the power of the Rebellion in the Mississippi Valley, and cut off all hope of success in the West. After the battle at Nashville the remnant of the Army of the Cumberland went to Texas, there to assist in wiping out the last relics of armed rebellion on the sunny plains of the South.

With the end of 1865, the last of the Army of the Cumberland was mustered out, after an existence of more than four years as a military organization in the field.

The faint sketch of the campaigns and battles just given, conveys but a feeble idea of its services and toils. It affords no conception of the noble and heroic actions of the distinct regiments, brigades, divisions and *corps* which comprised the army, nor of the brave and chivalric deeds of individual officers and men, which cast a halo of brilliancy always about its pathway. The exploits of the old army were great in themselves, and great in their consequences, and abounded with brilliant examples of high courage and devoted zeal. They should "neither be disfigured nor forgotten," but are worthy of enduring fame, and a conspicuous place in history. Says Napier, in reviewing the Peninsular war, " much injustice has been done, and much justice left undone, by those authors who have hitherto written concerning this war." The same may be said in respect to the war of the Rebellion. Its history has not yet been fully or truthfully written, and perhaps never may be ; but whenever it is, great credit and high renown must be allotted to the Army of the Cumberland, as one of the Grand Armies of the Republic, for its gigantic strokes toward the suppression of the Rebellion. The graves of the dead lie thick along its southern pathway, mute, yet solemn and convincing testimony of its prowess and devotion to the cause of the Union. It will be held, in after times, as no small honor to have fought for the Government, in the war of the Rebellion, and not the least to have followed the fortunes of the Army of the Cumberland.

PECULIARITIES AS A DISTINCT ARMY.

No sketch of the Army of the Cumberland would be complete, however hastily drawn, which merely traced its campaigns, marches and battles, but omitted to allude to the special characteristics which marked it. Your Society, in stating the objects of its formation, has given prominence to two of these characteristics, " *unanimity of loyal sentiment; and kind and cordial feeling.*"

The Army of the Cumberland was loyal to the Government, not only in the act of bearing arms in its defence, but in every thought, feeling, word, and action. There were no under-currents of doubt, complaint, disrespect or treachery toward the constituted authorities of the nation. There was no hesitation or misgiving about the justness of the war in which the army was engaged. Officers and men alike were inspired with an unswerving spirit of devotion to the national cause. A broad and intelligent patriotism nerved the hearts and steeled the swords of those who followed the banners of that army. This feeling, prominent from the first, grew with the growth and strengthened with the strength of the army, until it became a live, deep and abiding sentiment. It leavened the whole army as a mass, and gave surprising unanimity to its purposes and acts. No toil, hardship or suffering could overcome this sentiment; no enemy in the field, nor rebel sympathizers in the rear could shake it. When the enemy hurled his heavy columns on the front, he was repulsed by steady lines of bayonets, the sharp rattle of musketry, and the roar of well-manned artillery. When treason ran riot at home, brave words and glorious deeds came thundering back from the army in the field. This steadfast purpose was of great worth to the Government, and stood in lieu of thousands of armed men, in the North-west, who would otherwise have been required to protect the families and friends of the soldiers behind them.

The least faltering on the part of the " Army of the Cumberland," in loyalty to its flag, at one period, might have precipitated a civil war northward of the Ohio.   It is a matter of history that a secret, treasonable association existed in certain of the North-western States during the war, which numbered among its members many names of distinction, the object of which was to sow seeds of discord in the armies of the Government, to release rebel prisoners, kidnap or kill loyal officers, and promote the cause of the Confederacy by a counter-revolution in the North. It is known that systematic and artful plots were attempted to procure desertions from the " Army of the Cumberland," and to thin its numbers in every possible way.   To the credit of the men who composed that army, it may be said that, so far as they were concerned, all these treasonable schemes perished.   They scorned the approaches of treacherous northern sympathizers, and treated them with less regard than the open foemen, who met them in arms, fighting for the rebel flag,

The Army of the Cumberland was renowned for the kindness and cordiality of feeling which prevailed throughout all its organizations, and existed between its individual members. Harmony there always was, but more than this, there grew up that true friendship and real brotherhood in arms, which is bred only among brave men in the field, by common dangers and exposures.   This kindly feeling, commendable in all armies, must be remembered by you as a prominent trait in the Army of the Cumberland.   It existed to a great degree in all our Western armies, and is one of the pleasant memories of the war.   Friend-ships and attachments were there formed between officers and men, and individuals of both classes, which nothing but death can sever.   Every one who served in the old army can recall the respectful bearing, and unselfish attentions, which were the general rule of intercourse.   There was, too, a real cordiality and heartiness in all this, far above and exceeding the requirements of military authority or etiquette, which sprang from the spontaneous instincts of true men embarked in a common undertaking of peril and adventure. Jealousies, bickerings, or improper rivalries among officers, were almost wholly unknown; disagreements between different organizations never occurred. There was a faithfulness between subordinate and superior officers unusual in the experience of armies. Military law and usage ordinarily prevent open and improper comment, by subordinate officers or men, on the motives or acts of their superiors, but there are a thousand ways by which unfaithful service may be rendered and, for the time being, pass for true. Bad men infest every army, to a certain extent, and not unfrequently creep into official positions, where they can, for a while, find scope for arrogance or brutality. Happily, such examples were very rare in the "Army of the Cumberland." Its officers, as a class, were courteous gentlemen, and despised alike the brute, the "carpet knight," and the martinet. The rank and file of the army was composed largely of intelligent and energetic men, who became soldiers from the promptings of patriotism. They did not seek the army as a make-shift, or an occupation, and brought to it the earnest convictions and correct habits of successful and respectable citizens. Hence, there was less rancor towards the inhabitants of hostile territory, less plunder and pillage, less lawlessness, straggling and crime than is common in armies otherwise constituted. The kindliness of the Army of the Cumberland was not confined alone to its internal associations. It exhibited itself constantly towards an unprotected enemy. Moderation and justice marked its relations towards the helpless and innocent victims of the war encountered in its numerous campaigns. Now that the rougher passions, engendered by the war, are passing away, and the counsels of peace are to prevail, every soldier must feel gratified that such humane conduct marked the course of his old army. It is a pleasing reflection, in reverting to the unavoidable horrors of a civil strife, that the severities inflicted by any army fell far short of what the harsher laws of war justified.

Another feature of the Army of the Cumberland was the high military and moral discipline. This quality naturally followed, from the others alluded to, as well as from the character and labors of its different commanders. A high and stern code of discipline would be expected from such commanders as Anderson, Sherman, Buell, Rosecrans and Thomas; all of whom were educated to arms, and had made the business of war the study of a lifetime. They well understood the truth of the maxim, "*War is not a conjectural art,*" and constantly labored to promote that thorough discipline which alone can render armies powerful or effective. It is true discipline and constant duty that makes the soldier, and this is worth far more than exceptional acts of bravery. It is discipline which begets endurance, confidence, courage, and power, in an army, and without it numbers become ponderous and useless. Every soldier and officer of intelligence understands the advantage of discipline, and however hard its exact requirements may have seemed to raw volunteers, at first enlistment, they soon knew that, in war, it was but another name for safety and strength. It economizes life, insures success, gives rapidity, certainty and vigor to soldiery; without it, an army is little else than an armed mob, dangerous only to itself, and becomes a ready prey to stampede and defeat. The Army of the Cumberland attained an enviable proficiency in all the tactical knowledge, and other acquirements requisite for good service, but in addition to this, it cultivated and enforced a high order of discipline. Offences against good order became rare, and, when discovered, were promptly and severely punished. The officers were sustained and upheld by the men in the enforcement of all the rules of war. This sentiment, prevailing throughout the army, served to keep the men firm to their colors, and yet to preserve a good and healthful general discipline.

Another quality of the Army of the Cumberland was a great degree of military enthusiasm. The *morale* of the army was uniformly good. As a body, it always had zeal, spirit, hope and confidence. These qualities gave it not only endurance, but superadded enthusiasm. No reverses broke its spirit or diminished its zeal. Its tenacity and ability to endure reverses were sorely tried at Stone River. Its spirit and enthusiasm were brilliantly displayed, in contending against heavy odds, at Chickamauga. The officers and men, as a class, were always enthusiastic in asserting the justness of their cause, and in their steady belief of its ultimate triumph. This confidence gave the army great power in the conflict of battle, and rendered examples of bad conduct in the face of the enemy, either on the part of individuals or organizations, an exception to the general rule. A direct effect of this feeling was to prevent disquiet, homesickness—that bane of the volunteer soldier—desertion, and all the train of evil consequences which flow therefrom.

Another quality which was constantly observable in the Army of the Cumberland, was its *esprit de corps.* Pride in army organization is always a most desirable trait in military life. The officer or private who can sink all individuality in the name and success of his company, regiment, division, or army, is, by the same degree in which he does this, so much the better soldier. This pride of the soldier in the army to which he belongs, gives it force and vigor—ennobles the men, and operates as a strong incentive to individual valor. This animating spirit of the collective body was a conspicuous trait in the Army of the Cumberland. There were none of its regiments or batteries who were not chary of the good name of their army, and proud of the victories and services achieved by it.

These were some of the features of the "Army of the Cumberland" which were ordinarily to be remarked. They, however, by no means constitute all. They were qualities possessed in common by all our armies in the field, and it may be by others to a degree equal or superior to that of the one to which allusion is made. It is true that they existed in it, and by referring to this fact no invidious comparisons are intended.

TEACHINGS OF THE WAR.

The war of the Rebellion, like all sectional outbreaks, is not without its instructions. Results which follow a civil war are seldom apparent at its immediate close. Its teachings are not always impressed on the generation which has lived through the eventful scenes which spring from it. Time is required to soften the tone and passions of the contending parties, to heal up the wounds of the nation, and to show the permanent consequences which are produced. The late Rebellion is no exception to the rule. It brought about changes in our country and Government, and among our people, which will be as lasting as the Republic itself. It is impossible now to allude, in the most cursory manner, to all the revolutions in business, finance, political views, personal life and habits, which came from the war. They are many, and are full of instruction, regret, or foreboding, according to the temperament in which they are read, and spirit in which they are studied. Vast changes have, already, followed the war, and its teachings are grand, solemn and wonderful. It over-turned many of the accepted ideas of our people—not a few fundamental axioms in politics, and numerous preconceived notions in business and commerce.

One of the grandest effects which flowed from the Rebellion was the establishment of universal personal liberty in our country. The theory of our Government has always been that of complete individual freedom and protection, but yet, since its foundation, slavery and oppression had continually existed under its sanction.

At the commencement of the war, notwithstanding the boasted freedom of the United States, four millions of persons were held in bondage, used and traded as chattels, and subjected to cruelties such as were tolerated in no other civilized country. The war burst the shackles from these millions of poor creatures, and bade them look up, assert the intelligence the great Creator had given them, and strive to become worthy and useful citizens. It made our country not only free in name, but absolutely so. Henceforth the world may truly look to the United States as

> "—— the land of the free,
> And the home of the brave!"

With the war has gone the great curse of slavery, and with this are passing away those deep-rooted prejudices of caste and color which have been peculiar only to our country.

The war exploded the great Southern maxim of commerce, "Cotton is King!" This staple, hitherto, held high place, it is true, in all our great commercial relations, domestic and foreign, and gave to our Gulf States a certain power which was asserted to be supreme. Cotton, and its surroundings, and the ideas which cluster around its production, had much to do with bringing about the war; but, before it was fought through, the world learned that cotton was not all there was of the United States. Cotton, though a great power, as formerly used, was not "*King*"—the maxim, asserting it to be so, was a fallacy, but it required the war to teach us this fact!

Another truth, established by the Rebellion, was that all the chivalry and manhood of the nation was not compressed into that part southward of "Mason and Dixon's line." It taught us that there were valor, patriotism, and vitality elsewhere, and that too sufficient to preserve the Government, and to overturn the most powerful rebellion which has ever existed.

Another fact settled by the war was the mastery of the Federal Government. The claim of the supremacy of the State over the General Government in matters of conflict, and the doctrine of paramount allegiance owed by the citizens to the latter, were fully overturned. The falsity of such assumption is now understood. The right of secession is also abandoned, and will nevermore be asserted, at the point of the sword. The war determined the Federal Government as the great central controlling power which shall, for all time to come, regulate, within the limits of the written Constitution, the various States of the Union. Before the Rebellion, the great mass of citizens scarcely realized the existence of the Federal Government, or had any daily evidence of its being. It levied no personal taxes upon them, restrained their liberties in no way, nor exacted any thing from them. They knew that Congress held annual sessions, that a President was elected every four years, the Cabinet changed, that the Government transported their letters, and that it held a court in their State. The only officer with whom they came in contact was the postmaster. Comparatively few, away from the seaboard or the larger cities, had ever seen a custom-house, light-house, navy-yard, man-of-war, file of soldiers, or any thing else, except the national flag, which represented the physical being of the General Government. It laid its burdens so lightly on the citizen that they were hardly known. The war, however, taught our people the existence of a federal power, and its ability for self-protection, and the general defence.

These, and other similar lessons, were taught to our countrymen by the grim and horrid experience of the war. The soldiers also, who were engaged in it, survived its battles, and were honorably discharged, received an experimental tuition which they will not soon forget. They stood nobly to their colors in the tide of battle, and did not desert them in camp or march. Dangers, difficulties, or suffering could not drive them from their standards while there was a single armed foe in the field. Now that the war is over they do not propose to desert the cause for which they fought, for they still owe their Government allegiance and fealty. While they may no longer measure arms with an enemy, in battle array, they must still, as citizens, render homage and support to the constituted authorities. They naturally look for the results of their victory. As honorable soldiers they desire the return of peace, and the restoration of order as one of the first fruits. If this is not attained, then the war has been fought in vain, and all its carnage and cost have been made for nought. The survivors of the Union armies, with one accord, join their late Commander-in-Chief in his magnanimous and soldierly demand, " Let us have Peace ! " The people of the nation have re-echoed this demand, and have strongly emphasized it, by the recent election of our grand Chieftain to the Presidency of the United States. This great tribute to the soldier element of the country proclaims, in thunder tones, the determination of all classes to have that peace which is demanded by those who fought the war; as well as their intention to honor those who were engaged in it.

A further duty impressed on returned soldiers, by the education of the war, comes in the shape of an obligation to stand by one another. All other things being equal, there can be no wrong to the public in the soldier giving preference to his comrade, when his interests come in competition with the citizen who did not go to the war. He would be false to the acknowledged, though unpledged, ties which bind him to those with whom he has suffered and fought — false to the memory of his fallen companions — false to the associations which gather around and hallow his life as a soldier, if he did not do so. As soldiers, you kept the touch of the elbow when in line, so stand together now as citizens! The living public will honor you for such conduct, and posterity will not fail to praise your faithfulness.

Akin to this is another duty learned by the soldiers of the Republic,—to support none but loyal men for official stations. The man who took his life in his hand, and fought rebels in open arms, can not be expected, by the most charitable, to use his ballot to undo the work which his musket wrought. It is an insult to the soldier who has returned from the war, with an honorable record, and who has brains, to ask him to contribute to install unregenerate and unrepentant traitors, or their sympathizers, in place and power.

The war of the Rebellion was fought by volunteer soldiery. The policy of our Government has always been opposed to a large standing army. As a result of such course, the entire land force of the nation, at the commencement of the war, did not exceed fifteen thousand effective men — barely sufficient for light frontier service. Our navy, too, was small, and scattered over distant oceans. The Government was, therefore, necessarily compelled to call for volunteers, and to rely upon them for its support in the great contest before it. The army, small as it was, was divided in loyalty, and about one-fourth of the old officers went to the cause of the Rebellion; those remaining steadfast afforded material from which to officer the volunteer troops and largely to contribute to their education. The small force of regular troops, engaged in the war, proved themselves brave soldiers. All that martial science, endurance and valor could achieve, belongs to their history. It is the business, however, of the regular soldier to be brave and resolute — to fight gallantly. He is fitted by long preparation and exercise, by the study of the school and training of the camp. Such is not the case with our inexperienced volunteers. The nation is justly proud of the regular army, and of its valiant achievements. Another, and a peculiar pride, possesses our people as they turn to their volunteer soldiers. They are part of themselves, their fellow-citizens, their fathers, brothers, husbands, sons.

They are the immediate representatives of the state, county and neighborhood. They are "the Republic itself in arms!" They came, at the blast of the bugle, and roll of the drum, and ran, on willing feet, to their country's banner. They left their farms, work-shops, professions, homes and kindred, to fight back the foes of their common Government. They knew nothing of arms as a profession. Theirs was no mercenary service. Listening only to promptings of patriotism, they went forth to fight for their country, and then returned quietly to their homes, laid aside the garb of the warrior, put on the habiliments of peace, and resumed their former avocations. The war has demonstrated the fact that we now have a great and powerful Government, where every citizen can suddenly spring into a full-armed, effective soldier, and can as suddenly be transformed into a peaceful citizen.

You, of the Army of the Cumberland, and the volunteer soldiers of our other Grand Armies, have revealed the secret of the physical strength of the Republic. Our people now know the "mighty muscular power of our nation, and the nerves, tendons and fibres of our Government." We can now, as if by the wand of an enchanter, evoke great and magnificent armies. During the late war the calls of President Lincoln flashed, with electric speed, over the land, and, as at the blast from the wild horn of Clan Alpine's Chief, every "bracken, bush and stone" gave forth its

"—Warrior armed for strife."

But our volunteers have not only taught the lesson how easy it is to raise vast and powerful armies, but, also, the further and more important lesson, how easy it is to disperse them without violence or bloodshed. Your example, in quietly returning to your homes from the bloody scenes of four years' war, is full of meaning and instruction. The lesson to be learned from such conduct was not lost on the world. To-day the monarchs of Europe wonder how this is done. All civilization is astonished to know how *one million* of volunteer soldiers, who have fought to successful issue the most malignant civil war which time has yet recorded, have quietly stacked their arms and betaken themselves to civil pursuits. It is an irrefragable fact that this has been done, and that you, and your comrades in arms, have done it. The loyal volunteers of the United States have proven to the world the case with which our Government can raise armies, from her citizen soldiery, and then suddenly transform them to peaceful life. This element of strength is now as apparent as it is wonderful, and constitutes a grand bulwark of freedom among us. This ability suddenly to raise and disperse citizen soldiery, stands in place of immense armies and navies. It is like the fan of Paribanou, the fairy, in Oriental mythology — spread it, and the armies of powerful Sultans could repose beneath its shade — fold it, and it became a toy in the hand of a lady.

This host of veterans which has just disappeared from camp and field, is ready to spring up again at the sound of the trumpet. Now that peace is spreading her healing wings over the country, the vast military strength of the Rebellion has become added to that of the Government. If war with a foreign power should make occasion again to summon our countrymen to arms, we can now rally, in a common cause, from the survivors of the two late contending armies, two millions of such tried and trusty soldiers as fought the terrible battles of the Rebellion. This subtle but wondrous power is now with us. The nation feels it — the world knows it!

While the war cost many lives, and millions of treasure, it educated the nation to arms, and developed the martial taste of our people to such extent as to leave no apprehensions for the

5

future. Every loyal soldier laid down his arms at the termin-
ation of the Rebellion with the solemn, though unuttered
pledge, that he would seize them again on the first call of his
country, and again wield them in its defence.

With all the horrors, destruction, and expense of the war, it
was not without some good. In our point of view it operated as
a great field of improvement to those who passed through
its dangers and turmoils, and survived. Many of the rough,
boisterous, and untrained men of the country were disciplined by
the service. Many were there taught their first lesson of sub-
ordination, thoughtfulness, cleanliness, and systematic personal
habits. The lessons of the camps sometimes savored of vice,
but yet more frequently of virtues, and the conduct of the
thousands of soldiers who have quietly returned from the war,
and have since become honored and reputable citizens, shows
that their training in the field was not harmful, but improving.

CONCLUSION.

Gentlemen of the Society of the Army of the Cumberland!
Since first entering the service of your country you have seen
all the vicissitudes and hardships of a soldier's life — the camp,
the march, the battle, and the victory. You have borne
yourselves bravely and successfully, and have exceeded the
expectations of your countrymen. You endured the trials
of your new life without murmur. Hunger and thirst, exposure,
sickness, fatigue, have not daunted you. You encountered your
country's enemy around the church at Shiloh ; you toiled nobly as
one of the besieging armies at Corinth ; you rolled back the
advancing tide of battle at Perrysville ; you wrested victory from
the enemy amidst the tangled cedars at Stone River ; you held at
bay his compact hosts in the dark and bloody valley of the Chicka-

mauga; you endured the memorable siege at Chattanooga; you contributed part of the heroic column that stormed Lookout Mountain; you formed the centre in the memorable assault on Mission Ridge; your dead lay thick on every battle-field from Dalton to Atlanta. Many of you stood in solid ranks at the murderous battle at Franklin, and moved upon the enemy at the crowning victory at Nashville. Part of you "marched down to the sea" with our great leader, Sherman, while part made that other and terrible winter march in pursuit of a flying enemy, without which "the march to sea" would not have been so fully vindicated as one of the grandest exploits in war. Your record has been a glorious one. You can point to numerous pitched-battles in which your army was engaged singly with the enemy, and many others in which it bore a conspicuous part. Your services have been no trifling matter, no mere "fun mustering," but constant and deadly grappling with "foemen worthy of your steel." The long and toilsome marches you have made, the mountains and rivers you have crossed, the various routes you have traversed, the weary miles you have made, the fortifications you have built, all these I have not attempted to relate. The world knows these facts, for they have already passed into history, and have become great and startling truths. While you have been toiling on, and risking your lives in battle, you have not only been exalting yourselves, but unconsciously carving an undying fame. It is to be spoken to your credit, noble soldiers, that your army has not sullied its reputation by any base or unmanly actions. It wears no dishonorable scars. It has not recoiled in battle, nor faltered when the charge was sounded. In this respect you have a common repute with your fellow-soldiers of all the other grand armies of the Union—a glorious national heritage, which has been wrought out by gallant soldiery, and to which you have contributed.

One fact must not be omitted. Many of your regiments

became veterans in the volunteer service. The stripes of honor, added to the uniform worn by them, indicated that they were not only United States volunteers, but, further and higher than this, *veteran volunteers!* The additional title was no meaningless thing. It proclaimed to the world that those who enjoyed it had trod the wine-press of affliction, had been tried in the furnace of battle, and that three years of experience and faithful labor had been consumed before they gained that honorable distinction. The day that your veterans, having fulfilled their first enlistment, again entered the service, was the crowning day of their glory. Less patriotic or determined men would have shrunk from this second trial. To their noble purpose, to the re-enlistment of thousands in all the great armies of the Union, our country owes its safety and integrity.

The pleasure of every greeting among soldiers is commingled with sadness. In looking over the representation here of those who once composed the Army of the Cumberland, in vain we seek many well-known and familiar faces. Why came they not from the dangers of the battle to mingle with us to-day? Too well we know. The great record of battles furnishes the sad response, and points us to the heroic dead. It recalls to memory those who fell gloriously in battle, and rendered up their lives to their country—their souls to their God. We may deplore them, we may grieve for them, but our lamentations will not avail. Others there were who fell by the wayside in weary marches, or whose eyes grew dim and spirits fled from camp or hospital, and whose names adorn no battle-roll. Disease, the great destroyer made sad havoc in your lines. His victims far exceeded those who fell in battle. Many a comrade who escaped the perils of the field, driven from his place in line, came home "to die amid his friends and kindred— ending life where it began." Honor, then, to our patriotic dead!

Others, too, there were, not numbered with the dead, who, stricken by disease, or bullets of the enemy, have returned to drag out a life of disability and suffering. Honor, also, to them! Strong and manly soldiers once, their wounded limbs and shattered bodies are to be revered and held doubly precious.

But our sorrows to-day may not be wholly for the dead. Their names are

— "Freedom's now, and Fame's."

Our sympathies rather go out for the living. The nation mourns her warriors slain, and weeps over the rivers of blood which have reddened its Southern plains, but our personal and effective sympathy must be for the friends and relatives of the fallen braves—most of all, for the widow and orphan of the slain. While we can not but lament the dead, who manfully fought their last battle, it is the living that should call out our active condolence and future care.

Let the nation and the state, while, out of their abundance, they labor to perpetuate the memory of the dead, also make haste to provide for the needs of the living. Let it be a matter of individual duty with us all to care for the wants of the soldier's family. As God has given to each of us, so let him give of his substance to the widows and orphans of our gallant dead.

The stalwart returned soldier should have place, employment, and honors. The wounded and helpless should have home and comforts. The widow of the soldier, and his fatherless children, should not beg bread. His orphan should have education, and the state and kind friends should hover around him, like ministering angels, to nurture, instruct and guard him.

I leave to linger with you these parting injunctions which are caught from the spirit and purpose of your Association; and, again wishing you the return of many such joyous reunions, I bid you

HAIL! AND FAREWELL.

BADGE OF THE SOCIETY

OF THE

ARMY OF THE CUMBERLAND.

ORATION OF MAJOR-GENERAL J. D. COX.

MY OLD COMRADES: I feel, very sensibly, the difficulty of expressing fitly the feelings which must fill the heart of every member of the Grand Army of the West at such a reunion as this. We have met our old comrades of the *corps* and subordinate army organizations, since we parted at Raleigh after our last review as a separate army in the presence of Grant and Sherman (names that need no titles); but to-day the Army of the West meets, by its representatives, for the first time in the garb of peace. To-day, in the presence of the same commanders, for whom our love and admiration have not grown cold in the interval, we meet to renew our pledges of comradeship and brotherhood, to mingle our regrets for the honored dead, and our congratulations with those who have survived.

The years which have passed since that memorable April, 1865, by carrying us further away from the great and exciting events, then just ending, enable us to take a juster and more comprehensive view of the war itself, and of our own share in it; and though no true soldier need apologize for the honest pride with which he may have imitated the ancient hero in exclaiming, "*quorum pars magna fui,*" all will frankly admit that a distance of three years reduces somewhat the proportions, and tones down the coloring one used to give to the achievements of his own command as compared with other portions of the army. The soldier in the ranks naturally believes that his own regiment is the flower of the army, and is peerless in discipline and courage. This faith is so important a condition of success, that he would be an unwise commander who would discourage it. The emulation which grows out of the same elements of pride and self-confidence, shows itself in the division, the *corps*, or the army organization as well. In the larger unit it has much of the same value as in the smaller, and contains the same fallacy. We have all felt its influence, and know that there was none of us who did not feel a deeper thrill of pride and pleasure when he saw the flag bearing his own *corps* emblem moving to the front, than in looking upon any other banner that floated over the advancing host.

I said that time has modified these feelings somewhat. God forbid that either our interest in the cause for which we fought, or our personal satisfaction and pride in our own share of the work, should diminish! But I think that year by year, as the past recedes into the distance, the feeling will grow more and more general, and less individual; more an army feeling, and less that of a corps or division; more a national feeling, and less a local or sectional one. Looking back at our fathers' deeds in the old War of Independence, we hardly care now to inquire whether they served with Gates or Green, with Lafayette or with Schuyler. We are are satisfied with their glory in being members of the old Continental Army which established the Republic. In like manner our sympathies have been growing wider, and our appreciation of our comrades' work has been enlarging; the attraction has been extending the circle of its influence until we who have had our regimental reunions, our corps and subordinate army reunions, have felt the impulse to assemble, not as the Army of the Cumberland, of the Tennessee, of Ohio, or of Georgia, but as the Grand Army of the West, with which our posterity will be proud that we were identified, when our subordinate divisions shall have been forgotten by all but the diligent student of history.

And if our brothers of the Grand Army of the East could be with us, our welcome would prove that we have no jealousy of their splendid career, and hold it the dearest and most precious of all our honors, that we were a part of the great patriotic host — a unit in sentiment, peers in courage, and rivals only in honorable deeds — the army that saved the nation! Therefore, although I am here as the deputed representative of the Army of the Ohio, I shall not detain you long with any thing which may be peculiar to that organization, but shall hasten to the inquiry, how an army society may be made to produce some durable results, by throwing light on the history of the war, or by thorough and scientific criticism of its events.

The Army of the Ohio, which last bore that name, was organized in the summer of 1863, prior to General Burnside's occupation of East Tennessee, and consisted at that time of the Ninth and Twenty-Third Corps, and a cavalry corps, besides detached garrisons and troops in various posts of the Department of the same name. After the terrible winter of 1863-64, following the memorable siege of Knoxville, the Ninth Army Corps returned to the East and resumed its old position in the Army of Virginia, leaving the Twenty-Third Corps, with the cavalry and detached troops, to continue the army name. The regiments of which it was composed had nearly all been newly organized in the spring of 1863, but were made up, in considerable part, of officers and men who had seen much service in the earlier part of the war. Its regiments came from Ohio, Indiana, Illinois, Kentucky, and East Tennessee; and during the first year of the new organization had had the benefit of the systematic discipline and firm command of General Hartsuff. Thence, after a brief interval, it passed into the hands of General Stoneman, and, finally, just before the opening of the spring of 1864, it received as its permanent commander, General Schofield, whose presence here to-day prevents me from speaking of him in the terms of admiration and deep-rooted confidence which every member of the Army of the Ohio had learned to feel, long before the Government had done justice to his services in the field, or recognized the administrative sagacity which is now so fitly employed at the head of the War Department.

The winter which ushered in the year 1864, and the camp at Strawberry Plains, in East Tennessee, was the "Valley Forge" of the Twenty-third Corps. The raising of the siege of Knoxville was after the wagon roads to the Ohio river, two hundred miles away, had become impassable from the fall rains. No railroad communication existed; neither food nor clothing could be procured from the distant depots of supply; the surrounding country was exhausted, and our men were left to shiver in their rags, their frames debilitated by rations so reduced in quantity and quality that we shrunk from estimating the small proportion they bore to the regulation allowance. The minute account of that winter campaign, and a just tribute to the patriotic heroism of the men who, in the midst of all their sufferings, re-enlisted by whole regiments for a new terms of "three years, or during the war,"—is a tribute the Army of the Ohio owes to its heroes of the rank and file, and would be a military memoir which would give the proceedings of an Army Society real value to the future historian.

The 1st of May, 1864, found the Army of the Ohio taking its place as the left wing of the Grand Army, and preparing to cross the Georgia line as the campaign of Atlanta opened. Our first union with the combined army was in front of Dalton, where we made the demonstration on the enemy's works east of the ridge, whilst Thomas attacked Buzzard's Roost and Rocky Face, and McPherson was moving through Snake Creek Gap for Resaca. When the Army of the Tennessee had completed its movements, and we were ordered to withdraw from the menacing but exposed and isolated position on the extreme left, retiring in line of battle, over ridges, where the quartz rock seemed never to have lost its original sharpness of angles, and through ravines, tangled, and almost impassable, the enemy's skirmishers following closely our steps, the officers and men of the Cumberland Army, from the crags above, watched the movement, and their applause of its steadiness and precision was grateful to our hearts as a proof that our efforts to cultivate discipline and *aplomb* had not been in vain, and that we were received as equals by the men who had fought at Stone River and Chickamauga. Other compliments, subsequently received, may have sounded better in general orders, but none were ever more satisfactory to the recipients than when we were told, with hearty voice, in rough camp phrase, that our comrades of the other armies were convinced we " would do to tie to."

Our initiation was complete, and the bloody conflict at Resaca followed quickly, where we left many a brave fellow by the banks of Camp Creek. Then came the crossing of the Oostenaula, the new concentration about Kingston and Cassville, with the accompanying combats, the crossing of the Etowah, and the advance on Kenesaw and Marietta. Sometimes on the right wing, sometimes on the left, constantly on a flank, we shared with the Army of the Tennessee the rapid work of the campaign, the solid masses of the Cumberland usually occupying the centre, and giving momentum to the whole.

At the crossing of the Chattahoochie the Army of the Ohio had the post of honor, and the brilliant strategy of our General-in-Chief was not balked by any lack of skill or dash in the execution. It would be hard to select a more stimulating martial scene than the passage of that important river; or one in which all the details of dramatic effect were more complete. Beneath the cloudless skies of a warm and lazy summer day, the Twenty-third Corps marched silently under the cover of the ridges skirting the river, till Soap Creek was reached, where Colonel Buel's canvas pontoons were quickly framed and launched, the overhanging woods and tortuous course of the brook hiding the work from the enemy's outpost on the opposite shore of the river, behind whose precipitous hills Johnston lay, his attention fixed upon the masses of the great army encamped at the railroad-crossing several miles below. So unsuspicious of danger were the enemy's outpost, opposite, that a Georgia soldier of the detachment was writing a cheering letter to his wife at home, telling her to have no anxiety for him, as there were no Yankees within miles of them, when his writing was rudely interrupted, not to be resumed, and the half-finished letter was left to tell at once its pathetic story of household anxieties and troubles, and the completeness of the enemy's surprise. As if by magic, a long line of blue-coated skirmishers issued from the wooded hills into the bottom land; a regiment dashed into a difficult ford above; another, in the white pontoons, shot from the mouth of the creek, rowed by stout arms, that worked with a will; a few shots from the single cannon on the hill, upon the southern side; a rattling musketry fire from the covering skirmishers; the boats are over; the men are formed, and go up the slope on the run with bayonets fixed; capturing the gun, and meeting on the crest their comrades who had crossed by the ford; whilst the panic stricken outpost fly to Johnston's camp with the portentous news that the line of the Chattahoochie was broken. An hour's work of the nimble pontooniers puts down the bridge, and, before the enemy can move to resist the crossing, the whole *corps* is impregnably entrenched on the heights, and a *tête de pont* secured from which the army may move out at leisure.

Then came the closing in upon Atlanta, and Hood's well-conceived effort to crush our left, after making a *ruse* of withdrawing all his forces into the works of Atlanta; an effort which was foiled, though the loss of the noble McPherson made it a costly day to us. Sherman's headquarters were that day at the "Howard House" with the Army of the Ohio, and we love to remember how his usual nervous restlessness changed to quiet, smoothly moving work, and suavity of manner as the affair became serious.

My time will not permit even a hasty sketch of the operations about Atlanta; of the change to an aggressive policy on the part of the enemy, after Hood relieved Johnston; of the manner in which their forces were hurled against our earthworks, till, in the chaffing between pickets, the rebels began to say, with bitter humor, that they had about enough men left for "another killing." Still less can I follow up the interesting episode of the October movements, and the daring strategy of Hood in his march toward Tennessee, which might have succeeded with another opponent, and have brought our whole army north of the river, but which was met by a still more daring move, the march to the sea, for which English critics find no other parallel than Marlborough's famous march from the Low Countries to Blenheim on the Danube. At Rome, in Georgia, the Army of the Cumberland was divided; our Army of the Ohio going back with the Fourth Corps to operate against Hood, and the Army of Georgia was organized from the remainder of General Thomas' command. When we parted with Sherman at Rome, he expressed his faith that the march to the sea would be unimpeded, and that we who were remanded to Tennessee would find the fighting, if there was to be any. We found it, at Franklin and Nashville, and we will only say of it, that we did not mean that our comrades of the grand army should be ashamed

of us. Sherman knew into whose hands he had committed
the important task of foiling Hood; and Thomas and Schofield
were fully equal to their work: more than this, they would
not thank me for saying.

The nation was slow in gaining full knowledge of that
Tennessee campaign, and there is room for doubt whether
it is yet fully understood. The motives for the delay in
making the attack upon Hood, at Nashville, are perhaps pretty
well comprehended, and the result so brilliantly vindicated
the Fabian policy and the inflexible adherence of our commander, in that important battle, to what he knew to be right,
that words are not now needed on that point. I believe,
however, that the strategy of the enemy will, as a matter
of military science, be approved by the final verdict of competent critics, and it will be more and more clearly seen that
Hood's movements upon Nashville was not the random blow
of a madman, but a move in the military game which, though
of a desperate character, was wisely and boldly pushed, in
view of the desperate circumstances in which the Confederacy
was placed by Sherman's march upon Savannah. The game
was played of necessity for the whole or none, and we won
it, thanks to the God of battles, and to the courage and skill
of Thomas and Schofield, who had no child's play to deal
with. Hood's original movement against our line of communications, when we were at Atlanta, was a daring attempt to
transfer the theatre of operations out of Georgia and into
Tennessee again. Our chase of him to Galesville, in Alabama,
seemed to warrant him in believing he would be successful,
and he kept on through that state, always in reach of communication with the South, manifestly expecting us to follow him.
A mediocre commander would have done it; a timid one
would have put the whole army upon the railroad, and have
sought to head the enemy off before he could reach Nash-

ville. Either policy would have been a substantial success
for the Rebellion. Hood was, however, pitted against a
boldness and originality more than equal to his own. When
it became evident that the enemy could not be overtaken and
forced into a decisive engagement, the march to the sea, a true
stroke of military genius, was instantly determined upon, and
the Fourth and Twenty-third Corps alone were detached and
sent to Nashville to make head against Hood, until General
A. J. Smith's command, coming from the West, might restore
something like equality to Thomas' army, and enable him
to take the aggressive, whilst Sherman went into the very heart
of the Confederacy to take its life, and make its two arms
at Richmond and Nashville useless, if not powerless.

Hood's first daring conception failed, because it was met by
a more audacious and able one. When, then, he learned that
Sherman was back at Atlanta, it was too late to regain his
lost position, and the only possible means of bringing his
adversary back was by a *coup d'etat* against Thomas before
he could concentrate force enough to oppose him. Here our
game in Middle Tennessee became the dilatory one, and Schofield's work was to hold Hood back till Thomas had prepared
at Nashville to meet him. Hence our delay at Pulaski till
Hood had left Lawrenceburg, and the race to Columbia to
secure the crossing of Duck River, our infantry advance reaching the place just in time to save our cavalry from being
driven out of it. Hence, also, our delay at Columbia till the
last moment—even till one of the enemy's *corps* was in our
rear at Spring Hill, where, however, by some inconceivable
fatuity, Cheatham allowed us to make an unmolested flank
march, by night, within musket shot of his camp-fires. These
hair-breadth escapes were not rashly incurred, for General
Schofield had calculated the minutes, and knew that his veterans
could out-manœuver by night marches all the enemy's move-

ments in the short winter days; and, whether by day or night, we were ready for an attack. Every hour we stayed was gained for the concentration at Nashville, and the skill of our commander was turning our perils to the great advantage of the purposes of the campaign.

At Franklin we were obliged to offer battle, to give our trains time to ford the Harpeth, and Hood very rightly judged that if he could drive us into the river, nothing could stop his march to the Ohio. He delivered, therefore, a series of attacks, more pertinaciously obstinate and determined than any we had before experienced. The field was without obstructions, our defensive works were only a hastily constructed breast-work of earth, and it was the fairest possible test of the problem whether courage and numbers could, by a direct attack in front, take such a line from men of equal courage and discipline, armed with Springfield rifles. The result seemed to prove that the fire may be made too withering for any troops to preserve their organization under it. Breech-loading weapons would leave still less doubt of it. An event not included in the plan of our defence, seemed, for the first hour, to give the enemy reasonable hope of success, but though their repeated assaults obliged us to renew our fire at intervals till late in the night, at midnight we were unmolested in obeying our orders to withdraw, and complete our concentration at Nashville the following day, December 1, 1864.

Up to this point Hood's conduct of the campaign seems to me to have been on true military principles, and the risks he took to have been warranted by an ordinary calculation of the chances of war. Taking into account his great losses at Franklin, particularly the extraordinary fact of the death or disabling of thirteen general officers (a conclusive proof of the desperation with which the assaults were made), his policy in continuing the advance to Nashville may well be questioned. We must not forget, however, that he was ignorant whether our losses were not almost as great as his, and of the extent of the reinforcements Thomas might receive. The cause of the Confederacy was at such a pass that even a halt, whilst Sherman was in the heart of Georgia, would be ruin, and he was under a kind of necessity to keep up the appearance of aggressive action That his doing so imposed upon the country a false opinion of his strength, was plainly manifest in the nervousness every where felt and expressed at the delay in delivering the return blow at Nashville. Even the most competent judges at a distance began to question whether Hood were not master of the situation, and we may, therefore, fairly concede that he seemed to have ground for reasonable hope. Fortunately our commander at Nashville was a man of Washingtonian character and will, and knowing that his country's cause depended upon his *being* right and not upon his merely *seeming* so, he waited with immoveable firmness for the right hour to come. It came, and with it a justification of both his military skill and his own self-forgetful patriotism, so complete and glorious that it would be a mere waste of words for me to talk about it. Our choice of the anniversary of that memorable event for our reunion is itself a proof of our estimate of its importance. I have enlarged upon the events which led to it, because I think they have not been fully understood, and because the Army of the Ohio and its commander had a larger responsibility and a more personal interest in them. At Nashville we were relatively a smaller fraction of the national forces, and a description of its incidents comes more properly from our brothers of the Cumberland Army.

During our operations about Nashville, the cavalry *corps* of the Army of the Ohio was not idle. Under the command and leadership of General Stoneman, an expedition into Southwestern Virginia was made, which, for rapidity of movement, and completeness of execution, considering the inclemency of the season, was not surpassed by any expedition of the kind during the war. With the two divisions under his command, General Stoneman penetrated the enemy's country to Saltville, destroyed the important salt works there, together with much material of war; captured twenty-two pieces of artillery, and so routed and destroyed the enemy's forces under Breckinridge, that East Tennessee was never again troubled by a hostile presence. Again, in March, 1865, whilst we of the main body of the Army of the Ohio were engaged in operations, to which I shall presently allude, General Stoneman made another important expedition out of East Tennessee into South-western Virginia, destroying the railroads by which escape from Richmond was possible for Lee's army, and performing brilliant and valuable services which, but for the fact that it occurred during the general crash of the Rebellion, would have attracted universal attention. A little later, the same commander, with his dashing horsemen, had almost succeeded in capturing the person of Jefferson Davis, whose escort surrendered, but who himself, by changing his direction of flight toward the Atlantic coast, escaped for the moment, but only to fall quickly into the hands of General Wilson and his gallant troopers.

I have thus sketched the outline of the exploits of our cavalry *corps* to the end of the war for the sake of a closer connection of the narrative, and will now ask you to return for a moment to the operations of the Ohio army in Middle Tennessee.

No one who was there will be likely to forget the drenching winter rain-storm in which the Battle of Nashville ended; nor the chase after the routed enemy to the Tennessee river, by roads which were one deep and continuous mire, and through chilling alternations of rain and snow. Hardly was the river reached, when the Army of the Ohio received orders, at Clifton, not far above Pittsburg Landing, to proceed by river and rail to Washington, and thence, by sea, to the mouth of Cape Fear river,

in North Carolina. From a winter campaign in the valley of the
Tennessee, we proceeded without delay to another winter campaign on the Atlantic coast, some two thousand miles distant, by
our route of travel; and our Western troops had to add
to their experience the pleasure of being cooped up in trans-
ports at sea, during a storm, off Cape Hatteras. February and
March were occupied with the capture of Wilmington, the
advance from Newberne, the battle of Kingston, and in the
construction of railways from the coast to Goldsboro, where we
again met our old comrades of the armies of Tennessee and
Georgia, coming up through South Carolina to complete their
tour through the Confederacy. Again under our old chief,
we marched against our old adversary, Joe Johnston, and, at
Greensboro, on the eastern slope of the same mountain chain
whose western face had been so familiar to us a year before,
we had the honor of receiving the arms and issuing the paroles
of the only remaining army of the Rebellion. In these operations in North Carolina, we received into our organization of
the Army of the Ohio, the Tenth Corps, which had recently
done memorable service in the capture of Fort Fisher, and
that gallant body of men, under the command of General Terry,
was made free of the brotherhood of the Western army, though
they were Eastern men all, and had never served west of the
Alleghanies.

It would be pleasant to linger longer over these scenes,
and to touch upon some of the peculiar points of interest
in a campaign among the swamps of the Carolina coast, for
all who are represented here did not march through the Salk-
chatchie. My time, however, is too nearly exhausted to permit
me to do this, or even to attempt to portray the enthusiastic
joy of the meeting at Goldsboro, and the still wilder tumult
of rejoicing when, on the march to Raleigh, we got the news
that Grant *had* "fought it out on that line," and that Lee had

surrendered. The two great brothers-in-arms, who were almost brothers in blood by virtue of the singularly unselfish friendship which has honored them scarcely less than their great deeds, met at Raleigh and congratulated each other that, by God's good providence, the work begun at Donelson and Henry was accomplished, and that now they would be able to say, in tones of authority, to the men who had made war upon the nation's existence, "Cease your Rebellion!" The recent recognition by that nation of the fact that the remainder of the road to the permanent and enduring peace we long for, can be best marked out by him whose modest sagacity and heroism, whose unfaltering faith in his country's destiny, was our guide through the gloom of our great struggle, is proof to the world that Republics are not altogether ungrateful, nor do they require great trumpet-blowing of one's own merits to make them know a true leader when they see him. With the Administration of the country in such hands, and the Generalship of the Army committed to his twin-brother in renown and in patriotism, who will dare doubt that we "shall have peace?" The Republic longs most earnestly for unity of sentiment as well as for unity of government, — for unity of hearts as well as unity of territory, and we may rightfully hope that an administration in which the even justice of the civil ruler is meted out with the honorable courtesy which always marks the true soldier, will win back all American hearts to true allegiance to the nation.

I fear that my time is too nearly spent to permit me to say many things I desire to speak of. It has been impossible for me even to notice the many brilliant acts which characterized the career of the subordinate commands of our Army of the Ohio, much less to give the well-earned meed of praise to the individual officers and men who deserved it. I have tried to do no more than give a meagre sketch of what may be properly regarded the distinguishing features of the Army as a whole. Before closing my remarks, however, I would like to suggest a few queries regarding the use which may be made of an Army Society to illustrate and perpetuate the details of many events which will otherwise be in danger of being forgotten and lost.

Social gatherings have a great charm of their own, yet there may be danger that we shall be reproached hereafter with having neglected to preserve for our posterity the facts and reminiscences which will be invaluable material for the ultimate history of the war, but which will be lost forever, unless put into permanent form within the lifetime of those who are here present. The late Rebellion was the first great war in which rifled ordnance was used on a large scale for general purposes of the field as well as of the siege. It was also significant for the unprecedented use of intrenchments and earthworks as a feature of modern campaigning. It came in one of the revolutionary epochs in scientific invention, when the intelligent discussion of the questions which arose, carried on by those who were the eye-witnesses of the events which suggest the problems in the art of war, can not fail to be productive of increased knowledge of the art itself. Our nation may be so happy as never again to be involved in a warlike conflict, but the probabilities of peace will not be diminished by the spread of intelligence on the subject of military affairs.

The points in which a campaign in this country must necessarily differ from an European one, are extremely numerous. The features which marked this as a strife different from any other, either here or elsewhere, were scarcely less numerous. All of these deserve to be carefully and critically examined, and could we, in some permanent organization like those of the better historical societies of the country, meet for real business and discussion of such matters, or even, without frequent

large meetings, have an executive committee calling out and
publishing communications throwing light upon either the
theories or the facts, the transactions of such an association
could not fail to have lasting value to the world. Take only
a few of the many questions which would crowd upon us, as
examples of what I have referred to. To what extent is the
face of the country in the states where our most active campaigning was carried on, one which would be regarded
as impracticable for military operations in Europe?
Whether you consider the almost impenetrable thickets of
pine which we constantly met in Georgia, where it was frequently impossible for a horse to make his way between the
saplings, and where it was unsafe to neglect constant reference
to the compass to keep one's course and direction; or the
immense swamps of the Carolinas, where deployment of a line
was often a physical impossibility; would not the ordinary
rules of military science need a totally new construction and
application? Again, look at the almost total absence of any
roads better than a mere wagon track through a wilderness,
and the consequent dependence upon long and exposed lines
of railways for supplies, the country roads, even where only a
few miles of them were used, soon becoming mere quag-
mires; and was not this a new feature in war between
immense armies, calling for entirely new combinations and
expedients to surmount the difficulties? When you add to
these things the fact that the theatre of war was of such
enormous extent, and the movements of the later campaigns
on so vast a scale, in distance as well as in armament, as
to produce a combination of obstacles to be overcome, perhaps
quite unprecedented, must there not of necessity be room for
investigations abounding in interest, and details of the expedients invented, with their practical application, which would

be of immense value if they could only be preserved in some tangible and permanent form?

There are practical questions, also, with regard to arms and equipment, which are not yet settled. Were we right in adhering to the extent we did to the brass twelves, known as the Napoleon gun? Were not the three-inch rifled pieces proven to be equally valuable for throwing canister at short range as they were for throwing shell at long distances? and did not our experience prove that we ought to have rejected all but rifled artillery, even for light field work? With regard to small arms, also, have we had any satisfactory summing up of our experience as bearing upon the question of the balance between waste of ammunition and useless firing when breech-loaders were used, and the lack of rapidity in a pinch when Springfield or Enfield rifles were relied upon? We know that a wide divergence of opinion existed among us on this point, and the facts and theories ought to be brought face to face.

When we turn to the problems which were peculiar to the circumstances under which this war arose, we find queries arising of even greater interest than those I have referred to. What shall we say of the manner in which our great army was raised? Were we right or wrong in depending so long upon volunteering? Was the single battalion regiment the proper unit of organization? Was it wisdom or folly to try to preserve the old regular army organization, instead of scattering it at once to be used in leavening and instructing the whole volunteer force? What was the effect of allowing the regimental officers to be commissioned by the several states, and the promotion of the officers of the line to depend upon the state executives? How much more did the war cost us in lives and money, by reason of our system of constantly organizing new regiments, instead of filling up the skeleton battalions that were already doing duty in the field? The questions that troop up before us, when we reflect upon the subject, are legion, and I doubt whether we can say we have done our full duty by our generation, if we do not make some systematic effort to answer them.

In 1863, as Burnside was preparing his movement into East Tennessee, a friend put into my hands Kinglake's first volume on the Crimean war, then just published. Like many of you, probably, I was then pondering the problem whether the standing armies of Europe would not have been saved by their traditionary knowledge from many of the blunders through which we all had to learn our duty, when our vast army was so suddenly called into existence. I had been inclined to think that perhaps we were feeling our way bunglingly toward skill in arms, and paying dearly for our experience, by reason of lack of special education for our work. I think scarce any thing else could have so greatly increased my confidence and hope as the perusal of that single volume. It was not such a military history as a soldier would have written, and, as every body knows, the author seemed often to tell as if it were praiseworthy the very things a military man would have chosen to keep in the background. Perhaps that very thing constituted the value of the work. It showed that the traditions of standing armies do not and can not save the soldier from the necessity of learning his business by experience in the field, and that systems of administration based upon wars in Flanders will not do for an army landed upon the desert shores of the Crimea. It was a photograph of the daily life of the camp, in which our experience would enable us to discern at once that we had been at least as free from glaring blunders of administration, of strategy, or of tactics, as the combined army under Lord Raglan. I admit this is not saying much, and no one will mistake it for bragging; but it was to me a great comfort and ground of hope to find, by good testimony, that the inevitable imperfections and shortcomings of new troops, put suddenly in the field for the first time in their lives, were incident to all the armies of the great military powers of Europe, and were not peculiar to our own condition or system of organization.

The difficulties we had at the outset, and our modes of overcoming them, will, if fairly and faithfully told, benefit all who may come after us. It may save our posterity, some day, from paying quite so dearly for the lessons of experience as we were forced to pay. A near view diminishes something, it is true, of the general glitter which gilds a great campaign as it is narrated in ordinary history, but what is added in real human sympathy and interest more than makes up for the proverbial belittling effect of familiarity. We ought to be willing to be known and estimated for exactly what we were, and to be the first to criticise, calmly, our own part in a great event. We may thus render it a truly intelligible thing, instead of a marvelous romance, in which the general outline may be filled up according to each reader's fancy.

A full knowledge of all the circumstances of war will only make a civilized nation strive more wisely for peace : and as the improvements in the efficiency of arms make nations more careful how they invoke the judgment of the God of battles, so an acquaintance with all the cost and all the horrors which follow in the train of great military expeditions, may make a people more and more averse to strife, unless the cause be one as holy as that which called upon us in 1861 — the preservation of the Nation itself! With all our sad experience of comrades fallen, of a country desolated, of homes destroyed, of labors and sufferings of all kinds endured, and of unexampled burdens to be borne, I believe there is no one here who would hesitate one instant to draw the sword again to avert a like peril from our land. And should any emergency arise, (which God forbid,) that would call us again to enter upon a great conflict for national existence, I believe I speak the sentiments of all when I say that we would wish no better leaders, and could find no stauncher comrades, than we had in our old organization of the Grand Army of the West.

ORATION OF GENERAL COGSWELL.

Fellow-Soldiers: Four years ago, last Thursday, many of us here present, after a delightful and unmolested trip across the country from Atlanta, reached the rice swamps of Southern Georgia, and the outer gates of the city of Savannah, and there, dieting upon rice, after the luxurious chickens and sweet potatoes of Middle Georgia, we awaited the order to advance and take that city. But when, three days afterward, Hazen had foreshadowed, at McAlister, what would be the fate of Savannah, if Hardee should wait, that rebel commander, either not believing that this was the "last ditch" of the Confederacy, or else too much of a gentleman to welcome us to those "hospitable graves" we used to hear of, soon left our front, and Savannah gave up to us its keys. The Atlantic coast was reached at last, Sherman's great march to the sea was accomplished, and to military history was added a brilliant and most famous page. The beginning of the end of a wicked Rebellion had come, and the bright morning of peace was breaking in upon us.

More than three years and a half have now passed since we laid down our arms and were finally disbanded; since turning from the arts of war, we took up the better arts of peace. And although now "neither wars nor rumors of wars" disturb us, but peace, rather, is every where assured, and the old flag, more than ever now, the emblem of true nationality, liberty and valor, floats under every sky, respected and unassailed, yet are we, the former members of Sherman's armies, once more assembled at the call of our commanders. But it is to meet as citizens, quietly, and in peace, in a loyal city, with no clank of the sabre, no sound of the musket, no rumbling of the artillery, no wagons blocking up the roads, and with neither war nor panoply of war. We meet not because we are soldiers, but because we have been soldiers, and because here, and at this time, we want to revive the associations of our past; to recall to memory the experiences of the camp, the bivouac, and the field; to strengthen those friendships which are friendships only known to those who have fought by each other's sides, and which are not broken by every breeze that blows. We meet to refresh our memory of those deeds which go to make up the brilliant record of our countrymen in arms on so many fields of battle—in fine, we meet to bring again to mind that communion of exposure, of hardship, of daring, of pleasure and of pain, of glory and of victory, which has already made us, present and absent, brothers forever more. And as one of that fortunate and "goodly company," I am asked to speak for the Army of Georgia, for the left wing of Sherman's army, in its march through Georgia and the Carolinas.

My friends, it would be difficult for the ablest and most gifted to do justice to the merits of any army, or *corps*, or even organization of the great Union army of our country. Much more difficult, then, will it be for me, unused to such labors, to speak in fitting and satisfactory terms of that army, one part of which dates its record of service back to the glories of "Mill Spring," and the other to those "seven days" of heroic fighting on the peninsula. Each of the two *corps* of that army, having a record complete and independent of its own—both contemplated with pride and pleasure, both pregnant with glorious memories, both illumined by its illustrious and heroic dead, and both blended only to be made brighter, by participation together in the great military achievement of the age — Sherman's march — I feel as if mine was a double duty, and, for that reason, that I should be entitled to your charity and forbearance. If I should simply say, for the Army of Georgia, that it had tried to do its duty, wherever put, and that it was more properly for others to say how well that duty had been performed, perhaps I should then have said all that would become a member of that army in its behalf. Should I point you to its deeds, which are written in the war records of both the East and West of our country, it would be sufficient, and there its fame could rest, I think, safely and forever. But if I should conclude by saying that this organization had the honor to form the left wing of Sherman's army, and with its gallant comrade, the Army of the Tennessee, as the right wing, to march to the sea, and through the Carolinas; that at Raleigh it witnessed and stood ready to help enforce the surrender of the last army of the enemy this side of the Mississippi, that it marched thence to Washington, and was soon after disbanded only because there were no "new worlds to conquer"—it would seem as though then I should have said enough in its glory and in its praise. But when to this is added that the names of Thomas, Rosecrans and Buell, of Hooker, of Slocum and Howard, of Palmer and Williams, and Davis, and Mower adorn the rolls of that army, and that under such leaders, no troops could be but brave and serviceable, surely then I might stop, my task completed.

After the campaign of Atlanta, it became necessary for General Sherman to divide his army, sending one part back to Nashville, under General Thomas, to take care of Hood, and taking the rest with him to the sea, when the Fourteenth Corps, under Davis, and the Twentieth Corps, under Williams, in all about thirty-two thousand men, became known as the left wing of the Army of Georgia, and afterwards, at Goldsboro, as the Army of Georgia, under General Slocum. The

Twentieth Corps, which had served from the beginning with the Army of the Potomac, where it had shared in all the varied experience of that noble army, from Bull Run to Gettysburg, came west to Chattanooga in the fall of 1863, and joined the Army of the Cumberland. The Fourteenth Corps was at Chattanooga, forming a part of this army, to which it had belonged since the army organization, and, indeed, was the nucleus from which the Army of the Cumberland was reorganized in the early part of 1863. This *corps* had participated in all the battles of its army, from Stone River to Chickamauga, at which latter place, under a leader who never yet gave up a fight until he had thoroughly finished it, it had added to its record its brightest page. It had also shared largely in the victories of the West, aided in the pursuit to Corinth after Shiloh, and, in Kentucky, taking part in the battle of Perrysville, or Chaplin Hills. After the Fourteenth Corps at Chickamauga, after "Joe Hooker's fight above the clouds," after the efforts of both *corps* at Mission Ridge and Ringgold, after Resaca and Peach Tree Creek, after Jonesboro and the capture of Atlanta, it is needless to say that the "Acorn" and the "Star" became readily united in mutual sympathy and respect. If one could point to its Mill Spring, and Stone River, the other could point to its Antietam and Gettysburg. If one could mention its Thomas making his determined and successful stand at Chickamauga, the other could mention its Slocum performing the same good service at Chancellorsville.

The Fourteenth and Twentieth Corps were prepared to be friends, when they were united in November, 1864, and then, on the left, with the Army of the Tennessee on the right, and Kilpatrick's cavalry, they commenced to march towards the sea; the left wing moving in two columns from Atlanta, *via* Stone Mountain and Social Circle, to Madison, also *via*

Decatur, Covington and Shady Dale, and to Milledgeville *via* Eatonton; thence across the Oconee to Sandersville; to Louisville by the Georgia Central, as far as the Ogeechee, and by Farris' Bridge; thence to the works of Savannah itself, *via* Birdsville, Millen, Springfield, and also by way of Jacksonboro, Waynesboro, and the Augusta and Savannah railroad, capturing two of the enemy's gunboats on the Savannah river, destroying, as it marched, every railroad as it came across or along its path (in all, over one hundred and nineteen miles), burning all the cotton (about fourteen thousand bales), all the bridges, and all the hay, grain and fodder that were not consumed or carried with it, and taking from the country subsistence enough for an army twice its size. I have here a statement, made up at the time, of subsistence taken on the Carolina campaign, by a single brigade of this army, which may be interesting to you, and perhaps may refresh your memory as to the contents of our larder at that time. It is as follows, estimated in pounds: 21,200 flour, 40,388 corn meal, 52,426 salt meat, 15.900 bacon, 1,750 ham, 2.325 lard, 300 dried fruit, 1,108 sugar, 155 tobacco, 4,720 beans, 1,225 salt, 317,960 corn, 4 barrels of sorghum, 2,540 head of fowl, 531 head of cattle, 260 horses and mules, 2,409 bales of cotton destroyed, and 3 tons of fodder. I tell our friends at home that when they consider that this was but the collection of one brigade out of thirty-five other brigades in the whole army, they then can form some estimate of what was taken from the country on those two marches, *as well as some estimate of what was left.*

The left wing reached the defences of the city of Savannah on the 10th of December, where, with the Twentieth Corps resting its left upon the Savannah river, and the Fourteenth Corps on its right, it commenced its part of the investment of that city, and it is believed that during this march this army collected its share of subsistence (though it had not the experience in this line of the right wing), that it did its share of railroad and cotton destruction, its assigned part of marching and skirmishing, and at the end was ready for its part of the capture of Savannah. The Second Division of the Twentieth Corps occupied and guarded the captured city, and in regard to that occupation, and also in regard to the effect of this march upon the *morale* of the armies, General Sherman speaks as follows: "The behavior of our troops in Savannah has been so manly, so quiet, so perfect, that I take it as the best evidence of discipline and true courage. Never was a hostile city, filled with women and children, occupied by a large army with less disorder, or more system, order and good government." And 'twas here in Savannah that we learned of that victory, one of the most thorough and complete of the war, of which this day is the fourth anniversary—the great battle of Nashville—won by that indomitable soldier, who never yet lost a battle—that perfect master of his profession—George H. Thomas, together with the brave Armies of the Cumberland and Ohio. And we of the Army of Georgia were glad to see that the organization from which we had been taken—the Army of the Cumberland—was able to meet and cope with the great responsibilities devolved upon it, and add new lustre to its name. On the 15th and 16th of January, 1865, the left wing pushed over Jackson and Ward, to the South Carolina shores, opposite Savannah, and afterwards, at Sister's Ferry, crossed the remainder of its army, and commenced its part of the campaign of the Carolinas, moving to Purcysburg, Robertsville, Lawtonville and Allandale—and by Beaufort's bridge to Graham's Station, on the South Carolina railroad, which it destroyed as far as Johnston's Station; thence across the North and South Edisto; thence to the Santee river, opposite Columbia; from here

northward, crossing the Saluda at Mount Zion's Church, and
the Broad river, at Wateree Creek, to Winsboro, which it
reached on the 20th of February, and here destroying the
Charlotte and South Carolina railroad to Cornwall. We
moved over the Catawba river at Rocky Mountain Ferry, and
after a tedious march by way of Chesterfield, reached Sneeds-
boro; thence crossing the Great Pedee, this army moved to
Fayetteville by way of Love's and McFarland's bridges, over
the Lumber river. This Lumber river, as I remember it,
was a stream, seeming, at the time, the widest and most
vexatious we had ever crossed. Owing to heavy rains, it
was impossible to tell where it began, and before we had
reached the other shore we had about made up our minds
that we had struck it length-wise instead of cross-wise — but,
finally, the rains abated and the waters subsided, and landing
at last on the other side of this Jordan, we reached Fayetteville, March 11th. On the 13th we crossed Cape Fear
river, and on the 16th met the enemy in the battle of Averasboro, in which action the Twentieth Corps was particularly
engaged. It is, perhaps, sufficient to say of this fight that
we did not turn from our course, and that the enemy did.
Our loss was twelve officers and sixty-five men killed, and
four hundred and seventy-seven wounded — none missing;
while one hundred and twenty-eight of the enemy's dead were
buried by us; and one hundred and seventy-five prisoners,
three pieces of artillery, one caisson, and several ambulances
were captured. And now, crossing South river, on the
Goldsboro road, the whole of the enemy's force, once more
under their ablest General, Joe Johnston, was encountered by
the left wing, three days later, in the battle of Bentonville,
in which the hardest fighting fell upon the Fourteenth Corps,
the loss being nine officers and one hundred and forty-five
men killed; fifty-one officers and eight hundred and sixteen

7

men wounded; three officers and two hundred and twenty-three men missing; rebel dead buried, one hundred and sixty-seven, and three hundred and thirty-eight prisoners captured. It may be said of this engagement, that the enemy, though considerably outnumbering us, was handsomely repulsed and severely punished, and that a well-conceived plan of the enemy to crush the left wing of the army was completely defeated, and when, next day, the Army of the Tennessee, always sure to turn up when it was wanted, swung in upon his left and rear, that the last obstacle between us all and the final surrender was overcome.

From here, crossing the Neuse at Cox's bridge, this army moved to Goldsboro, where it rested a few days, meeting its old friends of the Army of the Ohio—with its well-earned laurels of the battle of Franklin—hearing of the good news of Richmond's fall, and then moving to Smithfield to learn of of the still better tidings of Lee's surrender, and the complete success of all military operations under General Grant; and thence to Raleigh, where came, on the 26th of April, that surrender of our enemy, which had been so fairly won, and the end of the war, which was so justly due. Starting on the 1st of May, the Army of Georgia marched up, by way of Richmond, to Washington, for the grand review, and then it disappeared to appear no more again, except in its appropriate place in history; living no more, save as it lives in the hearts and memories of those of whom it was composed; who will, while life shall last, hold dear its associations, and ever cling fondly to its name, and fame, and record. And if, during this period, from Atlanta to Savannah, Raleigh, and Washington, the two *corps* of this army achieved any thing that was glorious or victorious; if they performed any deeds which they now remember with gladness, and with pride; if they added to their fame or record; if they did their full measure of duty, wherever put; if, at Averasboro or Bentonville, they performed their part with gallantry and satisfaction; or did any thing worthy of brave soldiers, and true American soldiers, it was because they were united in purpose, sympathy, and respect, under a well chosen leader, brave and cool, faithful and impartial, Henry W. Slocum, and because they felt that they would be bravely supported on every hand by their associates and comrades of the armies of the Cumberland, the Ohio, and the Tennessee; conscious that each of these armies would perform its full share, and more; and because they felt and knew that they were a part of a well-regulated and "one stupendous whole," and that "whole" under the commanding eye of that great military genius of his day and generation, William Tecumseh Sherman.

When I call to mind the Georgia and Carolina marches, starting out that bright November morning, Atlanta in black ruins behind us, with its "pillar of cloud by day," and "its pillar of fire by night;" when I remember the foragers, with their useful, if not ornamental, teams and accompaniments; the pioneers, building the bridges and corduroying the roads almost as fast as we could march; the terrified gaze of the "chivalry" along our line of march; the friendly negro; the sweet potatoes, and corn, and sorghum, and chickens; the deep swamps; the occasional news and gossip from some neighboring column; the well-timed concentration of the columns; the different opinions we used to have as to our final destination, all of them doubtful enough to make us anxious to learn all we could, to study well the maps, and keep on guessing, and just about certain enough to make us feel every night that, at least, we were one day nearer our journey's end — a day's march just sufficing for a day's subsistence — the bummers always hungry, and, therefore, always efficient; how, if one mule gave out, we were sure to find two to take his place before the day was over; the strange and ludicrous contrabands, tumbling into our line of march, just in time to keep a joke or a laugh always passing down the line; the regular *reveille* an hour before morn, the low lands and causeways at the approaches of Savannah; not forgetting those railroads, nor the cotton destroyed, nor the houses vacated by their occupants, and how, after that, sometimes, the ground would seem to be vacated by the *houses* themselves; nor the stores buried in the earth, and unearthed by the foragers; when I remember all these, and the many, many other incidents of those two marches, grand and ludicrous, grave and gay, sad and joyous, the bitter and the sweet, the sunshine and the rain, the labor and the pleasure, the novelty and the complete success, and the great place in history which these two campaigns already take as wonderful and useful military achievements, and they all pass in review before my mind, as they do to-night, I stand in wondering admiration at the view, and, for one, I thank God that I was permitted to take a part in such great events.

But I look back to the waste and destruction which inevitably followed the track of our armies, and to the desolation which we caused with no feelings of exultation or boasting. Look at it as we will, it is no pleasant thing to see a people and a fair country visited with such heavy and severe punishments; to see a people, old and young, driven from their homes, as at Atlanta; burned from their shelter, but not by us, as at Columbia; stripped of their stores, their implements of husbandry and all their means of support; it was a sad sight to behold; it is a sad thought to dwell upon; but I solemnly believe that all the acts done by orders on those two marches were just and necessary, and that by reason of them, full as much as by any thing else, the war was ended, the shedding of fraternal blood was stopped, and the deluded people of the South made readier to accept the issue of the contest. And I venture to say that, when peace came, it was no where welcomed more gladly, or earnestly, or sincerely, than by the people whose lot it was to fall in the track of Sherman's army, in its march from the' mountains to the sea, and through the Carolinas. So, too, is sad the recollection of prison pens, and their starving victims—starved, too, in the heart of a country in which we found the richest supplies. So, too, is sad the sight of Union graves all over the land, of youth no generation could afford to lose, fallen in defence of their Government and their flag, which the bad passions of bad men had determined should be overthrown by a civil war, as unjustifiable and without cause as it was cruel, bloody, and unholy.

And here, my friends and comrades, I bring to a close my assigned part of this evening's entertainment—it is for the historian, in after years, to give our armies their just places in history. It was not expected of me that I should more than glance here and there, within the brief limit of my time, and I have but referred hastily and most generally to that army which was, for a time, the left wing of that command which, under Sherman, commencing at Chattanooga, marched over one thousand miles, fought over fifteen battles, besieged and captured two great cities from the enemy, took three State capitals, forced the evacuation of Charleston, destroyed more than two hundred miles of the enemy's railroads, overcoming large mountains and difficult rivers almost without number, smashing the shell of the Rebellion, and compelling the surrender of its old and hard-fought enemy—Johnston's army—and thus closing the last campaign of our great civil war; a war which called forth resources unknown to ourselves and surprising to the world. It came upon us when our Government was unfamiliar with large armies, and was not realizing the necessities of the hour; when our people were ignorant of arms and warlike ways; but a Government

honest and loyal, and a people brave and patriotic, soon made
themselves equal to the occasion, and before the war was
over, we saw a million and a half of men, armed and in the
field, fighting for the country they loved, and defending the
flag which they adored; with supplies in quantity and quality
unequaled by any government, or in any war; while the
noble women of the land, to every sick and wounded soldier,
provided the sweet comforts of kind nursing, together with
the choicest delicacies, in abundance, their hands could make.
No defeats dampening the ardor of the people; no disasters
weakening their faith; bearing the losses of their sons without
a murmur and without a waver in their purpose; each new
sacrifice but adding new zeal and vigor to their determination; suffering the blunders of their Government, and the
incompetency and inexperience of their officers without dis-
couragement, ever and always strong and inflexible in their
determination that their Government should live — "a Government of the people, by the people, and for the people."
And when the contest was over, we beheld the nation coming out of the civil war, unimpaired, and in all its former
majesty and beauty, "with not a star erased," and bearing in
its arms the lives and freedom of four millions of a new-born
people. Its sacrifices had been great, but its credit had been
strengthened, while the results of the war had proved that a
republican form of government could outlive the greatest peril;
commanding the respect of all the nations of the earth, and
proving, at last, that America was in fact, as well as in song,
"the land of the free, and the home of the brave "—with its
large armies disbanding, and pursuing the avocations of industry and peace at their homes; loving peace better than war,
and only loving war as a means of peace. Who can look
for a moment upon the teachings of that war without having
his faith strengthened, and his hopes brightened in the future

of our country? The nation is strong enough to be magnanimous to its conquered foe, while our people are earnest
and sincere enough, as they have so recently shown, to be
just to the demands of the future, and true to the lessons of
the past. And let us hope that by the experience of war we
have all learned to value the great blessings of peace. Though
the lesson has been stern, yet it has taught us to be pure
and high-minded as a nation, honorable and chaste as citizens.

Let us never forget those who fell fighting bravely at our
sides, nor those they left to mourn and feel their loss. And
let us all, " with malice towards none, with charity for all
(but), with firmness in the right as God gives us to see the
right," so act in the present, and teach our children to act
in the future, that never again shall a free and enlightened
American people be found divided against itself.

THE BANQUET.

In preparing for the grand reunion banquet of the evening of December 16th, it was inevitable that the soldiers of the Reunion Executive Committee should remember what the scenes of soldier communion had been during the long service of the Western armies in the field. How many times had the hard crust been broken, the insufficient and unpalatable meal been partaken, and wasted strength been but poorly replenished, because of the stern necessities, the cruel cost of martial duty! Of the two thousand men who might gather for festive commemoration in the reunion banqueting hall, how large a proportion had known the closest communion with hunger, disease, destruction, and death! Almost daily incidents of army life, had been the depressing burial dirge, the harrowing spectacle of mangled corses, or of comrades emaciated under burdens greater than flesh could bear, and the incessant recurrence of privations and hardships incident to all loss of the precious comforts, and sacred consolations of home. Not that there had been no cheer, and no festival in the camp, or on the march, or under the heavy shadows of dreadful battle. These men had kept the camp cheerful with an ingenious and persistent fortitude unknown before in the annals of military service. They had made every weary march with hopeful patience, from victory to reverse, as well as from reverse to victory, always seeing before the advancing and behind the retreating host the bright presence of justice, and with grand gayety almost of faith trusting *that* Divinity to shape the issues of conflict, while they rough-hewed them as they could. And even in the hours of great darkness, when the fiery lines of doubtful battle were joined, and the soldier only knew to do *his* duty, if possibly the wide and varied struggle might conclude in victory, there had been no lack of readiness to "put a cheerful courage on." The banquets of the camp, of the dusty or the muddy highway, and of fields that ran with blood, when constant courage had to make the best of war rations, and a brave spirit found high festival in what was really lean distress, could not but be brought vividly to mind when the reunion table was to be spread. It should be set, therefore, generously, in token of a long sacrifice ended, and it should be expected that the company to be gathered would be swayed by the old feelings with which, as soldiers, they had snatched hilarity on the hurried and toilsome march, and, for great courage's sake, had made jovial the frequent bivouac with death.

The large hall in which the reunion banquet was held was, in one or two respects, deficient in the requirements of the occasion,—the speeches could not be heard, and, at the supper, the available doors were found wholly insufficient for the ingress and egress of the waiters,—but its wide room, decorated as it was with familiar and famous battle-flags, admirably furnished what was most required—the space and scenery of a festive camp. Though the large company could not be served according to expectation, either with the rich viands of the ample feast, or with the after feast of reason and flow of soul, yet here were the associations of the never-to-be-forgotten war days, memories of the march, the camp and the battle wherever the eye turned, and these were men who had long known how to turn every occasion into good cheer, and to stir among themselves an enthusiasm of good fellow-ship. It was from these circumstances that the banquet was

more successful as a grand good time, such as the actual
camps had witnessed often, and the old, sacred banners had
before looked down upon, than as an occasion of speech-
making. Cut off, unavoidably, from hearing the responses to
the toasts of the evening, and thrown, to some extent, upon
their own resources, the great body of these men of our Western Armies made such high festival as they could, in the
fashion, somewhat, of the real days of the war. In other circumstances it might have been otherwise, and some harsh,
and mainly unjust reflections upon the occasion might have
been saved. But no one who rightly considers this scene, and
how these men had so many times made merry amid the desperate circumstances of war, compelling jollity to do service
with courage, will have any other reflection than that these
were our soldiers, over whom all the storms of the war had
swept, and in whose breasts had burned all the great passions
of the struggle against rebellion. Under such banners and
battle-flags as they had followed through the long course of the
war, hung now around these spacious walls, and amid the
thick-clustering memories of all the old days of heroism, let
the soldier have his brief hour of reunion enthusiasm. Eloquent speeches will survive the hour, and none will turn to
them with more interest than those who failed to hear them
when delivered. The occasion was worthy of eloquence, and
the responses made to the sentiments of the evening, will be
preserved by the soldiers of the Army Societies gathered at
the Banquet as an invaluable memorial.

Lieutenant-General WILLIAM T. SHERMAN presiding, the Banquet programme, after the feast, was as follows:

POEM: BY COLONEL GILBERT N. PIERCE.

I.

Halt the column, rest a moment,
  Stack the guns, the fires light,
Here is foraging in plenty,
  Let us bivouac here to-night.

II.

We have marched in separate columns,
  But have striven nerve and joint
That we all might meet together
  At this grand objective point.

III.

And we're truly grateful, thankful,
  That detachments all appear
Anxious for the work before them,
  Ready for the service here.

IV.

Georgia, Cumberland, Ohio,
  And the grim old Tennessee,
Answer to the call of Sherman,
  Father of the Family.

v.

So you keep your reputation,
   First in love, at feast or fray,
Siege of hearts or siege of fortress,
   Both were carried gallantly.

vi.

So said they, when at his bidding,
   Through the South the army went,
Sweeping like a whirlwind onward,
   Marching through the continent.

vii.

Oh! 'twas glorious, grand, heroic!
   Rushing over hill and plain;
With its mighty recollections,
   How the heart leaps up again,

viii.

How they cheered, and how they rallied,
   How they charged 'mid shot and shell,
How they bore aloft the banner,
   How they conquered! how they fell!

ix.

Fell! Ah, who shall tell their story,
   Those among the brave and best,
Who went down amidst the battle,
   Lyon, Ransom, and the rest.

x.

This the grateful pen hath written:
   Nations in their homage bow,

Myrtle weeps the fallen heroes,
Laurel crowns the living brow.

XI.

Wreathed with immortelles forever,
Men shall in the future tell,
Standing where he nobly perished,
How the brave McPherson fell.

XII.

Fell, amid the storm of battle;
Fell, while millions mourned his name;
Writing on a field historic
Epitaph of endless fame.

XIII.

Fell, ah soldier and civilian.
All of us fell down that day,
Weeping prostrate round the coffin,
Where the martial figure lay.

XIV.

This the cost of human freedom,
Weary hearts that long and wait,
Shadows, on a thousand households,
Sanctified, but desolate.

XV.

Ah! sometimes the friends who've left us,
Joined the army gone before;
Almost seem to bridge the river
'Twixt the near and further shore.

XVI.

But there came an end of fighting,
   Then was your employment done ;
What became of those battalions
   When the victory was won?

XVII

Let me point you to a picture —
   See a million soldiers there,
Flushed with triumph, and with weapons
   Flashing keen, and bright, and bare.

XVIII.

Vanished! Wondrous transformation!
   Where is now that mighty band?
Do they roam a vast banditti,
   Pillaging their native land?

XIX.

Ah! we point to field and workshop ;
   Let the world the moral see ;
There, beneath the dust of labor,
   Toil our veteran soldiery.

XX.

Ye were mighty in the battle,
   On the mountain and the plain ;
But you wrought your greatest triumph
   When you sought your homes again.

XXI.

Sought your homes in peace and quiet,
   Grasping with your strong right hand

Implements of honest labor,
　　Toiling to upbuild the land.

XXII.

He the noblest, truest soldier,
　　Who, when sounds of battle cease,
Mounts from war's uncultured desert
　　Upward to the plains of peace.

XXIII.

Chieftains who have saved a nation
　　Gain the gratitude of men,
But the mightiest of warriors
　　Smiled in *Peace* at Bethlehem.

XXIV.

Peace, you see, hath then her triumphs,
　　And, I hold, that we may reap
From the seed that we have scattered,
　　Thistles, tares, or golden wheat.

XXV.

We have still a work before us ;
　　Let each one his portion take ;
We must serve a while as sailors,
　　Standing on the Ship of State.

XXVI.

Not to fight, but more to brighten,
　　Polish smooth the good ship o'er,
Keeping taut and trim the rigging
　　Of our grand old seventy-four.

XXVII.

Veterans of a hundred battles
Clothed with honors, decked with scars,
Step aboard the good old vessel,
Spread the canvas, man the spars.

XXVIII.

You have kept the ship from sinking,
Carried her past thundering fort;
Take the helm, until you guide her
Surely, safely into port.

XXIX.

When our old commanders lead us
Who was there to say "I can't?"
That expression left the service—
Mustered out, *discharged* by Grant

XXX

Let the silent man of Shiloh
Still the factions angry roar,
Till the mighty wave of Freedom
Rolls unvexed from shore to shore.

XXXI.

Till our brothers, though they wander
North or South, can safely stand,
Writing, speaking, preaching, praying,
What they will throughout the land.

XXXII.

"Long live Liberty and Justice,"
Crush the fetters, break the chain!

8

Let this watchword, if it need be,
  Echo through the land again.

XXXIII.

Not in malice, but in mercy,
  Not in anger, but in love,
Asking what we grant, and only
  Granting what our hearts approve.

XXXIV.

Then the North and South, united
  With the East and West, shall be
Friends, in peace or war together,
  Children of one family.

XXXV

Then "our country," God preserve it!
  With its beauteous flag unfurled,
Reaching out, shall raise the helpless—
  Be the Mecca of the world.

XXXVI.

Comrades! Ye who in the battle
  Stood together, firm and true,
At the shrine of this Reunion
  Dedicate your loves anew.

XXXVII.

Ye are like the trees left standing
  When the fierce tornado's past;
Let the boughs of those remaining
  Twine together firm and fast.

XXXVIII.

Thus combined 'gainst wind and weather,
  Ye will have the strength of all,
And united brave the tempest,
  Or together nobly fall.

XXXIX.

Grand old army! Brave commanders!
  Grim survivors of the fight,
Warm your hearts at memory's altar,
  Press each other's hands to-night.

XL.

And when sounds the last assembly,
  When the guard has gone his round,
May you pitch your tents together,
  On some happier camping ground.

Song by the Glee Club ; — " *The Star Spangled Banner.*"

First Toast ; — *Our Country.*

Speech of General A. H. Terry :

Comrades : To speak fitly on the theme of our country's greatness would require the gift of tongues. Were the great story of her progress fitly told, assembled nations should be the audience, and Time himself should stay his course to listen to the tale.

That in the lapse of but two and a half centuries, a few feeble colonies, planted on the very verge of the continent, struggling against privation and famine, and scarcely able to maintain themselves against the attacks of hostile savages, should have expanded into a nation of forty millions of people ; that the vast wilderness should have been subdued, and in its midst stately cities, the home of commerce and the arts, should have arisen ; that the untrodden primeval forest should have yielded to fields white with harvests which feed the hungry millions of the lands from which our forefathers came ; that great highways, unparalleled in extent and in number, linking together even the two oceans, should have been constructed ; that broad rivers, thousands of miles from the sea, then nameless and unbroken save by the solitary canoe of the red man, should bear upon their bosoms countless fleets ; that the great deep itself should have become white with sails bringing to our ports the productions of every clime ; that the whole land should have become dotted with institutions of charity and learning, and with the temples of religion ; that here should have been founded the first great empire, based on the acknowledgment of man's equality with man, seems more like the fabled work of the slaves of the lamp in the Arabian tale, than a sober chapter in the history of mankind.

Well may the Old World, cramped and fettered by the traditions and institutions of the past, stand amazed at the gigantic progress of the New. No where is this stupendous progress more plainly visible than in the region in which we are met together—the illimitable West, a land of majestic streams, of boundless prairies, bordering on vast inland seas, blessed with a kindly climate and unsurpassed fertility of soil. Here the energy of our people has produced its most astonishing results. Less than half a century ago, where now stands this imperial city, stood a lonely frontier post, beyond the outermost verge of civilization. Now look around— churches, schools, costly mansions, huge warehouses and busy factories arise on every hand. An hundred avenues of commerce, stretching out on every side, bring us the harvests of ten thousand fields to be exchanged for the products of Europe, water-borne to this great mart. Soon the great national highway, overleaping alike the desert and the mountain range, promises to bring the riches of the oldest of the continents a tribute to the feet of this young giant of the West. And yet this city is but the type and the embodiment of the spirit of that vast region of which it is the centre and the beating heart.

How shall I fitly characterize the people of the West, their frankness, their generosity, their hospitality, and their kindly warmth,—how describe their devotion to their duty and to their country! Let the thousands of nameless graves which lie scattered from the Ohio to the Gulf, and from the Arkansas to the Potomac, answer the latter question. Do not think that I intend to do injustice to other portions of our country, or that I seek to exalt one section at the expense of others, for I know full well that in all this unparalleled achievement those others have borne their part. They have sent forth their best, their bravest, and their strongest, to these Western plains, and it is they and their children who have done this work. It is the blood of the East that courses through Western veins, and here, in the two greatest and best who sit among us, are the living proofs of what that blood, under genial Western influences, can produce.

There is, alas! one stain in the fair picture of our country's prosperity and happiness. The South sits in sackcloth, mourning and refusing to be comforted; but, purified by her suffering, and regenerated through sorrow, she will yet arise, and, hand in hand with those whom she has deemed her enemies, she will press forward with no unequal steps in the great march of civilization.

But why should we speak of sections or of parts? Henceforward there shall be no sections and no parts, but, bound together by ties which shall never be sundered, welded together by the fierce heat of war's dreadful furnace, the nation starts forward with renewed strength in her majestic course—one homogeneous whole. Hereafter no man will say, I am of the West, or of the East, of the South, or of the North—all such distinctions will be merged in the common title of American citizen. Great name! Greater than that of Roman citizen in Rome's most triumphant days. In other lands men strive to segregate themselves from the mass, and groping backward among the dusty and worm-eaten records of the past, seek for ancestral honors and dignities wherewith to deck themselves and establish a fancied superiority over their fellow-men. Here, standing on the broad platform of equality and fraternity, and surveying the glittering record of the high achievements of our race, each gathers to himself a share in them all, and proclaims it his birthright in the single phrase, I, too, am an American citizen.

The idea of duty to our country is not an unfamiliar one to those who are assembled within these walls. All here have proved their devotion to it in days of toil, of suffering, and of danger. But it is not alone amid great convulsions that that devotion should be manifested. The national life is made up of the individual lives of its people, and every man, however humble his sphere of action may be, contributes his quota to the nation's good or ill. Men of science tell us that, in the material world, no force is ever lost. The beam of light, darting from its source, flies onward in the depths of space through all eternity. A word is spoken; it is but a breath, a little movement of the air, and in a moment, to our dull senses, it is gone forever; but it is still living; the vibrant atmosphere still records it, feebly and more feebly as time passes, but on the ear of the Omniscient it is forever sounding. To that ear the quivering atoms still echo the words of innocence spoken in the garden before the fall; still shudder at the sounds of " crucify him, crucify him," which were uttered in the city of David more than eighteen hundred years ago. So is it also in the world of action. Men can not, if they would, live for the present alone. Every action has its consequences, and every consequence its consequences. Every deed is a link in the great chain of cause. When the places that know us now shall know us no more forever; when even the stones which the hands of affection shall raise to mark our last resting-places shall have crumbled into dust; when our names shall have perished from the memory of man, our undying actions will still live, affecting for good or for evil the generations yet to be. Our hands are upon chords which stretch far down through the coming centuries, and as we shall touch them, so will they resound. They might have resounded with the clank of chains, and the despairing cries of an enslaved and a down-trodden people. Let us be glad in the belief that they will resound with the great anthem of the free. Let us then, by our

love of country, by our sense of duty to our country, strengthened
by the recollections which we have here renewed of common
effort, when our country's peril was the greatest, and her need
was the sorest, resolve to so live that our every act shall be a
mite cast into the treasury of our country's welfare, to do that
which in us may lie to rear here the altars of truth and of justice,
and to fix firm and deep, on the everlasting rocks, the foundations
of that great fabric of liberty which shall not only shelter us and
our posterity, but shall be the refuge of the oppressed of every
nation and of every clime.

Song by the Glee Club ; — "*Unfurl the Glorious Banner !*"

Second Toast ; — *The President of the United States.*

Speech of General R. P. Buckland :

Fellow Soldiers: General John M. Palmer, who was
to have responded to this toast, being unavoidably absent, I
am called upon, without due notice, to take his place. I wish
to say, by way of apology, that I have not willingly taken upon
myself the risk of undertaking to satisfy your expectations ; nor
do I expect to do so. But having received a peremptory order
from superior authority, without an opportunity of declining,
I am before you to respond, as best I may, to a toast which
was designed to call out, for the benefit of this great audience
of heroes, the well-known eloquence of the distinguished
Governor elect of this State.

The Constitution of the United States vests in the President
the executive power of the nation, and makes him the
Commander-in-chief of the Army and Navy of the United
States. It is, therefore, peculiarly appropriate, on this occasion,
that we who formed a part of that great army which so recently

saved the life of the nation by conquering its enemies on a hundred bloody fields, should pay proper respect to the officer to which belonged the responsibility of organizing that army, and developing the resources which enabled it to win the victory. We can not forget how nobly that great responsibility was discharged by the lamented Lincoln. Unlike kings and emperors, who elevate themselves to power by trampling upon the rights and liberties of the people, the President of the United States represents the executive power of a free people, and is entrusted with that power by their free choice, to enforce, not his, but their will; to execute the laws which they make through their representatives assembled in the Congress of the United States. It is a high and an honorable trust, to which it is the right of every American citizen to aspire; and it has been said that every American, at some period of his life, has entertained expectations of becoming President of the United States. However that may be, we are honored to-night by the presence of one distinguished gentleman who has not been disappointed in that regard, and we are also honored by the presence of several others whose great services in the field entitle them to the highest place in the affections of the American people. May they in due time receive their reward.

The American people, grateful to General Washington for his successful services as the leader of their armies in the war for American Independence, expressed their gratitude and appreciation of his patriotism by electing him the first President of the United States; and he, in return for their confidence, rewarded the people, and honored himself, by a faithful execution of the trust. And now the American people of to-day, equally grateful to General Grant for his great services as the leader of their armies, suddenly brought into the field to defend and preserve the national Government, following the example of their fathers, have embraced the first opportunity to express their gratitude to him, and their faith in his patriotism and unerring judgment, by electing him to the exalted position first occupied by Washington. It is the ardent hope of every patriotic citizen that the administration of General Grant may be as successful as that of General Washington in healing up the national wounds, and laying the foundation of long years of peace and prosperity.

The most eminent men of the nation are selected to fill the Presidential office, but no man, however exalted for talent, or however distinguished his services as a general, or as a statesman, can add to the dignity of the office; for the reason that the office is the concentration of the sovereign executive power of all the people of the nation. A man may be elevated to that office who is wanting in ability to perform its high and arduous duties, or who may prove faithless to the trust, but such a misfortune would only disgrace the man. It would not in the least disparage the dignity of the office; nor should it lessen our respect for its legitimate authority. The prosperity of our free Republican institutions depends upon the disposition of the people to enact only just laws, and then to respect and obey them, whoever may be, for the time being, intrusted with their execution. It is, therefore, a duty, on all occasions like this, to pay proper respect to the President of the United States.

And now, my friends, in closing these remarks, I have only to express my sorrowful regrets that among so many of you who expect to be, and so many who deserve to be, so few ever will be President of the United States!

THIRD TOAST; — *The Army and Navy of the United States*—While each is ever ready, by its own resources, to sustain the national honor, may they always stand shoulder to shoulder, as on the Mississippi, in promoting the prosperity and preserving the union of our common country. — Sentiment proposed by Admiral D. G. Farragut, U. S. N.

Speech of GENERAL JOHN M. SCHOFIELD:

FELLOW SOLDIERS: I regret my inability to fitly respond to your toast, "The Army and the Navy." But I am more than compensated by the presence of so many of those gallant soldiers who, in war and peace, were and are always ready for the discharge of every duty. I rejoice to see here, also, a goodly number of the gallant officers of that volunteer navy which bore so honorable a part in many of the memorable operations in which you were engaged, and I regret that Farragut, Porter, and other naval heroes are not also with us to-night. I may well leave it for those gentlemen who are to respond severally for the armies represented here, to make in the aggregate a fitting response for the army at large, and the navy, for the gallant armies of which they will speak are fair types of the whole; but while I leave it for others to recount, as well they may do with honest pride, the events of the past, I may be permitted to dwell for a moment upon the present, and indulge in hopes of the future.

We see in the fraternal union which we now enjoy, an exhibition of the peculiar character of the army and navy of the United States, as distinguished from those of other great nations. Drawn together by a patriotic sense of duty in our country's hour of peril, and held together through long years of desperate war by that bond of duty which alone is capable of thus binding men to each other, we find engendered by our martial union, ties of affection and respect, which have only been increased during nearly four years of peace. Although scattered from the mountains to the sea, and from the lakes to the gulf, at the call of our honored chief we assemble around this festive board, to pledge each other anew that, whether in war or peace, for our country's honor and weal, we will stand shoulder to shoulder until the great battle of life is ended.

The Grand Army of the Union has not been disbanded— it still lives in the true, stout hearts of its soldiers, and even when they have passed off the stage of life, its spirit will exist in their sons—yea, and in their daughters. As with the individual man, so it is with the nation. When from the dictates of an honest heart the nation puts forth its full strength to accomplish a great good, the heart is thereby enlightened and purified, the strength increased, and the life prolonged. In this increase of strength and vitality, the nation feels that its grand army and navy, whose deeds are the nation's pride, are not things of the past, but that they still live.

Music by the Band ;—"*Red, White, and Blue.*"

Fourth Toast ;— *The Army of Georgia.*

Speech of General H. W. Slocum :

Mr. Chairman and Fellow-Soldiers: On behalf of the officers and soldiers of the Army of Georgia, both present and absent, I thank you for the compliment paid to that organization. I regret the absence of Generals Davis, Williams and Mower, who, as corps commanders in that army, acquired the most enviable reputations as soldiers, and to whose gallantry and efficiency the organization was, in a great measure, indebted for the good name accorded to it at the close of the war. I am glad to see that several of its division and brigade commanders are present. On our campaigns these officers were frequently in a strife for the honor of taking the head of the column, and, when brought into action, they were always, of course, in advance of the commander. Now, it is an old and established rule that "those foremost in the fight should be first at the feast." Under this rule, they are entitled, on this occasion, to speak for the Army of Georgia, and that honor I shall cheerfully accord to them.

This is the first meeting of the officers and soldiers of the Western Armies that I have had the pleasure of attending since our final review in Washington; and this reunion has been to me one of the happiest events of my life. It is always a pleasure to a soldier to meet a comrade who has borne with him the dangers and hardships of a campaign—recalling to mind with him the scenes of the past—the two together again fighting their battles over. It is true that the remembrance of nearly every scene is tinged with sadness, for scarcely an event can be called to mind which is not associated with the loss of some gallant comrade, whose bravery and devotion to his country we can but feel should have been rewarded by his being permitted to enjoy with us the present hour—the pleasure of beholding a Union restored—a country saved. But in this conviction who can say that those of us who survive, reap in reality any more glorious harvest than those who themselves fell beneath the sickle of death? A nation's tears are the tribute paid to their memory— tears that perennially water the laurels they wore, and will keep them fresh and green long after we have passed off the stage.

To-day we have been permitted to meet—not a single comrade, but thousands of them, from all parts of the country, most of whom we have not met since the disbanding of our armies. In addition to this, good tidings are brought us from absent comrades, scattered over nearly every state—tidings proving that the war has not injured or demoralized the young men who carried it to a successful close. We are told that the great mass of the soldiers, having returned to civil life, are struggling with difficulties as successfully as they did while in the army. General Sherman closed his report on the campaign through the Caro

linas with these words: " In conclusion, I beg to express, in the
most emphatic manner, my entire satisfaction with the tone and
temper of the whole army.   Nothing seems to dampen their
energy, zeal, or cheerfulness.   It is impossible to conceive of a
march involving more labor and exposure; yet, I can not recall
an instance of bad temper by the way, or of hearing an expression of doubt as to our perfect success in the end."   In saying
this, the General did but justice to the officers and men of his
command, and I have never entertained a fear that men of whom
these words could be truthfully spoken, would fail of success on
returning to their homes and entering upon the peaceful avocations of life.

To most of our soldiers the army was a good school.   It
taught not only lessons of patriotism, but of perseverance and
energy.   The man who has fought four years to save his country,
has had his love of country burned into his soul by the ordeal of
fire, and he who, in the dead hour of winter, has uncomplain-
ingly forded wide rivers, and constructed roadways through
almost impenetrable swamps, will not be apt, in civil life, to
succumb to ordinary difficulties.   Speaking of war, Burke says
it suspends the rules of moral obligation, and what is long
suspended is in danger of being totally abrogated.   Civil wars,
he declares, strike deepest into the manners of the people.   They
vitiate their politics; they corrupt their morals; they pervert
even the natural taste and relish of equity and justice.   By
teaching us to consider our fellow-creatures in a hostile light, the
whole body of our nation becomes gradually less dear to us.
The very names of affection and kindred, which were the bond
of charity while we agreed, become new incentives to hatred and
rage.   In her hour of trial, when enemies at home and abroad
were predicting and desiring her utter destruction, our country
found defenders in her own sons.   The patriotism of our people
was not displayed on the battle-field alone, but from nearly every

city and town came money as well as men, and the money came at a time when the lender evinced patriotism as well as faith in loaning to the Government. The final victory of our arms was a triumph for the advocates of a republican form of government throughout the world; and now, to complete our triumph, to gladden the hearts of our friends in every land, to make our victory doubly dear and brilliant, we should struggle to avert the evils which, we are told, always follow civil war. Let not the war vitiate our politics, corrupt our morals, or pervert our taste for equity and justice, and our victory will be more complete and more grand than any in the world's history.

As to the best method of averting these evils, the most patriotic men may at times differ. As on the great march to the sea, we sometimes found *corps* diverging from each other, and occasionally a body of troops, either from a defect in our maps, or from the ignorance of our guides, would be found on the wrong road, yet having a common objective point, all would be concentrating; so, in the efforts of patriotic men to secure the nation's welfare, however much their guides may temporarily differ, all who earnestly desire peace, prosperity, and the preservation of their country's honor, must ultimately be found marching in the same direction. Our annual meetings serve to keep fresh in our minds, and in the minds of our people, the events of the war, and I would not have one page in the history of that struggle obliterated, but I would use it to strengthen our devotion to the country, and our determination to countenance nothing in politics, nothing in business, nothing even in social intercourse, which does not tend to the country's weal. The grand idea which animated our armies during the strife was to place our national character in the high niche to which its illustrious ancestry entitled it, and to show the world that the descendants of Washington, Gates, Green, Hamilton, and the fathers of the country, are capable of defending and preserving the free institutions we inherited from them. Now that the war is over, and the victory won, let us continue to emulate the glorious example of the revolutionary patriots, and devote ourselves to achieving new renown for our country by our devotion to the arts of peace. We have learned in the rough school of war to discipline and master ourselves, and we shall, by the application of this knowledge to the pursuits of civil life, gain bloodless victories, not less important than those achieved upon the tented field.

FIFTH TOAST ; — *The Heroes of the Rank and File.*

Speech of GENERAL S. A. HURLBUT :

COMRADES : It is just and becoming, Mr. President, that an assemblage like this should render honor to the Rank and File, and I am glad that the pleasant duty of responding to this toast has fallen upon me. No such body of men, in my judgment, were ever assembled as the volunteer army of the late war. History fails to give us such examples, for history has never yet had to deal with such a people as this. The mother was worthy of her sons, and the sons of their mother, for the army was the child and representative of the nation. No troops ever stood for the honor of their flag, for the safety of their country, so thoroughly identified with the sentiment of the people, as did this Army of ours, which sprung into sudden and terrible life at the cry of the imperiled nation, fought through the long war with such singular tenacity, accepted, endured, aye, welcomed severe discipline as a necessity of success, and, having acquired the skill, steadiness, and unity of impulse of the veteran, yet at the end disappeared without a ripple in the great current and mass of the citizenship from which they sprang. To the eye of the stranger, toward the close of the war, one million of trained and disciplined soldiers hung over the future of the nation, pregnant with all evil and disquiet, as the Alpine avalanche impends over some sleeping village. But when the summer air of peace breathed softly over the land, this thing of terror silently dissolved into its elements,—with no torrents, no rush of waters—in many gentle streamlets, each of which made glad again some long desolate home. No other people could have produced such an army; no other people could thus have absorbed them when their task was done, without perceptible shock to the commonwealth.

From all ranks, pursuits, and modes of life they came, these heroes of the Rank and File. The sun-burned plowman, the apt mechanic, the swart artisan, the pale student; from all trades, all professions, all industries they came — many earnest, thoughtful, devoted; some moved by the wild spirit of adventure; some for the mere excitement of the battle and the march; some of high culture and education; some with but little of either; a strange, wild gathering of apparently discordant elements. Yet, under the fervent heat of love for an insulted country, and with the strong current of military discipline, they grew into the columns that swung with Grant round the beleaguered Vicksburg, and at Champion Hills and Jackson made vain the boastings of the Gibraltar of the Mississippi; they pried into that living rock which withstood Thomas at Chickamauga; they shattered Hood at Nashville; and they became that plow of God, which, in the hands of Sherman, scarred the deep furrows of their march through the mountains, from Atlanta to the sea. They also formed that barrier of fire and steel on which Lee leaped to ruin at the heights of Gettysburg; they were that relentless giant hand that forced the Army of Northern Virginia from the Wilderness to Petersburg and the Appomattox, and shook the sheltered remnants of the Confederate armies from the iron fingers, the paroled prisoners of the great Republic. Pittsburg Landing and Shiloh taught us early

9

to respect the personal manhood of the Rank and File. It was somewhat awkward and unscientific fighting, but they struck hard in that strange and deadly conflict.

It has always seemed to me, Mr. President, that the courage, endurance and steadiness of our private soldiers had in it something of the miraculous. With no rank to incite, with no promotion probable, with no future ambition, no hope even of special personal mention, they went forth to exhausting marches, to dreary midnight watchings, to the trench and the rifle pit, to the line of actual battle, to the storming column, to face death in all forms, to endure disease, to suffer the slow agony of the prison pen, ready to live when life was but endurance, ready to die when to die was duty. For these great actions and this great endurance, there must have been some efficient cause, and, as I read it, that cause was the love of country and the love of home. They could not come back dishonored, and they all meant to come home, and bent all their powers and energies to finish the work quickly and well and be again at home. No man of us who has worn the insignia of rank and command, but owes a free and hearty tribute to the Rank and File. Every badge of authority, from the bar of the subaltern to the quadruple star that worthily rests on the shoulder of the General of the Army, is the representative and the creature of the heroism of the Rank and File, mute but glorious witness to the self-denial of their lives, and the gallantry of their deaths. As the engineer uses and guides already existing forces, so this heroism of the Rank and File was the vast living power which it was consummate generalship to mold, direct and control. All honor, then, to our comrades, the living heroes of the Rank and File. All credit to the dead who died for us and our country.

> " On Fame's eternal camping ground
>   Their silent tents are spread,
> And glory walks her solemn round
>   In the bivouac of the dead."

SONG by the Glee Club; —" *Sherman's March to the Sea.*"

SIXTH TOAST; — *The Army of the Ohio.*

Speech of General MILO S. HASCALL:

FELLOW-CITIZENS OF THE ARMY, AND GENTLEMEN OF THE BOARD OF TRADE OF CHICAGO: Having recently been selected to respond to the toast which you have just heard read—" The Army of the Ohio"—in place of the distinguished Secretary of War, its former commander, you will readily appreciate the diffidence I feel in undertaking to fill the place of one at once so illustrious, and so well calculated to do the subject justice. I promise you, however, that my remarks shall possess at least one merit, which, according to a distinguished authority, who has done us the honor to be with us this evening, surpasses all others, and that is, they will be very brief.

That distinguished soldier and citizen, who was the orator for the Army of the Ohio, last evening, at the Opera House, did the subject such complete justice that little else need, or could be said, if the occasion and the time rendered it proper to indulge in extended remarks. After what he has so well said in regard to the organization and campaigns of the Army of the Ohio, I will only further add some allusions to some of the noble spirits that offered up their lives during the different campaigns in which we were engaged. First and most prominent on the list of our departed heroes, stands the name of General William P. Saunders, who fell a short distance in front of the fort that now bears his honored name, at Knoxville, Tennessee. Of him it can be truly said, that he was the idol of our army. No one who was present at the time Longstreet was closing in upon Knoxville, will ever forget the almost reckless daring he manifested during the three days that Longstreet was closing in upon and investing the city. General Saunders had only two days before received notice of his promotion to the rank of Brigadier-General, a promotion that General Burnside was obliged to have made, in order to get a proper commander for the cavalry of his army. He was immediately assigned to the command of the cavalry, and ordered to detain the enemy as long as possible, to give the infantry time to construct defensive works about the city, which was, at the time, almost entirely destitute of any kind of defences. For two days, on the south side of the Holston river, General Saunders was engaged in this work, constantly at the head of his command, and the works then being tenable on that side, his command was transferred to the Knoxville side of the river, with orders to make a stubborn resistance in the direction of London, from whence Longstreet was rapidly advancing with the main body of his army, preceded by cavalry. It was here that Saunders made some of those desperate charges, and engaged in hand-to-hand conflicts, such as are rarely witnessed, and there, in plain view of the fort that now bears his illustrious name, with fighting in front of him, fighting to the right of him, fighting to the left of him, fighting in the rear of him, and himself wielding his sword with invincible bravery, there, I say, far in advance of any of his command, and entirely unappalled by the danger and clangor that surrounded him, the fatal bullet struck him which ushered his spirit into the presence of God. Another desperate charge recovered the dead body, and we had in our possession all that was mortal of the gallant, heroic, and equally modest Saunders. The enemy then immediately closed in and completed the investment and seizure. The same night, at about midnight, we buried him quietly and privately, it being impossible, on account of the proximity of the enemy, and the arduous duties of the hour, to have a formal funeral. I have seen many noble dead, but never such heartfelt sorrow as pervaded that little funeral procession, not exceeding two dozen, and all officers high in rank, as not a man could be spared from the trenches. We were all forcibly reminded of the circumstances of the burial of Sir John Moore, and some of the verses of that beautiful poem are so strictly and truthfully descriptive of this burial, that I can not refrain from repeating them here :

> " Not a drum was heard, not a funeral note,
> As his corse to the ramparts we hurried;
> Not a soldier discharged his farewell shot
> O'er the grave where our hero we buried.
>
> We buried him darkly, at dead of night,
> The sods with our bayonets turning;
> By the struggling moonbeam's misty light,
> And our lanterns dimly burning.
>
> No useless coffin inclosed his breast,
> Nor in sheet nor in shroud we wound him;
> But he lay like a warrior taking his rest,
> With his martial cloak around him.
>
> Few and short were the prayers we said,
> And we spoke not a word of sorrow;
> But we steadfastly gazed on the face of the dead,
> And we bitterly thought of the morrow.
>
> Slowly and sadly we laid him down,
> From the field of his fame fresh and gory;
> We carved not a line, we raised not a stone,
> But we left him alone in his glory."

Numerous other brave spirits yielded up their lives during this siege. Among the number, the gallant and accomplished Colonel Comstock, of Michigan. But time admonishes me that I must hasten on. Passing by the other numerous engagements and hardships which the Army of the Ohio endured, the next

serious engagement we had was at Resaca, where General
Schofield lost a distinguished member of his staff, and the
Second Division lost very seriously in officers and men, and
the Third fared not much better. From this time on until the
fall of Atlanta, the Army of the Ohio was almost constantly
engaged, being all the time on one or the other flanks of the
army, and constantly fighting into new positions. The Army
of the Ohio can justly claim credit for making the flank movement on the 1st of July, 1864, which caused the evacuation
of Kenesaw Mountain and Marietta, and the Second Division
of that army was the first to drive the enemy inside the fortifications near the Howard House, at Atlanta, and the first to
establish its batteries and commence the shelling of the city.
I would fain follow the army in Atlanta, describe its desperate
engagements at Franklin and Nashville, and its memorable
achievements after being transferred to North Carolina, and till
the close of the war, but time will not permit. The glorious
achievements of the Army of the Ohio were not accomplished
without serious losses. Our list of dead include the names of
the gallant Saunders, Colonel Comstock, Colonel Lowry, of the
One Hundred and Seventh Illinois Volunteers, Captain on
General Schofield's staff, and Capt E. D. Saunders, A. A. G.,
on General Cox's staff, besides numerous other officers, and that
long list of less noted but not less gallant and honored dead,
who fill the unmarked graves all over the rebellious states. All
great achievements cost great sacrifices, and the peace we enjoy
to-day has been no exception to the rule. On the other hand,
we find, with our Army of the Ohio, that "peace hath her
victories no less renowned than war." The country has not
been slow to appreciate the exalted character of the services
of the Army of the Ohio, or the splendid ability of its leading
men. The United States at large, with one voice, has appropriated our Schofield and made him Secretary of War. The

great State of Ohio, almost before he was out of the field, took up our statesman, General Cox, and conferred upon him the highest honors in her gift, and the little State of Rhode Island has served our gallant Burnside in the same manner. The great states of Ohio and Michigan have made our Generals Sherwood and Spalding the keepers of their great seals, and my neighbors in Indiana have this fall taken up our General Packard and made him the successor of the illustrious Colfax in Congress; while our inevitable General Jack Casement has spanned the continent with railroad iron, made his "everlasting fortune," and been elected to Congress from Wyoming, though he declares that he can not waste his time in small matters till he gets the Pacific Railroad done. We have numerous other evidences of the esteem in which our Army is held, but time forbids further allusion to them this evening.

SEVENTH TOAST;—*To the Memory of the Heroic Dead.*

In the absence of General John A. Garfield, who was to have responded to this sentiment, and for whom the duty and the honor of special commemoration of the heroic dead were reserved until it was too late to make any other arrangement, there was no speech in response to the seventh toast.

MUSIC by the Glee Club;—"*Pleyel's Hymn.*"

EIGHTH TOAST;—*The Army of the Tennessee.*

Speech of General JOHN A. LOGAN:

FELLOW COMRADES: The toast, "The Army of the Tennessee"—The Army of the Tennessee—the child of patriotism, born amidst revolution, came forth with all the energy and vigor of youth, without a furrow upon his brow, or a scar upon its manly form; with the flag of the Union, the emblem of our unity, our glory and our strength, in one hand, and the sword of eternal liberty in the other, upon the bended knee, they swore that this land should be made free. The Army of the Tennessee, the first to win a victory, that went trembling o'er the wires, that gladdened every heart in this land, and filled every soul with joy. The Army of the Tennessee is without much written history — yet it has a grand history. Its history was written from the time it commenced its march from Shiloh to the end of the war by the swords of veterans and the blood of traitors. Its course was onward, its course was upward. From Donelson to Shiloh, from Shiloh to Corinth, from Corinth to Vicksburg, and around it, were many bloody battles fought, and there the haters of this glorious fabric of ours had their blood drunk by the sands of their soil, and at the same time many, too, of our own patriotic brothers breathed their last and were remembered by the relations of the dead. I remember well—but I shall not attempt to go into details—many of the incidents of this war. I do remember one in particular, at the battle of Baker's Creek, before Vicksburg was invested. The Army of the Tennessee went into battle against the combined hosts of treason, singing:

> "John Brown's body lies mouldering in the grave,
>   And his soul goes marching on."

On the march of the Army of the Tennessee, from Vicksburg, after forty days investment of that proud stronghold (where many, I am sorry to say, of the flower of this country were mown down by the enemy), we separated, a portion taking their march to Black river — a portion afterward to the Kenesaw — assisting in relieving the army of our gallant Thomas when so hardly pressed by the enemy.

From thence they marched with Sherman to the sea. As I said, they gained the first great victory, and they were in the last battle, where the last gun was fired, at Benton's Cross-Roads.

The Army of the Tennessee — no better than other armies, but equally as good. The Army of the Tennessee — not more valiant than others, but equally as valiant. The Army of the Tennessee — with no more pride than others, but equally as much. The Army of the Tennessee, with no more patriotism than others, but equally as much. It was an army, it is to-day an army composed of patriots left, who would to-morrow respond to the tocsin of war, on the call of our country, as freely as it did at first.

The Army of the Tennessee had several commanders. Why, my comrades, you know (and of course you do, for you were of it,) that the President elect, of whom all men who are patriots are proud, was the first commander of the Army of the Tennessee! You know that the brave and gallant Thomas was once a General in the Army of the Tennessee! You know that it was commanded by the gallant Sherman! And you all know it was commanded by the lamented McPherson. And of him, permit me, my comrades, to speak. His tongue is silent in death; his body is cold. He can not speak for himself. McPherson, McPherson is dead; but yet lives in the memory of every man that ever served under him.

He was a gentleman, by nature made. He was an educated man, by his country's gift. He was a noble man, with his bosom full of generosity. The milk of human kindness welled up in that frame of his, a fountain wide and deep. His magnanimity was as broad as the area of his whole country. His generosity had no confine, and the gifts of his nature were as bright and as gleaming as the sun's beams at noon-day. If you want to know the correctness of the page left by that man; if you want to know the brightness of his history, go and stand by the tomb

of McPherson; there wait until the rainbow shows itself in the
sky; then see the rays of the sun play across its variegated hues,
and fall upon the dew-drop of the velvet rose that there grows
upon his grave—emblems of the purity of his life. Upon that
scene cast your eyes, and then remember that this is emblem-
atical of the bright page and reputation of that gallant soul that
is gone.

Now, my fellow-comrades, I only speak of these men of the
Army of the Tennessee because they come to my mind. It had
other noble men. All who belonged to it were noble men, and I
love them all. I love that man now prostrated with disease con-
tracted during its many fatigues and battles—the man you all
know, the man of integrity, the man inspired with patriotism,
the man worthy to be at the head of the nation. I speak of John
A. Rawlins.

It was, too, afterward commanded by Howard. He has a
history in this war going to prove him that noble man we all
know him to be.

Of myself, who commanded the Army of the Tennessee, I
shall not speak.

But, my fellow-citizens and comrades, there are others to be
mentioned besides those whom I have mentioned. I can not call
them all by name, but let me say this: Among all our heroes of
our compatriots and brothers in arms and officers who sleep,
to-day, the sleep that knows no waking, let their memories be
fresh at all times, and let them live and be ever green in the
recollections of us who survive them. But there are others still;
who are they? The poor but gallant soldiers who carried the
musket! That man who carried the knapsack and the rifle, in
the Army of the Tennessee, to whom, to-day, we all owe the
reputation we made.

He fought our battles; many of them we left behind as we
marched along, and you all remember the little mounds we used

to see, as we marched along, dotting the place where the private soldier sleeps for ever. There are none to speak for them to-night. Those who are left we love and respect, and the memories of those who are dead we revere. When they passed away, though not having, in the din of battle, that opportunity of meeting their God that others might have, yet, in my judgment, their ascension robes were made doubly white on account of their patriotic devotion, by that God who judges all.

There is a God, and whenever I hear any thing said (as I often have,) by persons speaking of the merits of the army, and of those who passed away without enjoying the privileges that are accorded to men at home, I remember what was related by that old German poet, once upon a time, and this is it.

When God conceived the majestic idea of making man, He called the three ministers who constantly wait upon His throne about him—Truth, Justice, and Mercy. He said, "Let us make man." Truth said, "Oh, God, make not man; he will pollute Thy sanctuary." Justice said, "Oh, God, make not man, he will trample Thy laws under foot." But Mercy, upon her bended knee, with streaming eyes, said, "Oh, God, make man, cast him from Thy plastic hand on earth, and I will guide him through his life down the path of time; I will care for him in all his trials, in all his troubles, in all his vicissitudes; and when the final day shall come of rendering accounts, I will return him to Thee, borne beneath the hollow of my hand, the child of mercy as Thou didst give him to me." So it is with the patriotic dead.

Now, my fellow-comrades, in conclusion, let me say this. In speaking of the army, the short time that we are allowed here to-night (and as you all know I never make any preparation when addressing you or any other body of men, never writing a speech, but always saying that which comes to my lips), assembled together as we are, the Army of the Tennessee, the

Army of Georgia, the Army of the Ohio, the Army of the Cumberland, and others represented here—we can but remember that we have been soldiers; and we are soldiers yet! if our country needs our services. Let us meet together on all occasions as soldiers, as countrymen. Let us come together in a kindly spirit. Let us do away with all bickering and prejudice. Let us meet as soldiers. We have fought for one common cause, for one common country, for one common flag, for one common Constitution. And when separating, let us separate in the same way—with kindly feelings toward all—no matter what our politics may be, or what our prejudices may be, or what we may feel, or what we may think. Let us, as we have always done, renew our allegiance to the Government that gave us birth, to the flag that protected us, and the Constitution that preserved us. Let each and every one of us to-night register an oath high up in heaven, that each and every star upon the old flag, shining now as brightly as the stars that deck the plains of heaven, shall always give the same light that they have given—that never shall there be a particle of their brightness or their glory and luster in any way dimmed, darkened or obscured by the hand that treason may raise against this Government. Our sires look down from heaven and say, we freed a nation, ye have freed a world—

> Above your deeds in the celestial glee,
> The bells of Heaven ring out their jubilee,
> Men of the Army of the Tennessee.

Now, my fellow-comrades, I have said more than I intended to say, much more, and you will kindly pardon me.

I thank you most heartily for the kindly manner with which you have listened to me, and ask of you the same consideration of those who are to follow me.

NINTH TOAST;—*The Widows and Orphans of our Fallen Comrades.*

Speech of GENERAL T. J. HENDERSON:

COMRADES: Of all the memories of the late rebellion, there is none so full of sorrow and sadness as the memory of our fallen comrades, and the Widows and Orphans left behind them. And yet it is one of the pleasing recollections of the terrible strife through which we have passed, that they have never been forgotten. Here to-night, amid all these festivities, surrounded by all the magnificence and splendor of this great occasion, and in this august presence, I am proud that the loved ones, the Widows and Orphans of those who nobly fought and bravely fell, and whose graves were found all along the lines of our many marches and battles, are not forgotten, but, on the contrary, live in all our memories, and share in all our sympathies.

Comrades, it is one of the sacred duties we owe the gallant dead, never to forget those who gave up their husbands and fathers to help fight the battles and win the victories which have made memorable not only our own deeds, but our country's fame. What sacrifices they made; what sorrows they patiently bore; what painful anxiety they endured while sitting at the window, and watching for the coming back of those they loved, but watched in vain, we may never know, but we can commend them to the sympathy and support of a grateful and a patriotic people. We can cherish their memory in all our associations, and in all our lives. We can bear to them the consideration that their husbands and fathers nobly died while defending the old flag—that they gave up their lives that the nation might live. We can tell them of their gallant deeds. We can point them to their country's glory. Above all, we can preserve the great, free government, the rich legacy bequeathed to us by our fathers, and now made more precious by the blood of our fallen comrades, as an asylum for them and their posterity forever. And this is the richest reward we can offer them for all their sufferings and sacrifices. As we strew the graves of our fallen comrades with flowers, let us invoke our country's richest and choicest blessings upon their Widows and Orphans, and may their lives ever be lovely and pleasant.

TENTH TOAST ; — *The Army of the Cumberland.*

Speech of GENERAL GEORGE H. THOMAS :

FELLOW-COMRADES OF THE ARMY OF THE TENNESSEE, OF THE OHIO, THE GEORGIA, AND THE CUMBERLAND : We have assembled in this city where we have a grand reunion of the four armies which had the good fortune to serve together in the West, where we claim that we did some good duty. To wind up these interesting proceedings, we have assembled here this evening to unite together in a social banquet to testify towards one another our fraternal love, begotten amid hours of danger, and when we were attempting to discharge our whole duty to our country. These sentiments, I know, are entertained by the Army of the Cumberland and the three other armies. But as their representative to-night I wish to express to you again the fraternal feeling which we hold towards all of you. The cordial manner in which we have been received by the citizens of Chicago, should ever be remembered by us as a demonstration of their patriotic feeling. Therefore, I wish to tender to them, in behalf not only of the Army of the Cumberland, but of the other army societies here, our heart-felt thanks. As our time is limited, and there are several other speeches to make, you must excuse me from saying any more. I bid you good-night.

I am requested now to present a toast which was expected

from me at the close of the regular toasts this evening. I give you " The Citizens of Chicago. Their enterprise is proverbial, and their liberality no less so. The latter will be long remembered by the united armies of the Tennessee, the Ohio, the Cumberland, and the Georgia."

ELEVENTH TOAST ;—*The Cavalry Corps of the Military Division of the Mississippi.*

Speech of General J. H. WILSON :

COMRADES : In responding to the sentiment which you have just received, and which revives in my mind so many stirring recollections, it is not my intention to detain you by a recital of historic details ; but I should be false to the hardy riders, who never were false to me or to their colors, if I failed, in their name, to return their grateful acknowledgments for the graceful manner in which you have just complimented them.

It is said that a prominent general, in the early days of the Rebellion, offered a reward for a dead cavalryman ; and we are all familiar with the derisive cry : "Fight in front ! There goes the cavalry to the rear !" I remember hearing it upon one occasion which may have some significance among the potent but unseen influences which gave character to the war. It was on the night after the battle of Mission Ridge, while General Grant, accompanied by his staff and orderlies, was riding toward Chattanooga. As the cavalcade dashed by, a division of infantry, pushing to the front, made the gloomy forests of the Chickamauga re-echo with the old shout of derision. The laugh was on their side then, although the joke had become somewhat threadbare. Whether or not this incident brought to the mind of our chieftain a clearer perception of the necessity for cavalry which should persistently head and fight in the other direction, I can not say, but it is certain that the campaign about Chattanooga led to the selection of a cavalry leader whose name will live when that of Murat is forgotten—gallant Phil. Sheridan. Since the days of Mago, who, with his Numidian horse, overthrew the chivalry of Rome at Cannæ, no more splendid reputation has burst upon the world!

It was my good fortune to be selected for the work laid out by Sherman for the cavalry of his military division, and hence I feel it a sacred duty to allude briefly to its principal features.

At Galesville, in October, 1864, General Sherman in that frank and perspicuous manner so characteristic of the man, unfolded his plans and told me his wishes; turned over to my command the entire mounted force belonging to the armies of the Cumberland, the Tennessee, and the Ohio; gave me unlimited control of this splendid *corps*, and generously added: " Do the best you can with it, and if you make any reputation out of it, I will not undertake to divide it with you." At that time the bulk of this force was dismounted, and parts of it were scattered from South-western Missouri to West Virginia. McCook, Long, and Kilpatrick commanded the three divisions from the Army of the Cumberland; Upton and Hatch the two from the Army of the Tennessee; R. W. Johnson that from the Army of the Ohio; and Knipe, the last, made up principally of new troops from Tennessee and Indiana. Kilpatrick, with five thousand men, and most of the horses, went down to the sea with Sherman, while the rest of the force remained with Thomas to aid in the work of crushing Hood. The official reports have told how Hatch and Croxton kept watch and ward along the Tennessee for the six anxious weeks previous to Hood's passage of the river in his northward march; how they were reinforced by Capron and Hammond, and struggled to impede the hostile advance; and how at last Hood and Forrest received their first defeat at Franklin. You all know how the

country was held in suspense lest the rebels should press northward and flank us out at Nashville; while our imperturbable
commander, secure in his position of strength, was gathering his
force for a final and crushing blow. A cavalry officer himself,
he knew that cavalry without horses were like a sabre without a
hilt—powerless for offence, and dangerous only to him who
holds it. He therefore chose to wait while we gathered
horses. When the day of battle arrived we marched out with
twelve thousand men, nine thousand of whom were mounted,
and full of confidence; besides three thousand more who had
been sent in pursuit of Lyon.

I shall not detain you with the story of Nashville. Our comrades of the Army of the Cumberland know how Hatch, Knipe,
Johnston and Croxton burst through the rebel works, wheeling
grandly to the left, enveloping the hostile line, and, in conjunction with A. J. Smith's travel-stained veterans, supported by
those of Schofield's *corps*, swept the rebel troops from hill to hill,
capturing prisoners, guns and breastworks, till the darkness of a
wintry night checked their onward career. My comrades of the
cavalry have not forgotten how gracefully the gallant McArthur,
in admiration of their dashing assault, refused to contest with
them the honor of having been first to enter the rebel works, and
first to reach the rebel guns. That battle, with its splendid
rivalry between cavalry and infantry, was worth a lifetime of
ordinary service. No trooper went to the rear that day except
on a *stretcher* or in an ambulance. Pushing forward the next
morning, wheeling steadily toward Nashville, Hatch and Hammond pressed the goaded and desperate foe in flank and rear till
Hood, in the agony of despair, wrote to Chalmers: "For God's
sake, drive back the Yankee cavalry, or all is lost!" It was too
late. Step by step, up the deep slopes of the Brentwood Hills,
and through their tangled thickets, the dismounted troopers held
their way. Finally, when the infantry advanced to the assault of

10

the rebel works in front, they met the cavalry entering them triumphantly from the left and rear. This was too much for the rebel host. Broken and crushed, like grain between the upper and nether millstones, it fled ingloriously, under a pall of darkness, from the field. The many instances of personal daring that characterized the night fighting which followed—Spaulding's headlong charge in the dark, against rebel barricades; Hammond's gallant conduct at Hollow Tree Gap; the stirring affair at the West Harpeth, where Hatch, Coon, Hammond and the Fourth Regulars overwhelmed the rebel rear guard, and captured their last battery; the thousand cases of unrecognized and unrewarded valor which marked the terrible fifteen days of marching, bivouacking and skirmishing, without rations, and without forage, through a country already desolated by the march of contending armies; the almost human suffering of the starving, overworked horses, as they sank, by thousands, in the half-frozen morasses which lined our route, would require a Xenophon to depict them. We shall never forget the toil, exposure, hunger and suffering of that terrible winter campaign. But we were amply repaid for it all by the unstinted commendations bestowed upon us by our comrades of the infantry, but, more than all, by the consciousness of our duty done, against more than mortal odds. From that day forth, there was no word of ridicule for the cavalry, in the Army of the Cumberland. The new *corps* had bathed its guidons in blood, and was generously hailed as full brother in the field of honor.

The next two weeks were spent in cantonments along the banks of the Tennessee. Five divisions, in all twenty-seven thousand men, were collected, seventeen thousand of whom were mounted and ready for service. Knipe was sent to join Canby; Johnston, with three brigades, was left to keep watch over the rebels of Middle Tennessee; Hatch was encamped at Eastport, waiting to receive new arms and a remount, before following out a route marked out for him. The rest of the *corps*, nearly fourteen thousand strong, splendidly mounted and equipped, and nearly all provided with the best fire-arms ever put into the hands of a soldier—the Spencer carbine and rifle—began their wide-spread march through the desolate region of Northern Alabama. Concentrating at Elyton, Croxton was detached to move upon Tuscaloosa, while the main force, with the impetuous Upton in advance, headed boldly for Selma. Forrest, with Roddy, Armstrong and Crossland, were encountered at Montevallo, again at Randolph and Ebenezer Church, but were swept out of the way like chaff before the whirlwind. Marching twenty-five and thirty miles a day, with constant fighting, was a poor day's work. On the second day of April, Selma, the last Southern stronghold, was carried by storm. Thirty-two field guns, three thousand men and horses, and large quantities of valuable military property, fell into our hands, while Forrest and his generals succeeded in escaping under cover of night, by leaving their followers to their fate. I can not do justice to the knightly gallantry displayed upon that occasion by Long, Minty, Miller, and their devoted troopers. The chivalry of Spain, in their palmiest days, never excelled it. The field over which they advanced was as level and unimpeded as this floor, and was swept in all directions by the fire of sixteen guns. The works which they carried were a strong bastioned line, covered by a deep moat, and still farther out, by a stockade five and a half feet high. The attacking force of one thousand five hundred and fifty men and officers, in single line, faltered not, but, relying upon their trusty Spencers, dashed forward without a waver, scaled the stockade as boys play leap-frog; poured into the ditch, and clambered over the parapet defended by a force numerically greater than their own. Long, Miller, McCormick, Biggs and Dobbs, with over two hundred of their comrades, were stricken down; but Selma was ours, and "fairly won!" Pausing only long enough to bridge the swollen Alabama, we pushed forward toward Montgomery, raising the starry flag over the first capital of the Confederacy. Destroying the cotton, boating, and military stores, we continued our hurrying march toward the Chattahoochee ; LaGrange capturing Fort Tyler at West Point, and Upton the *tete de pont*, at Columbus. It is not too much to say that these actions were never surpassed for audacity and resolution. The attack on Columbus was made after nine o'clock at night. Upton, assisted by Winslow, Noble and Benteen, led his three hundred chosen troops, dismounted, elbow to elbow, like " Grenadiers of the Guard," straight against the breastwork that barred his road, and although three thousand rebel infantry, and fifty-two guns, throwing all kinds of missiles, did all in their power to hold them at bay, he swept every thing before him. Even the bridges, and the very guns for their defence, were captured before the bewildered rebels could retreat beyond them. The assault upon Fort Tyler was scarcely less remarkable, although it was made by daylight. When it is considered that the ditches of this work were impassable, that three bridges, on three sides of the work, were laid, and each of them used by columns which crossed the rebel parapets almost simultaneously, it will be acknowledged that both officers and men had passed by the days of half-measures in warfare, and were equal to any emergency. Night fighting is the crucial test of discipline, and it is no more than justice to say that Cromwell's Ironsides could not have met it better than did Upton's Division at Columbus. The cavalry learned there, at Selma and Nashville, one of the greatest lessons in warfare—that there is no cover so good as darkness, and no protection so complete as resolute courage in times of great peril ; that caution is the virtue of prosperity, but audacity that of great emergencies !

We tarried at Columbus thirty-six hours, burning and destroying, while the advance guard opened the road to Central

Georgia. Next Macon, with its garrison of major-generals and militia, fell an unresisting prize into our hands. A few days thereafter Croxton, who by a series of masterly marches had outwitted Jackson, burned Tuscaloosa, and fought Adams near Eutaw, making a wide sweep to the northward and eastward, rejoined us in the heart of Georgia, where we were stopped by something more difficult than rebel lines to break. I refer to the armistice which preluded peace. I need not explain to an assembly of soldiers, that there were sad hearts among us that day — sad and glad ones too — for while we all rejoiced as good citizens that the war was ended, it must not be forgotten that our columns were moving toward Virginia at the rate of forty miles a day, and that we had hoped within twenty days to unite our forces with those of Sheridan, and to measure our metal with his in patriotic rivalry. But the last battle had been fought, and there was nothing left for us but to gather in the fruits of our victory. Learning from rebel sources that Davis was a fugitive, and believing that he would be restrained by neither armistice nor capitulation, we took possession of railroads and telegraph lines, sent scouts throughout Northern Georgia, and detachments to all important points between Marietta and St. Marks. With Upton at Augusta, Alexander at Coosa, Winslow at Atlanta, Minty and Croxton at Macon and along the line of the Ocmulgee, with detachments on the Chattahoochee and the Flint, and McCook at Tallahassee, we barred all doors and patrolled all roads leading to the South and West. The first information of Davis' movements was obtained from a rebel citizen who had seen him at Salisbury; but this was soon supplemented and confirmed by the untiring zeal of Lieutenant George O. Yeoman, Acting Inspector General of Alexander's brigade. This gallant young officer, with a detachment of twenty men, all disguised as rebels, joined Davis' escort near the Savannah river, and by sending in couriers kept his commanding officers informed of all the movements of the rebel chieftain. It was upon this information that Croxton and Minty were directed to select their best regiments, the one to march eastward to the Oconee, and the other to march southeastward along the Ocmulgee. The story of the pursuit and capture has been told in detail. You have heard how Harnden, with the First Wisconsin cavalry, struck the trail at Dublin—thanks to the information given by a colored man—and how the Colonel and his men followed without food or forage for three days and nights, through swamps, morass, and forest, to the neighborhood of Irwinville, all the time gaining upon the fugitives, and all the time becoming more firmly convinced that he was on the right track; how Pritchard, with the Fourth Michigan, crossed the trail at Abbeville, and after skirting the Ocmulgee several miles further, turned also toward Irwinville; and how, in the gray of the dawn of the 10th of May, his troopers captured the President of the so-called Southern Confederacy, not booted and spurred, with his visor down, but struggling ungracefully in the encumbering garb of woman. What an ignoble and pitiful end! What more ignoble stain could the gallows fix upon such a man? How wisely Providence ordered events! In that hour the country was overwhelmed with sorrow for the untimely death of the beloved Lincoln; the colors of the nation were draped in black, and sadness had driven the smile from every countenance—when lo! the news of Davis's capture, in disguise, flashed across the wires, and spread with lightning speed. The effect was magical; it was the farce after the tragedy, and a laugh of derision followed the wail of mourning.

During six months of almost constant marching and fighting between the Ohio river and the Gulf of Mexico, the Mississippi and the Atlantic, these troopers never went round a place they should have gone through. They justly claim that they never got within sight of a gun that they did not take, whether posted in the open field, behind breastworks, or beyond streams; that they never made a charge which failed, and never lost a bridge of their own, nor permitted the enemy to burn one over which he was retreating. They captured nearly fifteen thousand prisoners, thirty-two stands of colors, five fortified cities, and two hundred and eighty guns. They burned, or helped the rebels to burn, two hundred and fifty thousand bales of cotton; destroyed railroads, bridges, cars, locomotives, foundries, ship-yards, factories, and military stores, as long as they could find them to destroy; after the surrender, they paroled fifty-nine thousand rebel soldiers belonging to the armies of Lee, Johnson, and Beuregard, and arrested the Postmaster General, Secretary of the Navy, Vice-President, and President of the Confederacy.

When the war ended, the seven divisions numbered thirty-five thousand men for duty; the three divisions under my immediate command, fourteen thousand, exclusive of three full regiments of colored troops, recruited and organized, clothed with rebel uniforms, and armed with rebel rifles, while on the march. They had twenty-three thousand head of horses and mules, were provided with three excellent batteries of horse artillery, among which were Robinson's Chicago Board of Trade Battery, and Battery "M" and "I" of the Fourth United States Artillery, they were fully provided with arms and ammunition, and in every way justified the praise of General Sherman, when he said "they were the largest and best equipped body of mounted troops that ever fell under his command." They were equal to any duty which could have been required of them, except that of lying still in the enemy's country. Motion was the first law of their existence, as well as the principal component in the measure of their utility; they required all the surplus product of one county to support them one day. I believe that the best

cavalry is the best infantry mounted, and that mass or numbers,
into the square of the velocity with which either can go, is the
true measure of its working capacity. Forrest came near the
secret of cavalry, and, in fact, of all warfare, if there is any
secret, when he said to one of my staff officers: "Tell General
Wilson that I don't know much about tactics, but I *would give.
more* for fifteen minutes of the bugle on him than for three days
of tactics." I am glad to say that we never gave him fifteen,
nor five, nor one minute, but went for him all the time.

Neither the country nor the army appreciated the division,
brigade and regimental commanders of the cavalry *corps* at their
real worth. There were men among them fit for any command
that could have been given them, and, as a class, they were as
gallant and capable as ever drew sabre or wore uniform.   It
will always be regretted for their fame that the war did not
last six months longer. They were, with a few exceptions,
not yet turned of thirty.   Upton, Alexander, Winslow, Croxton, LaGrange, Watkins, Murray, Palmer, Kitchell, Noble,
Benteen, Young and Kelley, were of the younger set, while
McCook, Minty, Long, Kilpatrick, Hatch, Knipe, Coon, R.
W. Johnson, Hammond, Cooper, McCormick, G. M. L. Johnson, Atkins, Spaulding, Pritchard, Miller, Harrison, Biggs,
Vail, Israel Garrard, and Frank White, were somewhat older,
though still possessing the sinews of youth. Our grey-beards,
and we had but few, were Harnden—as sturdy as Burley of
Balfour, and Eggleston—the type of those who rode with Cromwell in Marston Moor. The rank and file were veterans in
service, but young in years, and I can aver with truthfulness that
I never saw their superiors for endurance, self-reliance and pluck.
After they were massed at Nashville they believed themselves
invincible. When armed with Spencers it was their boast that,
elbow to elbow, dismounted, and in single line, nothing could
withstand their charge. "Only cover our flanks," said Miller

before Selma, "and nothing can stop us!" In conclusion, it is my duty to add that I never saw one of them skulk before battle, or sneak to the rear after the action began. They seemed to know by instinct when the enemy might be encountered, and the only strife among them was to see who should be first in the onset. With a *corps* of such men, the more the better, properly mounted, armed and organized, nothing is impossible except defeat.

The clangor of war is over, and quiet reigns throughout the land; our chargers are converted into plow-horses, our guidons are folded tenderly away, our carbines and sabres hang rusting on the wall, our ranks are broken, and our troopers side by side gathering the victories of peace. The fire of patriotism yet burns brightly in their bosoms, and should, perchance, the bugles sound "to arms," they will rally to their standards and charge again for country, God and victory!

Music by the Band;—" *When Johnny Comes Marching Home.*"

Twelfth Toast;— *The Army of the Mississippi.*

Speech of General John Pope:

Mr. President and Gentlemen: As this is a reunion of officers belonging to organizations of Western troops, as they stood at the close of the war, and as I have not the honor to be a member of either, I had expected that I would be permitted to remain a silent guest, and avail myself of the privilege which your kindness and courtesy have conferred, to listen to the addresses of the distinguished officers who have spoken, and to renew with many of you the pleasant social intercourse which separation has so long obstructed. The toast just given, and the calls upon me, admonish me that more is expected, and I have not the privilege, even had I the inclination, to refuse to respond.

Of all the armies here represented, the Army of the Tennessee is the oldest in years and in organization. But two others had birth at the same time, and stood side by side with that army at the siege of Corinth. These two armies were the Army of the Ohio and the Army of the Mississippi. General Buell, the able soldier who organized and commanded the Army of the Ohio, during its whole existence (an army noted in its day for its organization, its discipline, and its efficiency) is not here present, to speak in fitting terms in its honor; but General Thomas, the most renowned of its soldiers, whose name and fame are inseparably connected with it and its successor (the Army of the Cumberland), sits on my right, and is, no doubt, both ready and willing to respond in its behalf.

Of the Army of the Mississippi, which it is my highest honor to have organized and commanded, it seems appropriate that I should say something, and I trust you will bear with me if I seem extravagant in the few remarks which I shall make. The official life of the Army of the Mississippi was not long, but it was long enough to inscribe on its banners "New Madrid," "Island No. 10," and "Corinth," "Second Corinth," and "Iuka;" long enough to bear on its rolls such names as Schuyler Hamilton, C. S. Hamilton, Plummer, and Kirby Smith; long enough to give to the Armies of the Tennessee and Cumberland such renowned soldiers as Rosecrans, Sheridan, Stanley, Mower, Granger, Corse, Palmer, Elliott, Noyes, Fuller, Sprague, Wager Swayne, Morgan, and many others; long enough to contribute to these armies (mainly to the Army of the Tennessee), some of their best and most distinguished regiments. An organization which gave such deeds and such soldiers to the country, should not be suffered to be forgotten amongst men, and I esteem it a privilege that it has fallen to my lot to recall to remembrance its brilliant record. Of the pain and reluctance with which I found myself separated from that army in the midst of its successful career, by orders which I could not resist, and of what afterward befell, it perhaps does not become me to speak, except to say that in time of trial and misconception, confronted by difficulties which the country seems yet little to comprehend, I was strengthened to endurance by the knowledge conveyed in a thousand assurances that the sympathy and confidence of that army went with me through all. But a few months after the evacuation of Corinth the organization of the Army of the Mississippi was broken up, and its commanders and its regiments absorbed in the Armies of the Tennessee and Cumberland. From that day their fortunes were identified with those armies. In the great campaigns which swiftly followed; in their toils and perils; in their victories, and in their fame, the old regiments of the Army of the Mississippi bore their full part, and have their full share; but I do not doubt, indeed I know, that even now, assembled here to recall and to enjoy the remembrance of their later achievements, and the fame of their latest army organizations, they look back with affection to the old Army of the Mississippi, and remember with pride and pleasure its brilliant history.

The War of the Rebellion, with all its brilliant deeds, and its heroic sacrifices, has been consigned to history, and its vivid impressions are fast fading from the minds of men. It seems eminently proper, then, that the gallant soldiers who played their part in this great war, and to whom the Government to-day stands indebted for its life, should meet together from time to time to keep alive the memories of the past achievements, and the cordial brotherhood which binds them together. But let us hope that the next reunion of the Western armies may embrace all those who at any time served in the armies of the West. Let us remember the many gallant officers wounded at Belmont, Donelson, and Shiloh; at Pea Ridge, at Island No. 10, at

Corinth, and at Perryville, and, because of their wounds, never able to rejoin their commands. Let us be mindful of the many officers separated at an early day from the Western armies by orders or other circumstances which they could not control. Let us recollect the numerous and widely dispersed forces serving in Missouri and Arkansas who played their part manfully in the field to which they were assigned. None of these belong to the army organizations here represented, and yet there is not one of them who did not feel an equal interest in the career of the Western armies, and does not feel an equal pride in their splendid achievements. Not as guests, but as members in full brotherhood, these men should be welcomed at any future reunion of the armies of the West.

The cordial harmony, and the earnest good feeling so plainly manifested among the large number of officers who have taken part in this reunion, sufficiently demonstrate that neither widely separated homes, diversity of pursuits, nor differences of political opinion, have sufficed to weaken the strong friendships formed in stirring scenes of war, and cemented by so much glory and so much grief. It is to this feeling of personal regard among the members of the great armies which have so lately been re-absorbed into the bosom of the people that we are indebted for much of our immunity from personal and political bitterness and distrust, and as these great armies once saved the life of this nation by the power of their arms, it is by no means improbable that they may yet preserve it from further civil strife and convulsion through the influence of the personal attachment and confidence formed during the war, and strengthened and perpetuated during these army reunions.

THIRTEENTH TOAST; — *Our Sister Armies of the East, the South, the Gulf, and the Frontier.*

Speech of General THOMAS C. FLETCHER, of Missouri:

COMRADES: The fame of our sister armies is enrolled in the Capitol; their deeds are preserved in the record of the events of the time. The glory they shed upon American arms will grow brighter and brighter as time shall reveal more fully all the causes which contributed to our final victory. On the most thrilling pages of the history of the great American War, there will be found inscribed the deeds of the ARMY OF THE EAST. Its fame can not be added to by any proceeding here on our part. It first taught the vaunting Southerner to respect the valor and the manhood of the men of the North. It exhibited first, and perhaps in highest degree, the persistence and power of endurance which distinguish the American soldier. Defeated, crushed, hurled back; broken and bleeding, they rallied again and again, and were taken back by successive leaders to fight the bravest and best of the troops of the South. Roman and Grecian heroism will fail to claim the attention of the generations of the future, when they shall read the story of the brave and true men who were nerved by faith in God, and in the justice of their cause to do the deeds of the Army of the East. Their deeds are history. No eulogy from me can add to their glory. No eloquence can add to the force of the plain facts of that history. '

And our SISTER ARMY OF THE SOUTH! Who would attempt the useless task of weaving a wreath of rhetoric above or about the chaplet of glory with which it crowned itself in the contest with the strong, well organized, desperate and well supplied enemy, on his own soil, and aided by the very climate, which was to him healthful, but full of disease and death to

the stranger? We can only leave for the history of the Army
of the South our testimony, as actors with it in the great general
struggle for liberty and law, to the noble part it bore.

What can be said of the Army of the Gulf that has not been
said of the Sister Armies of the East and of the South?
When exultation gives place to the calmer enjoyment of
the results of great achievements, then all the means which
contributed to the final success are looked for and appreciated.
The history of a nation is usually but the story of its wars ; the
first version, what the armies say of themselves, the later one,
what they say of each other. We need not wait for the reason-
ing and philosophical study of the coming time to trace out the
deeds of our Army of the Frontier, and to speculate as to its
importance in the causes which contributed to the grand results of
the war for liberty and the Union. The Armies of the Tennessee,
Cumberland, Ohio, and Georgia lead it here by the hand as a
sister to the very presence of the future, and before witnesses
whose name and fame will outlive that of Cæsar and Bonaparte,
and fade from freedom's scroll only with the name of Washington—they proclaim our Army of the Frontier full sharer
of their glory. Though comparatively few in their numbers,
they were strong in their faith, and with heroic hand wrote "the
fiery gospel in rows of burnished steel" all over the prairies,
and along the river shores where the hand of the savage wielded
the scalping-knife in Confederate service for the cause of slavery
and rebellion. And where superior forces opposed, and lurking
foes did foul murder in the name of war, through the valley
dark with the terror and blood of neighborhood deadly strife,
they led the patriot citizen up to the inspiring heights of new
hope. Tradition, story, and song will hand down to the
posterity of the brave and noble Union men of Southwest Missouri and Northern Arkansas the names and memory of our
Army of the Frontier, and on the smoke-dried cottage wall

will smile their pictures brave and bright. They made historic the hills, and prairies, and fords, where they met the enemy, at Cane Hill, Prairie Grove, Bentonville; and in numberless engagements they bore the flag in triumph, kept over twenty-five thousand of the enemy constantly employed, and made continued marches, the rapidity and heroism of which were not exceeded in the war. The gallant little army went in its greatest proportions, like its distinguished leaders, Schofield, Herron, and Blunt, to win new glory on other fields, in other army organizations, and to join the swelling tide that, under Providence, was directed by Grant and Sherman in the course that swept away the Confederacy.

SONG by the Glee Club ;—"*America.*"

FOURTEENTH TOAST ; — *The Loyal Citizens who sustained us at Home while we fought the Enemy at the Front.*

Speech of GOVERNOR OGLESBY :

SOLDIERS : "The loyal citizens who supported you at home while you fought the enemy at the front," are listening with silent but attentive ear to what shall be said here to-night. In the presence of this august assemblage of our national patriotic brotherhood ; in the presence of the soldiers of the Republic, the loyal people have no report to make, except to say, God bless the noble soldiers who fought for and saved the nation. Outside of these walls, to-night, there is peace. A cautious, patriotic, and appreciative people know who to thank and to honor for this priceless boon. Quiet and dignified in the hour of victory, they calmly survey the field, and place the laurel where only it belongs, upon the brow of the brave. How proud the loyal citizens are of the good men assembled here — men who have offered their lives for their country. The tattered and battle-worn flags hanging about this hall to-night, shield and protect you now, and bear witness to your heroism and devotion in the days of the fearful strife of battle. In the name of the loyal people, who wish to be silent when the soldiers are about to speak, I will say that one and all of you, from the honored private to the commander-in-chief, are borne forever, and affectionately, in their hearts. Thus responding for the loyal masses; thus speaking for every man, woman and child in the grand old Republic, I bid you welcome, and in their names, hail with delight your presence here to-night."

FIFTEENTH TOAST; — *The Loyal Women of the United States.*

Speech of Colonel J. M. BROWN:

MR. CHAIRMAN, AND COMRADES OF THE GRAND ARMIES: The toast just proposed deserves an abler respondent than I can hope to be. It is our recognition of the heroism, the loyalty, and the self-sacrifice of the women of America, who gave to the country all that they hold dearest. If absolute loyalty is to be honored; if the love of country and abnegation of self is to be approved and reverenced by us; if disinterested labor and sacrifice, that counted not the cost, is worthy the gratitude of truly grateful hearts, then are the women — the loyal mothers, wives and sisters of our common country — those whom we, the soldiers of the Republic, in our hour of reunion, should honor with the truest, the sincerest gratitude of soldiers' hearts.

What sacrifice on the country's altar was more dearly purchased than the life of the husband who left his widow desolate? What can comfort the heart of her, whose only boy died that the nation might live? Who can count the tears of her whose hope in the coming years poured out his blood that the tree of our liberties might be watered therewith? If we who survive feel the moistening eye and the thickening throat as we recall the names and features of our comrades who have gone before, how ever present the sorrow of those whose staff and hope have departed, whose joys and whose loves lie buried in a bloody grave! Sir, we made our sacrifices. We marched and bivouacked. We fought. We triumphed. For us there is the consolation of victory gloriously earned. We who survive find in these reunions, and in our country's approval, the reward of our trials, our dangers, and of our hardships. But the loyal women of the United States have no rewards that find their expression in occasions like this. Theirs was for each an individual devotion; the sorrow of each is her own burden of grief. We who have fought this fight well know the power that woman's aid lent to the fallen Confederacy. We have seen too often how female resolution supported the failing spirit of the disheartened Confederates. We have seen how woman's power was potent against the right, and how men, in a wrong cause, were nerved by it. But we have all of us seen, as well, the power of the loyal woman's influence. All of us have felt the animating spirit of the wives, and mothers, and sisters, who gave their dear ones to the country, and whose zeal flagged not while the country was imperiled. Who is there here of all the great armies, who does not recall with tenderest memories the blessing of her who sent him forth to do battle for the right? Have we not abundant cause to thank "the loyal women of the United States," that we entered the conflict strong in heart, and persevered to the glorious end? But the loyal woman's mission did not end with the gift of husband, or son, or brother, to the Republic. Her care and prayer were constant and efficacious. The whole world stood amazed at the prodigies of benevolence

II

wrought, through woman's hands, by our unparalleled Sanitary Commission. The blessings distributed by that benign charity are only known to us, fellow-soldiers, who saw and shared, in the hospital, the bounties which our loyal women, with laboring hearts and open hands, so freely furnished. To the loyal women of our country, then, let us give the praise which every soldier's heart feels to be so justly their due. Their patriotism first sent husbands, sons and brothers to the national armies—their love and devotion followed us in our campaigns, and in battle; their care was ever vigilant for us when sick and wounded; their prayers ever ascended to heaven for our safety and for the right.

Music by the Band;—"*Home, Sweet Home.*"

Sixteenth Toast;—*The Armies of the Republic in War and in Peace;*—The Rebellion called them into existence—its overthrow converted their swords into ploughshares, and their spears into pruning hooks. By quietly disbanding and returning to the avocations of peace, they have astonished the world no less than by their prowess in the field.

Speech of General M. F. Force:

Comrades: "Peace hath her victories no less renowned than those of war." Those tattered colors thickly clustered around these walls speak to us with mute eloquence. They are whispering from every fold the story of our four years' toil. Our pulses beat fast as they recall these campaigns, battles, sieges. But the proudest achievement they call to mind, is the army's quiet muster out, and return to the pursuits of peace.

They who bore these colors were no army of mercenary troops, or of subjects fighting only for their monarch's glory, or their own. They were born a host of citizens, with homes to leave, and homes to return to, taking up arms only from profoundest impulse of duty, and glad to lay them aside when the occasion was over. Those citizens, independent men who looked the world in the face, and acknowledged no man a superior, self-reliant men who pushed through the world with their own wits and their own strong arms, men accustomed to have a voice in the control of public affairs, seemed at first unruly material out of which to make an army. Yet, in a few months, swarms of such citizens were transformed into a vast, smoothly working machine ; or rather one .great living being, with one central brain, and moving in every part responsive to the will of the commander as the very muscles of his body.

The very trait which makes the American an independent citizen, made him an obedient soldier. He yields respect to law, not as a power which can enforce obedience, but as an authority to which reverence is due. So when he learned that military discipline is a part of the law, that military command is a function given by law, and military obedience is a duty prescribed by law, that moment he became a soldier, yielding implicit and prompt compliance to orders, not with the mechanical obedience of routine, but with an intelligent instinct which often anticipated· orders.

So citizens learned the arts of war without forgetting the ways of peace, and when the time for disbanding came, it was easy to lay aside the musket and return to the plow. When that time came, some even in the field doubted the results of sudden emancipation from discipline. Many at home who had only heard of the desolations of war, were apprehensive. When the fields of war disgorged a million men, and the roads leading north shook with the tread of discharged soldiers, some at home seemed to see a cloud sweeping up to scatter disorder through the land. The cloud came. It spread over the whole country, but only to dissolve into gentle rain, permeating, enriching

the land. A million soldiers disappeared. In their place
appeared a milllion busy citizens, on every farm, in every work-
shop, and office, as if they had never known war. These men,
keeping the promise many made at the muster out, "we will
now go home, and in our own lives give an example of that
obedience to law which we have enforced in others," present a
rarer spectacle than any shock of arms. Each one thus faithfully doing the duty that he has before him, no matter how humble
the sphere of his daily toil, no matter how secluded the hamlet in
which he lives, is, in his own place, as truly noble as Washington at Valley Forge, or Grant at Appomattox.

SEVENTEENTH TOAST; — *The Loyal and Patriotic Press.*

Speech of General CARL SCHURZ:

SOLDIERS: I think I shall confer a favor upon this assembly if I refrain from making a long speech. I can not, like
our Commander-in-Chief, the President elect, plead that I am
entirely unaccustomed to public speaking, but I can hardly find
fault with you if, on an occasion like this, you can not accustom
yourselves, very easily, to quiet listening. The toast I have to
respond to is: "The Loyal and Patriotic Press!" I think I
can improve upon the sentiment: The union of the men of the
pen and the men of the sword! The men of the sword have
valiantly and gloriously carried out and enforced the ideas
and principles for long years advocated by the loyal and
patriotic men of the pen. That is their highest glory. The
men of the pen will never become tired of sounding the
praise of the patriotic men of the sword. And now they
are battering, with the formidable artillery of printed letters,
the citadels of ignorance, prejudice and disloyalty which the
men of the sword have still left standing. The union, then,

of the men of the sword and the men of the pen; of the men of action and the men of thought, of intelligence and power. As long as that union lasts, the Republic of the United States will be safe.

EIGHTEENTH TOAST;—*Our Invited Guests.*

Speech of Governor EDWARD SALOMON, of Wisconsin:

MR. PRESIDENT, AND GENTLEMEN OF THIS ARMY REUNION: With diffidence I rise before this assemblage of laurel-crowned soldiers. I see before me the great and world-renowned commander of those armies, whose brave and distinguished officers are united upon this festive occasion. Gracefully he wears upon his brows his high, well-earned honors. Here, too, is the old brave commander of the Army of the Cumberland, all covered with glory and renown, whose equestrian figure will grace the National Lincoln Monument at Washington, if the voice of his old command and that of the nation is heeded, but whose fame will outlive all monuments of stone or metal. Then I behold that distinguished and energetic commander of the Army of the Ohio, who now so ably wields the power of the War Office; and hosts of others of great distinction, whose names are well known to fame, are here assembled. On all sides, indeed, I find myself, surrounded by men upon whose daring, valor and fortitude, a few short years ago, depended the fate of this great American Republic, and who, with their comrades in arms, on land and water, saved it from destruction. It is an impressive scene, and one which crowds the memories of our great national struggle so thick and fast upon me that language fails me aptly to express my feelings. And then, foremost among your invited guests (for such I take him to be, although most emphatically one of your number) there is that man who, above all others, is the idol

of the American people, on whom rested the supreme command
of all the Union armies during the last years of that fearful war,
so happily brought to a successful close by his indomitable
energy and great generalship, and who, chosen soon to assume
the highest position in the gift of this free people, stands before
them as their second Washington. You have assembled here,
Mr. President and gentlemen, to renew the memories of the past,
the recollection of your deeds, and of the scenes through which
you passed when battling for the preservation of the Union; and
we, your invited guests, have gladly come here to enjoy with you
the pleasures of this reunion, and to do honor and homage to you
and to those bright deeds of valor indelibly written by you upon
the pages of American history. In one sense, the guests which
you have invited represent the people of this nation outside of
your organization. With pride and interest that people look
upon this reunion, and follow your proceedings here.

"Either *with* the shield or *upon* the shield return," was the
last word of the Spartan mother to her son when he went forth
to do battle for his country. You, gentlemen of the army,
returned "*with the shield;*" returned victors, and your mother-
country is proud of you, and glad to see you rejoice in your
deeds! In behalf of your invited guests, and of all the loyal
people of this land; nay, in the name of all lovers of liberty
every where, I would fain take each one of you by the hand, and
in one warm pressure renew what my tongue fails to express—
the gratitude of this free people for all you did and suffered for
your country's cause. That integral and substantive part of the
Union forces known as "Sherman's Army," has quite a history
of its own, a glorious record of brave deeds and able generalship,
which will be handed down from generation to generation.
"Sherman's March to the Sea," will be a phrase whose significance will be known to every American school-boy, and at the
Christmas table the very children will know what a splendid

Christmas gift was made by General Sherman to President Lincoln, in 1864. That march, and that Christmas gift, were "the beginning of the end" of the war! But, Mr. President, it is not for me, here, further to dilate upon the glories of Sherman's army. They are better known to you than me, and have been spoken of by eloquent lips. In the world's history there have been many wars, but none more sacred, none whose purpose was purer and holier than this great war for the preservation of the Union; and well may you, gentlemen of the army, be proud of the memories of that war, and commemorate them on occasions like this. You have also assembled here, however, to renew the friendships formed in those trying struggles and scenes, when, side by side, you suffered, and fought, and bled to uphold our country's flag. Thomas Moore somewhere most truly says that

> 'The love born of sorrow,
> Like sorrow, is true."

So it is with your friendships of the war. They were born in the nation's greatest agony and trials, amid the carnage of battle and the sorrows and deprivations of the field, and they have been sealed by the death of three hundred thousand of our country's youth and manhood. Such friendships must live; they can not die but with their possessors. Permit me, Mr. President, and gentlemen of the army, in conclusion of these few remarks, to express to you this sentiment:

> "May friendship die,
> And hatred live,
> *Never* in your hearts.'

NINETEENTH TOAST ; — *The South — Let us have Peace.*

Speech of General DURBIN WARD :

MR. PRESIDENT AND FELLOW-CITIZENS : We are here in peace, recalling to mind the friendships and the glories of an era of war. Around me are the heroes of a hundred fields. In the bivouac, the march, and the battle we lived, struggled and triumphed together. Many of our comrades in the long and weary "*tramp, tramp, tramp,*" perished by the wayside ; many pined to death in the prison or the hospital, and many went down gloriously on the gory field, while the din of battle chanted their requiem in the "diapason of the cannonade ;" while we, some bullet-riddled, scarred and maimed, some developed and strengthened in every fibre of physical and moral manhood, have emerged from the deadly clouds of war into the glad sunshine of peace, and meet to-day as brothers to feed anew in the altars of our hearts the holy fires of an undying patriotism. And now, my comrades, when "grim-visaged war hath smoothed his wrinkled front," and even the re-echoes of the conflict are fading from our ears, let us not forget the significance of the struggle, or the grandeur of the achievement. Remember not merely the feats of valor, or of military genius — these are in no danger of passing out of mind ; they are already blazoned forever upon the illumined page of history. But, grand as they were, the great cause for which we fought was grander still. The splendor of our victories are surpassed by nothing before in the history of the world ; but their glory is enhanced by the nobleness of the cause in which they were gained. They fought for a nation's life ; they achieved a nation's peace and grandeur. It is this peace and grandeur — it is this peace and this glorious destiny which patriotism enjoins us to constantly remember, and transmit with grateful hearts to the keeping of our children.

It is a severe but just commentary on the dominion of passion and prejudice over reason, that great and revolutionary changes in political organizations are rarely made except through bloodshed. The internal convulsions of Rome, the overthrow of feudalism, and the consolidation of monarchy in Europe, the Reformation, the era of Cromwell, and the French Revolution are notable examples in other countries. Nor are we an exception. Our national independence was baptized in blood, and our Federal Union consolidated in the fiery furnace of war. Political theorists had doubted or denied the perpetual obligation of our national compact, and asserted the freedom of the States to withdraw at pleasure; and, sad as was the ordeal, our institutions, like those of other nations, had to be tried by the dread arbitrament of force, and their perpetual covenant sealed in blood. The political growth of our nationality was stunted, and crippled by the heresy of secession, and our national escutcheon was stained by the sin of slavery; from the heresy and the stain alike the triumph of our arms has forever relieved our national future.

But these are not the only great achievements of the war. The political thinker and the humane enthusiast may have made one or the other of these the load-star of his action. But higher, and deeper, and holier than all else in the popular heart, was that mysterious, half-religious sentiment of patriotism, worth more to a nation than all the dogmatic catechisms of the politicians. Our country! our flag! fired the heart and nerved the arm of the American soldier, as his faith and its symbol, the cross, inspired the heroic crusader. The chief good of the war, then, was the lofty, the sublime patriotism it cultivated. The Constitution of the National Government, the rights of the states, and the balance of power between them, are the adaman-

tine walls of our political structure. But the people make and
unmake ; they are the Government itself, and on their wisdom
and patriotism alone the whole superstructure finally rests.
Should the mightiest nation on earth menace the rights, or seek
to overthrow our Government, would not millions of soldiers
equally from the North and the South rush eagerly to the front
in the nation's defence? The South! *Let us be friends!*
We have conquered the South, but we have not vanquished them
to servitude. We have only redeemed them from secession and
war to union and peace. Who that took part in the strife does
not know that even in its darkest hours, a love for the old flag
lingered in the breasts of the rebels themselves? When most
defiant, did they not model their national and state governments
mainly on ours? In their maddest moments they remembered
with love the old forms of institution, and copied their very flag
from our own. Like lovers parted by a sudden quarrel, the old
affection between the sections was secretly cherished by each, and
was stronger than either knew. In returning again to the open
arms of the Union, the defeated South has nothing to conquer
but its wounded pride, and our own magnanimity ought to make
that no dificult task. We have gloriously proved we knew how
to make war; let us now magnanimously show we know how to
make peace. The victory of arms is ours. All that stood in the
way of peace and union is buried in the grave of the past. Let
its only epitaph be, "To err is human; 'tis Divine to forgive."
The victors can afford to be generous, and the truly brave are
always magnanimous to the disarmed. The merciful terms of
Grant and Sherman to their conquered foes do them as much
honor as their grandest victories. Nay, they are their grandest
victories.

Fellow-soldiers, in the heat of conflict we may have felt the
animosities of civil war, but we ever stanched the wounds of a
foe, or cooled the dying lips of even an enemy. And now, in

he hour of victory and peace, we are called on to bind up the wounds of a conquered section, and teach them to cultivate friendship by cultivating it ourselves, to reciprocate the esteem and confidence cherished by our common ancestors. As the ocean which has been tossed by the storms of a season, but then returns to its accustomed tides, so the passions of sectional strife do not at once subside with the storm, but will, ere long, be called to sleep in the quiet ocean of national peace, whose only sectional uses shall be the emulation of brothers in the service of a common country. Sprung from the same noble ancestry, nurtured to love the same free institutions, speaking the same language, inspired by the same religious faith, and heirs to the same glorious national heritage, who can doubt that a few years will make us all, of every section, proud alike of our free institutions and national glory, and equally fired by the loftiest national patriotism? The impetuous Southerner, goaded by imaginary wrongs which a false theory had taught him were real ones, struck for what his mistaken zeal clothed with the dignity of "rights," and gallantly he fought for them while resistance was possible, and the same ardor will nerve his arm in the national service, now that the elements of national strife are buried forever in the grave of the "Lost Cause." Men of the South, if we are but true to ourselves, how gloriously looms up the national future! The graves of your Revolutionary sires are sacred soil, no less in our affections than in yours. The services of your great men in times past, in peace and in war, are as dearly cherished by us as by you. Your ancestors and ours went hand in hand to the council-boards, and stood shoulder to shoulder on the battle-fields of the Revolution. You and we were once friends in peace and war. Your valor and ours were the common price of our vast dominion and of our common glory. Once more "let us be friends." The great future is ours and yours, and with it the hopes and the destinies of a common country. If we would make that future peaceful and grand, let us, as soon as possible, bury the animosities of the late war, and vie with each other in developing to the utmost the spirit of brotherly love and national patriotism. We have the finest institutions, the richest sources of national wealth, of any people on earth, and we need but peace, fraternal confidence, and wise counsels to be the ruling power in the family of nations, and at the same time the home of the freest and happiest people the world ever saw. Counseled by the lessons of our Divine Master, let us bury the " dead past." Nerved to the arduous duties of the " living present," and inspired by the stirring hopes of a magnificent future, let us strike hands with all of every section who " keep step to the music of the Union," and, in the spirit of a catholic patriotism, send greeting to the whole country, universal amnesty and perpetual friendship.

Song by the Glee Club;—" *Shall Old Acquaintance be Forgot?*"

LETTERS.

THE following letter of invitation, and the replies appended, form an interesting part of the General Reunion Report:

COMMITTEE ROOMS, ARMIES TENNESSEE, }
CUMBERLAND, OHIO AND GEORGIA, }

CHICAGO, *November* 30, 1868.

SIR ; — The soldiers of the Western armies represented in the Armies of the Cumberland, the Tennessee, the Ohio, and Georgia, feeling that the best memories of their lives are connected with those years which they spent in the successful effort to vindicate the integrity of their government and country, and obedient, as of yore, to the call of their old leader, LIEUTENANT GENERAL SHERMAN, will assemble at Chicago on the fifteenth and sixteenth of December next, to renew again in social intercourse friendships formed, and to perpetuate the ties which so closely bound them together, in the hour of peril and danger to their common country.

You are respectfully and cordially invited to be present and participate in the observances of the occasion.

An immediate reply, addressed to GENERAL A. C. DUCAT, Secretary of this Committee, will be thankfully received, and will facilitate the necessary arrangements for the reception of those who accept this invitation.

We have the honor to be, very respectfully,

Your obedient servants,

JOHN MCARTHUR,
F. T. SHERMAN,
A. C. DUCAT,
JOHN M. CORSE,
W. B. SCATES,
JULIUS WHITE,
A. C. MCCLURG,
WM. E. STRONG,

} *Committee of Invitation.*

WASHINGTON, *December* 14, 1868.

GENERAL ; — Please express my thanks to your Committee for their kind invitation to be present at the Army Reunion at Chicago, and my regret that I can not avail myself of it.

The gratitude of the whole people follows the brave soldiers who saved the Republic, one and indivisible. Even the gallant men whose cause was lost will yet find, welcome to generous rivalry in service to our common country, that their loss was not loss, but exceeding gain.

Yours, very respectfully,

S. P. CHASE.

GENERAL A. C. DUCAT,
        Secretary of Committee.

NEW YORK, *December 7th*, 1868.

DEAR SIR ; — I am in receipt of your favor of the 2nd instant, inviting me to be present at the Reunion of our Western Army, on the 15th, and hasten to answer you that, while nothing could give me more pleasure than to meet with those who composed that gallant Army,—whose march was always onward, and whose movements I once watched with so much anxiety and interest, when my duties called me to the Upper Mississippi,—still the numerous engagements I have already accepted, and the very inclement state of the weather, render it impossible for me to comply with the request.

I regret this the more, inasmuch as I have always advocated the constant reunion of those of both branches of the service, as the best mode of establishing that good-fellowship and harmony which always should exist between such as have endured together the privations of war; which was particularly the case in our recent Rebellion.

As I shall not, therefore, be able to make the speech you desire, permit me to give you, in its stead, the following sentiment:

"The Army and Navy of the United States—While each is ever ready, by its own resources, to sustain the national honor, may they always stand shoulder to shoulder, as on the Mississippi, in protecting the property and preserving the union of our common country."

I am very truly yours,
D. E. FARRAGUT,
Admiral U. S. Navy.

W. E. STRONG, Esq.

———

DEPARTMENT OF STATE, WASHINGTON, D. C.,
December 7, 1868.

GENERAL A. C. DUCAT,

    Chicago, Illinois:

DEAR SIR;—I have received the invitation with which you have favored me, to the Reunion of the soldiers of the Western

Armies, to be held at Chicago on the 15th and 16th of December instant.

It ought not to be necessary for me to express, at so late a day, my exalted appreciation of the honorable and heroic services which the soldiers of the Western Armies have rendered to the Republic. It can hardly be necessary to say that it would be very inconvenient, if not impossible, for me to visit Chicago on the happy occasion referred to. I am sure that it is unnecessary to say that I sincerely regret my inability to accept the invitation, and while I earnestly hope that the meeting may be a happy and useful one,

I am very truly yours,

WILL. H. SEWARD.

ATTORNEY-GENERAL'S OFFICE, WASHINGTON,
 December 12, 1868.

SIR ;—I have had the honor to receive the kind invitation of your Committee to be present at the Army Reunion, at Chicago, on the 15th and 16th instant.

I have the good fortune to have formed the personal acquaintance of some of the celebrated soldiers who will make up your numerous and brilliant company upon this interesting occasion, and it would give me the greater pleasure to look upon the whole array of the brave defenders of our constituted liberties who shall answer to the call of their former leader, General Sherman.

So long as it is and must be easier to serve than to save the state, so long must all the professions and employments of life pay homage to the citizen soldiers who by war have maintained, that they and we in peace may obey, the laws and constitution of our country.

But necessary attendance upon my duties here will deprive me of this pleasure, and I can only send my good wishes for the general joy of your whole company.

I have the honor to be your obedient servant,

WM. M. EVARTS.

———

WASHINGTON, *December* 15, 1868.

GENERAL GEORGE H. THOMAS:

Please present to the officers and soldiers of the great Union Armies my sincere congratulations on the circumstances under which they now reunite at Chicago. May the influences of this reunion tend to establish and perpetuate fraternal feeling among all who now honor and sustain the flag, however they may have been heretofore divided.

HUGH McCULLOCH.

———

HEADQUARTERS DEPARTMENT OF THE MISSOURI, ⎫
CAMP SUPPLY, CANADIA RIVER, ⎬
INDIAN TERRITORY, *December* 5, 1868. ⎭

GENERAL McCLURG, *Chicago:*

MY DEAR GENERAL;—I am in receipt of your note of November 15, to-day, and deeply regret my inability to attend the Reunion of the armies of the West, in your city, on the 15th instant, on account of the Indian troubles in my department. I have asked Generals Sherman and Thomas to make my regrets. I had set my heart on being present at this meeting, and feel very sad over my disappointment.

Yours truly,

P. H. SHERIDAN,
Major-General.

12

ATLANTA, GEORGIA, *December* 8, 1868.

GENERAL;—I have to-day received the printed letter of invitation to be present at Chicago, on the 16th inst., to attend the Army Reunion to be then held; and I regret extremely that my public duties are of such a nature as to render it impracticable for me to accept.

I regret this the more, as it would have afforded me great pleasure to meet my brother soldiers of the Western armies, and to have interchanged with them those friendly courtesies and feelings of mutual respect and kindness which I trust will ever characterize the utterance of our nation's soldiers, whether they come from the West or the East. Earnestly and sincerely hoping—indeed feeling satisfied—that your Reunion will be productive of much pleasure, and of beneficial results in the future, I remain, with great respect,

Most truly yours,

GEORGE G. MEADE,
Major-General U. S. Army.

GENERAL A. C. DUCAT,
Secretary Committee, Chicago, Illinois.

————

WASHINGTON, D. C., *December* 11, 1868.

GENERAL A. C. DUCAT,
Secretary Committee, Chicago, Illinois.

MY DEAR GENERAL;—I have the honor to acknowledge the receipt of your communication of November 30, extending an invitation to me for the Army Reunion, to be held at Chicago on the 15th and 16th of December next.

I feel highly gratified by the compliment, and regret that it will not be practicable for me to attend.

I am, very respectfully, your obedient servant,

W. S. HANCOCK,
Major-General U. S. Army.

U. S. NAVAL ACADEMY, ANNAPOLIS, MD.,
December 5, 1868.

DEAR SIR;—I have the honor to acknowledge the receipt of your kind invitation to be present at the Army Reunion, to take place at Chicago on the 15th and 16th of December. It would afford me great pleasure to be present, but both my health and duty prevent the acceptance of your invitation. It would be a pleasant sight to me to witness the meeting of comrades who had marched and fought together for so many long years, and I should be much gratified to meet the many gallant officers of the Army of the Tennessee, with whom I was associated at Vicksburg, Red River, etc. My connection with the different branches of the Army of the Tennessee was always most agreeable to me; and, although I hope none of us may ever live to witness a renewal of the fraternal strife that has so marred the best interests of our country, yet if any party should attempt to break up this glorious Union,—the only asylum that I know of for those disposed to be free,—I trust that the army and navy will be found fighting shoulder to shoulder, as they always have done, under the flag which the armies of your reunion so gallantly carried to victory.

· Hoping that you will have a most pleasant time, and that this will not be the last occasion when the gallant officers of the army will meet in fraternal union, I remain,

Very respectfully and truly yours,

DAVID D. PORTER,
Vice-Admiral.

WILLIAM E. STRONG, Esq.,
Sec'y Executive Committee Armies of the Tennessee, etc.,
Chicago, Illinois.

HOBOKEN, NEW JERSEY, *December* 9, 1868.

GENERAL A. C. DUCAT:

GENERAL;—I have the pleasure to acknowledge the receipt of the very courteous invitation to be present at the Army Reunion to take place at Chicago on the 15th and 16th December.

It is with sincere regret that I find myself prevented, by business engagements, from accepting the invitation of the Committee, for I should no doubt find among the soldiers of the Western Armies many of my comrades of the Armies of Western Virginia, and of the Army of the Potomac, and I should be only too glad to embrace the opportunity of extending my acquaintance among the soldiers of the gallant Armies of the West.

With my sincere wishes that the reunion may, in every respect, be a most pleasant one, and that it may tend to strengthen still more the close ties of fellowship uniting the soldiers of all the Federal Armies,

I am, most respectfully, your obedient servant,

GEO. B. McCLELLAN.

NEW YORK, *December* 8, 1868.

GENERAL A. C. DUCAT,

     Secretary, etc.:

DEAR GENERAL;—I have been honored with your invitation for the 15th and 16th of December, and regret extremely that my health will prevent my participating in your rejoicings at Chicago.

I have the honor to be, very respectfully,

Your obedient servant,

J. HOOKER,
Major-General U. S. Army.

HARTFORD, CONNECTICUT, *December* 11, 1868.

GENERAL ; — I have received the invitation to attend the meeting of the soldiers of the Western Armies who belonged to General Sherman's command. Nothing would give me greater pleasure than to meet these soldiers, among whom are many of my old companions in arms, and to witness the greeting of their old commander by them.

But my engagements will not permit me to leave here now, and with thanks for your invitation, and best wishes for the entire success of the Reunion,

I am, respectfully yours,

W. B. FRANKLIN,

Former Major-General U. S. Volunteers.

GENERAL A. C. DUCAT,

Secretary, etc., etc.

———

UTICA, *December* 12, 1868.

GENTLEMEN ; — I am sorry I can not accept your invitation to attend the Reunion of the soldiers of the Western Armies, — Cumberland, Tennessee, Ohio, and Georgia, — at Chicago, on the 16th instant. As many of the regiments sent out from New York, while I was Governor of that State, served in these armies, I feel a personal as well as a national pride and interest in this gathering.

It is not necessary to speak of the respect and admiration in which the soldiers of the Republic are held by its citizens ; and foremost among you will be the distinguished General, now at the head of our armies, who won his first laurels as one of the leaders of the Armies of the West.

His election to the office of President of the United States, bears witness to the fact that, in addition to regard for his other merits, the patriotic services of the soldier are held in honorable and grateful remembrance by the American people.

I have the honor to be,

Truly yours,

HORATIO SEYMOUR.

To the COMMITTEE OF INVITATION.

WASHINGTON CITY, *December* 10, 1868.

GENERAL A. C. DUCAT,

Chicago, Illinois:

DEAR GENERAL;—The beautiful circular issued from your committee rooms, is just received by me. I would gladly obey the call of my old leader, General Sherman, and be present with you at Chicago on the 15th and 16th inst., to renew in social intercourse friendships formed, and to perpetuate the ties which so closely bound us together in the hour of peril and danger to our common country, but an engagement entered into some time since will prevent me from going. The most cordial greetings I receive are from soldiers, now civilians, who have served with us during the war; and I know that my own heart goes out towards a soldier, wounded or crippled by bullets from the enemy, or towards a family left helpless by the loss of a father upon the battle field, with more genuine sympathy, and a more earnest desire to assist, than it does towards others.

A short time ago, a young man who had lost his right arm and right leg in the service, came to my house late at night utterly destitute; his family were comparatively helpless, and dependent upon him for support; he had pawned every thing he possessed that was valuable; had earnestly sought employment up and down the streets of New York; had petitioned politicians; and, having failed in all his efforts, finally come to me utterly crestfallen and discouraged. The Secretary of War and others were able to assist him, and did so, and he went back to his home with a happy heart.

I believe, if the sympathies of the multitude for poor soldiers who have been crippled, or rendered useless for employment requiring physical effort, shall ever grow cold, that at least their old companions and officers who may be in good circumstances, with health and strength, will never fail to labor earnestly and actively in their behalf.

Trusting you may have a pleasant and profitable reunion, and one never to be forgotton, I remain, with great regard,

Your faithful friend,

O. O. HOWARD,

Brevet Major-General, U. S. Army.

———

WASHINGTON, *December* 11, 1868. ·]

GENERAL A. C. DUCAT,

Secretary Committee Invitation:

GENERAL;—I have had the honor of receiving the invitation of the Committee to the Army Reunion at Chicago on the 15th and 16th inst. The associations of the field gave rise to friendships far different from those formed under the usual conditions of life, and it would be a source of very great gratification to me to meet the gallant soldiers of the Western armies, and I regret sincerely that it is not in my power to be present and participate in the enjoyments of the reunion.

I have the honor to be, very respectfully,

Your obedient servant,

A. A. HUMPHREYS,

Brevet Major-General.

St. Paul, Minnesota, *December* 17, 1868.

General A. C. Ducat:

Sir;—On my return to this place, after an absence of two months, I found awaiting me the entirely unexpected honor of an invitation to attend the meeting of the soldiers of the Western armies at Chicago on the 15th and 16th inst.

I was at Chicago on my way to this place on the 15th, wholly unaware that an invitation had been sent me, and, although my duties did not permit my stopping to participate in the observances of the occasion, I should not have failed to express my regrets (had I known of the invitation,) that my time was not at my disposal, so that I might accept the courtesy extended.

I take this my first opportunity to acknowledge the honor of being invited, and to express my thanks for having been remembered on such an occasion.

Yours, respectfully,

G. K. Warren.

New York, *December* 9, 1868.

General;—I regret that ill health deprives me of the pleasure I anticipated in attending the reunion at Chicago on the 15th and 16th inst. Let us ever cherish the associations of our glorious struggle. I trust it may not be long before we shall see a grand reunion of the societies of all the armies.

With grateful acknowledgements to the Committee of Invitation, and to yourself,

I remain, General,

Very sincerely yours,

D. E. Sickles.

General A. C. Ducat,
Secretary Committee Invitation, Chicago, Ill.

The Western Union Telegraph Company,

NEW YORK, *December* 12, 1868.

GENERAL WM. E. STRONG,

    Secretary Executive Committee, Army Reunion:

Gratefully appreciating the honor, I regret to state that ill health prevents my undertaking the journey, and compels me to decline the distinguished part at the banquet assigned me in your kind letter of the 8th inst. All honor to the heroic armies of the West, and their illustrious leaders!

    Very respectfully,

        D. E. SICKLES,

        Brevet Major-General U. S. Army.

———

WASHINGTON, D. C., *December* 9, 1868.

GENERAL;—Please accept my sincere thanks for the invitation to be present and participate on the occasion of the reunion of the societies of the armies of the Cumberland, Tennessee, Ohio, and Georgia, and my regrets that I will be unable to avail myself of your kindness.

    Most respectfully,

      Your obedient servant,

        W. N. BARNES,

        Brevet Major-General U. S. Army.

GENERAL A. C. DUCAT,

    Secretary Committee, Chicago, Ill.

WASHINGTON, *December* 11, 1868.

GENERAL A. C. DUCAT,
   Corresponding Secretary, Chicago:

GENERAL;—I deeply regret that circumstances over which I have no control will prevent me from participating in the observances connected with your glorious Army Reunion.

Please accept my warm thanks for your cordial invitation.

I have the honor to be, General,

   Very respectfully, your obedient servant,

   S. P. HINTZELMAN,
   Brevet Major-General U. S. Army.

———

NEW YORK, *December* 12, 1868.

GENERAL;—I had the honor to receive, yesterday, the invitation of the Committee to be present at the reunion of the armies of the Tennessee, Cumberland, Ohio, and Georgia, at Chicago, on the 15th and 16th inst.

It would give me sincere pleasure to take part in the reunion of soldiers of the war; to meet again the many with whom I have been more or less intimately associated in the service; and to make the acquaintance of many more whom I know only through their reputations acquired during the war; but I am compelled by circumstances to deny myself the gratification of greeting them in person on the occasion.

   Very respectfully and truly yours,

   A. G. WRIGHT,
   Brevet Major General U. S. Army.

PRINCETON, W. VA., *December* 20, 1868.

GENERAL A. C. DUCAT:

DEAR SIR;—I beg to acknowledge the receipt of the invitation to be present at the assembling of my companions of the Western Armies at Chicago. The invitation only came to hand by last mail, thus utterly putting it out of my power to have been present.

I am assured that the reunion was full of stirring reminiscences, and have a sad regret that I could not have been with you, and enjoyed my small share of them.

Thanking the Committee for their kindness, and yourself, personally,

I am, very truly yours,

D. N. COUCH,
Major-General late U. S. Army.

———

WASHINGTON, D. C., *December* 12, 1868.

GENERAL A. C. DUCAT,
Chicago, Illinois.

GENERAL;—Many thanks for your kind invitation to be present at the reunion, in Chicago, of the Western Armies, on the 15th and 16th of this month. I regret extremely that my duties are such as will render it impracticable for me to be absent from Washington at that time. I shall ever retain the most agreeable reminiscences of my service in the West, and feel sure that the friendships formed while in the field will be permanent and lasting.

With great respect, I remain
Your obedient servant,

JOHN G. PARKE,
Brevet Major-General U. S. Army.

WASHINGTON CITY, *December* 11, 1868.

GENERAL A. C. DUCAT,

    Secretary Committee Invitation:

GENERAL;—I have the honor to acknowledge the receipt of an invitation to be present and to participate in the observances of the Reunion of the Western Armies, at Chicago, on the 15th and 16th instant. Not having been personally a participant in any of the great field struggles of the West, under Grant, Sherman, or Thomas, names immortal now, I am especially thankful for the invitation, which, however, my current duties will not allow me to accept. Permit me to propose to the Army Reunion the following sentiment: *The grand fraternity of the great Generals of the Western Armies.*

      Very respectfully, your obedient servant,

           A. B. EATON,

        Brevet Major-General U. S. Army.

———

BROOKLYN, NEW YORK, *December* 7, 1868.

GENERAL;—Yours of the 30th ultimo, conveying the polite invitation of the Committee on Army Reunion at Chicago on the 15th and 16th instant, is just received.

I regret that my duties will prevent my attendance. Many acts were performed by the Western Armies, in the late conflict, which the pen of history will render immortal, and which have sunk deep into the grateful hearts of loyal people of the whole country.

      Very respectfully,

           SILAS CASEY,

        Brevet Major-General U. S. Army.

GENERAL A. C. DUCAT,

    Chicago, Illinois.

BROOKLYN, NEW YORK, *December* 9, 1868.

GENERAL A. C. DUCAT,

    Secretary Committee Invitation, Chicago, Illinois:

GENERAL;—I have the honor to acknowledge the receipt, to-day, of the invitation to attend the Army Reunion.

I greatly regret that circumstances will prevent me from having the honor and pleasure of attending.

       With high respect, your obedient servant,

           ST. GEORGE COOKE,

           Brevet Major-General U. S. Army.

WEST POINT, NEW YORK, *December* 8, 1868.

GENERAL A. C. DUCAT,

    Chicago, Illinois:

MY DEAR GENERAL;—Your very kind invitation to be present and participate in the Army Reunion, at Chicago, on the 15th and 16th instant, is duly received. Although I can not claim to have belonged to either of the glorious organizations which are to assemble in your city on the 15th and 16th, to fight their battles over again, yet I do claim to have organized and sent forward to them, more troops from Illinois and Indiana than any other one officer, and should not, therefore, feel like a stranger in a strange land amongst them, in your great city, for doubtless some of them would recognize in me the individual who first made them *hold up their right hands* and " solemnly swear to bear true faith and allegiance," etc., and would be willing to accord me the honor of having performed the initiatory step of making them great men. I wish I could be with you, but I regret to say I can not. I have just returned from a leave of absence, and have not the conscience to ask for another leave so soon ; so will have to content myself with the newspaper reports of the speeches and good things which will be said upon the occasion.

And with my best wishes that you may have a glorious good time,

I am, General, very truly,
Your obedient servant,
L. G. Pitcher,
Brevet Major-General U. S. Army.

———

Fort Sullivan, East Port, Maine, }
December 18, 1868. }

General A. C. Ducat,
Secretary Committee of Invitation,
Armies Cumberland, Tennessee, Ohio, and Georgia.

General;—I have just received your invitation, dated 30th November, to be present at the meeting of the soldiers of the Western armies represented by the societies of the Armies of the Tennessee, Cumberland, Ohio, and Georgia, in Chicago on the 15th and 16th of this month, and to participate in the observances of the occasion.

I feel sensible of the high honor conferred upon me, and deeply regret that even had I received the invitation in time it would have been out of my power to accept it. It would have been very gratifying to me as one who, although a Western man, served throughout the war in the Army of the Potomac, to meet as comrades in a great cause our fellow soldiers of the Western armies in social intercourse, and to unite with them in doing honor to their illustrious comrade, and in recalling the memory of the great deeds they performed under his leadership; but my engagements would have made it impossible for me to go to Chicago at this time.

Very truly yours,
Henry T. Hunt,
Brevet Major-General U. S. Army.

WASHINGTON NAVY YARD, *December* 12, 1868.

DEAR SIR ;—With many thanks for the flattering and cordial invitation to participate in the observances on the occasion of the Army Reunion at Chicago. I regret very much that my duties oblige me to decline the great pleasure.

Your obedient servant,

R. BREESE,
Commander U. S. Navy.

GENERAL A. C. DUCAT,
    Chicago.

———

WASHINGTON, D. C., *December* 10, 1868.

GENERAL A. C. DUCAT,
    Secretary Committee Invitation, Chicago, Ill.

GENERAL ;—Cordially approving of the perpetuation of the fellowship and friendship which grew up among the officers and soldiers of our patriotic armies, I should delight in participating in the intercourse of your annual meeting.

I had the honor, in some of their darkest and also some of their most glorious hours, of doing what I could as a member of the general staff of the armies of the United States, to alleviate their sufferings, repair their losses, and secure their triumphs.

These are among the most agreeable recollections of a long military service. I regret that I am unable to visit Chicago on the 15th and 16th inst.

I beg of you, whom I well remember at Chattanooga, where we counseled together upon the situation, and the measures necessary for success, to give my most cordial greetings to our brother officers, and to assure them of my pride and pleasure in having been with them.

I am, very respectfully, your obedient servant,

M. C. MEIGS,

Q. M. General. Brevet Major-General U. S. Army.

————

WASHINGTON, D. C., *December* 11, 1868.

GENERAL A. C. DUCAT,

Chicago, Ill.

SIR ; — I have the honor to acknowledge the receipt of an invitation to attend the reunion of the Western armies at Chicago on the 15th and 16th of the present month.

I regret very much that my engagements forbid my being present on this interesting occasion, especially as it would afford me the pleasure of meeting the honored members of your societies, many of whom I am proud to remember among my early and most valued friends.

The object of your reunion can not be too highly appreciated, and it should commend itself to all of our citizens, who should be proud of the deeds of those armies which contributed so largely to the preservation of our Government.

I have the honor to be,

Very respectfully, your obedient servant,

A. B. DYER,

Brevet Major-General, Chief of Ordance.

————

WASHINGTON, *December* 11, 1868.

GENERAL A. C. DUCAT :

DEAR SIR ; — I am just favored with the receipt of your Committee's invitation to the great military reunion at Chicago, the 15th inst. I desire to tender my acknowledgements for the honor of the invitation, whilst I must beg of you to accept the expression of my sincerest regrets that official engagements, just now pressing upon me, will not permit my acceptance. Be assured I am with you, in spirit, most cordially, though it was not my good fortune to be permitted to participate with you in the perils and glories of the active field.

I am, with much regard,

Your obedient servant,

B. W. Brise,

Paymaster-General U. S. Army.

Washington, *December* 11, 1868.

General A. C. Ducat,

 And Gentlemen of the Committee:

Gentlemen;—I have the honor to acknowledge the receipt of your invitation to attend a meeting of the soldiers of the Western Armies, at Chicago, on the 15th and 16th of this month, and regret that I shall not be able to be with you. It was not my fortune, during the war for the suppression of the Rebellion, to serve in either of the distinguished armies you represent. Yet I watched with deep interest your splendid feats of arms, and felt a soldier's pride in every victory which crowned the heroic efforts of that portion of the Grand Army of the Republic. Having three times crossed the continent with Western troops, and tasted with them the luxury of mule and buffalo bull meat, I never had a doubt but that your armies would overcome all obstacles and force which might oppose them; and when you cut loose from your base and swung out from Atlanta, when the whole country was anxious, watching the pillar of cloud by day, and fire by night, that marked your course, I never for a moment doubted that you would arrive safely at the sea.

13

I will not occupy your time by making any thing like a detailed reference to the achievements of your armies, but I must say that your organization seeks the accomplishment of an object worthy of the brave men of which those armies were composed, and that it has my entire sympathy and hearty wishes for its success and perpetuity.

I have the honor to be, gentlemen, with high regard,

Your obedient servant,

W. H. EMORY,

U. S. Army, Late Major-General of Volunteers, Commanding 19th Army Corps.

BRISTOL, ILLINOIS, *December* 13, 1868.

GENERAL A. C. DUCAT :

DEAR SIR ;—It has been a most earnest desire on my part to be present in Chicago at the time of the gathering of the armies, but a sickness that has now laid me aside for two weeks, forbids it. I am suffering from an attack of acute bronchitis, and have not left my quarters for a fortnight.

Please express to any of our old comrades my regret at not being permitted to meet them, and assure them of my continued interest in their welfare.

Yours, most truly,

JOEL GRANT.

NEW YORK, *December* 14, 1868.

GENERAL ;—I very much regret that the invitation to be present at the Army Reunion at Chicago reached me so late that I was unable to alter engagements made for this week. It would have given me much pleasure to be present. I should have been glad to meet again the friends with whom I had been associated du'ring the war, and to have made the acquaintance of others so well known to us all, but whom I have not had the pleasure to know personally.

Yours truly,
J. C. FREMONT.

GENERAL A. C. DUCAT,
  Chicago.

WASHINGTON, *December* 13, 1868.

DEAR GENERAL ;—I am in grief that I am compelled at this last moment to give up going to Chicago. Tell all our Cumberland boys that I regret more than I can tell. But our work here has accumulated so that I can not get away. Write me, and let me know what kind of a time you had.

Ever yours,
J. GARFIELD.

WASHINGTON, *December* 12, 1868.

GENERAL A. C. DUCAT ;—Your kind invitation to attend the reunion of the Western Armies, was received some days since, and I have delayed to reply until the last moment, hoping to find a way to accept the same. I deeply regret that I am compelled to decline.

To meet with the noble assemblage of men who will doubtless be with you on this great occasion, I should heartily enjoy. To hear them recount anew their experiences and triumphs for liberty's sake, would add new force to the admiration which I, in common with all their grateful countrymen, cherish toward them. To recall the glorious deeds of our sainted dead, whose self-sacrificing patriotism is the marvel of the whole civilized world, would yet more exalt and hallow their sacred memory. To assist in the expression of our common pride in the glory of our national arms, would be with me a labor of love.

It is the proudest memory of my life that I was permitted to be a part of the mighty past, and that my tongue and hand were the instruments to call into action many of the immortal heroes whose names were not born to die; and especially do I feel interested in this reunion, for it is in very deed the marshaling anew of the genius and prowess which first lifted the clouds of adverse fortune from the nation's horizon, and revealed the nation's redemption. One name we may mention without danger of being considered invidious, for his glory is ours. He moved into the mighty arena, and order sprang from chaos. He spoke victory into being. Lately, with the foresight of a prophet, and the authority of a predestined ruler, looking upon the new gathering of discordant and stormy elements, he said, "Let us have peace," and the storm recognized its master and straightway accepted the situation.

In closing, I can only renew my thanks for the invitation tendered, and my regrets that I can not be with you. Congratulating you upon the happy prospects for our beloved country, so near at hand, and wishing you entire success in the objects for which you meet,

I am, General, with profound regard,
Your friend,
RICHARD YATES.

To GENERAL DUCAT,
  And the Committee.

ALBANY, *December* 7, 1868.

DEAR SIR; — It would afford me great pleasure to participate in the festivities of the reunion, at Chicago, of the soldiers of the armies of the West; a pleasure which would be enhanced by the privilege of seeing so many whose names are honorably identified with the defence of the country. Official duties incident to the close of my term of office are so pressing as to prevent me, greatly to my regret, from being with you.

Very respectfully,
R. E. FENTON.

GENERAL A. C. DUCAT,
Secretary Committee Invitation, Chicago, Ill.

NORWICH, CONN., December 12, 1868.

GENERAL A. C. DUCAT,
Corresponding Secretary:

DEAR SIR ;— I thank you for your invitation for the 15th and 16th inst., and regret that I can not join in your congratulations on that interesting occasion.

Permit me, however, to claim the privilege of being closely allied and deeply interested in the soldiers who composed the Army of the Union, and to say that no language that I can use can express my appreciation of their services.

I am, with great respect,
Your obedient servant,
WM. A. BUCKINGHAM.

WASHINGTON, December 11, 1868.

GENERAL ;— I have the honor to acknowledge the receipt of an invitation to be present at the reunion of the Western armies which will assemble at Chicago on the 15th and 16th of this month.

Having had the good fortune, as Governor of Minnesota, to aid in sending into the field many noble regiments which shared in the dangers and glories of the armies of the West, it would afford me sincere pleasure to participate in the observances of this very interesting occasion. But I regret that the requirements of public business will probably prevent my attendance.

Yours, very truly,

ALEXANDER RAMSEY.

EXECUTIVE DEPARTMENT, INDIANA, ⎱
December 18, 1868. ⎰

GENERAL A. C. DUCAT,

Secretary Committee Invitation, Chicago, Ill.

DEAR SIR;—I have the honor to acknowledge the receipt of the communication of your Committee of the 30th ultimo, inviting me to be present and participate in the Army Reunion to be held at Chicago on the 15th and 16th days of the present month.

Allow me to assure you that I deeply regret that official engagements will prevent me from enjoying the pleasure and honor of participating in the observances of the occasion.

Trusting that the reunion may more than realize the expectations of the gallant and patriotic soldiers who may participate therein, and to whom the Republic owes so much, and with many thanks to the Committee for the kind invitation,

I have the honor, General, to be,

Very respectfully, your obedient servant,

CONRAD BAKER.

LINCOLN, *December* 15, 1868.

SIR ;—Your favor of the 30th, containing the invitation to attend the reunion of the armies of the West, was this day received. The delay results from the fact that the capitol of the state has been recently removed from Omaha to this place, and, probably, from a temporary stoppage of the mails from the recent storm.

Nothing would have afforded me greater pleasure than to have been present at your reunion to-day, to meet the heroes of the battles of the Mississippi Valley, and of Sherman's march to the sea.

May this reunion cement more firmly the bonds of fellowship between the glorious men of the armies of the West, and cause the fires of patriotism to glow with renewed ardor over the entire length and breadth of the Union restored by their valor.

> I have the honor to be,
> Very respectfully yours,
> DAVID BUTLER,
> *Governor of Nebraska.*

GENERAL A. C. DUCAT,
  Secretary Committee.

———

NASHVILLE, TENN., *December* 10, 1868.

MY DEAR GENERAL ;—I am compelled, by imperative professional engagements, to deny myself the pleasure of attending the reunion of the Western Armies this year. Present my best wishes and most cordial greetings to our old comrades.

> With regrets and regards,
> Very truly yours,
> G. P. THRUSTON,
> *Late Brevet Brigadier-General U. S. Army.*

ALBANY, *December* 7, 1868.

GENERAL A. C. DUCAT,
  Chicago, Illinois:

I regret that a pressure of official engagements will not admit of my acceptance of your invitation to be present at the reunion of the grand old Armies of the West, on the 15th and 16th of the present month.

Wishing you, in every respect, a joyous and happy meeting,

    I am, respectfully yours,

      S. E. MARVIN,
    Adjutant-General State New York.

———

TRENTON, N. J., *December* 11, 1868.

GENERAL A. C. DUCAT, .
  Chicago, Illinois:

GENERAL;—I have the honor to acknowledge the receipt of an invitation from your Committee to be present and participate in the Army Reunion, at Chicago, on the 15th of this month. I have delayed reply, hoping it might be possible for me to be with you, to meet many of my personal friends and old comrades. I find, however, that my official duties just at this season will deprive me of the pleasure. While I regret my own inability to be present, I add my most earnest wish that your gathering may be successful in cementing a union of men of tried loyalty, and at the same time an honor to yourselves, a glory to your country, and a sure preventive to treason in future.

    WILLIAM S. STRYKER,
    Adjutant-General New York.

DesMoines, *December* 12, 1868.

General Arthur C. Ducat,

   Secretary Committee, Chicago, Illinois:

Sir ;—I have delayed my answer to your invitation to be present at the " Reunion" of the Armies of the Tennessee, Cumberland, Georgia and Ohio, at Chicago, on the 15th and 16th instant, hoping that I should not be compelled to decline it; but duties here will deprive me of the honor and pleasure of the occasion.

Iowa has her pride in her share in those armies and their exploits. Their history is a part of our State's history. Many an Iowan will boast of his share in their victories, and his children and grand-children will remember and repeat the proud boast of the gallant soldier.

May all of you survive for many more happy reunions! Long may you live in the memories of a grateful people! And may your example, your patient endurance on the march and amid other sufferings, your gallant bearing and bravery on the battlefield, and your patriotic devotion at all times and on all occasions, be so impressed upon the hearts and very fibres of all coming men, that if emergencies ever shall arise, they will be worthy imitators of your deeds.

   With great respect, very truly yours,

      N. B. Baker.

NOTE.

THE following is a complete list of the sub-committees under whose special charge the various features of the Reunion were prepared:

FINANCE COMMITTEE.

Colonel JOHN MASON LOOMIS, *Chairman.*

General John M. Corse; General Theodore F. Brown; General M. R. M. Wallace; Major G. S. Hubbard, Jr.; Colonel L. H. Whittlesey; Colonel C. W. Davis; General James R. Hugunin; Major George Mason; General W. Scott Stewart; Colonel Samuel B. Raymond; Captain D. C. Bradley; Colonel Lyman Bridges; Captain R. P. Derrickson; Colonel J. B. Sweet; Major J. G. McWilliams; Captain Lyman A. White; Captain E. V. C. Klokke; Colonel C. Fitz Simmons; Colonel J. M. Woodworth, M.D.

COMMITTEE ON BANQUET.

General WILLIAM E. STRONG, *Chairman.*

General John McArthur; Colonel W. W. Wheeler; Colonel Huntington Jackson; Major S. B. Eaton; General C. T. Hotchkiss; General J. H. Ledlie; Colonel R. A. McFeeley; Colonel Henry Howland; Major A. H. Boyden; Captain J. P. Rumsey; General R. W. Smith; Colonel C. H. Dyer; General H. N. Eldridge; Captain W. H. Gale; Captain John W. Gregg; General John B. Turchin.

COMMITTEE ON RAILROADS AND TRANSPORTATION.

General I. N. STILES, *Chairman.*

General Joseph Stockton; Major O. A. Schultz; General J. R. Hugunin; Colonel Levi P. Wright; Colonel W. Stubbs; Captain Harry Pease; Captain A. C. McMurtry; Captain Chris. Miller; Captain O. H. Morgan; Lieutenant Fred. Fake; Lieutenant C. F. Schuman; Lieutenant John W. Rumsey.

COMMITTEE ON INVITATIONS.

General JOHN McARTHUR, *Chairman.*

General F. T. Sherman; General A. C. Ducat; General John M. Corse; General Walter B. Scates; General Julius White; General A. C. McClurg; General William E. Strong.

COMMITTEE ON RECEPTION.

General J. D. WEBSTER, *Chairman.*

General John McArthur; Major E. Powell, M.D.; General George W. Smith; General C. T. Hotchkiss; Major Lu. H. Drury; General R. W. Smith; Colonel W. W. Wheeler; General W. Scott Stewart; General A. C. McClurg; Lieutenant Caleb Blood; Colonel John Mason Loomis.

COMMITTEE ON HALLS.

General A. C. McCLURG, *Chairman.*

General Joseph Stockton; General William E. Strong; General W. Scott Stewart; Colonel W. W. Wheeler; Major A. H. Boyden.

COMMITTEE ON DECORATIONS.

Major W. L. B. JENNEY, *Chairman.*

Colonel Lyman Bridges; General Ezra Taylor; General A. C. Ducat; Colonel G. I. Waterman; Colonel Nelson K. Towner; General A. E. Erskine; General Theodore F. Brown; Colonel A. Silversparre; Major J. A. Fitch: Colonel John M. Woodworth, M.D.; Captain George F. Robinson; Major E. V. C. Klokke; Lieutenant George H. Heafford.

COMMITTEE ON PRINTING AND BADGES.*

Major S. S. HART, *Chairman.*

Major S. B. Eaton; Colonel H. S. Brown; Major J. J. Spaulding; Major Samuel E. Barrett; Colonel Oliver Stewart; Major W. L. B. Jenney; Colonel L. H. Whittlesey.

COMMITTEE ON MUSIC.

Captain L. B. CHURCH, *Chairman.*

Major A. H. Boyden; Captain Henry Bennett; Major C. S. Moore; Major E. O. F. Roeller, M.D.

* It would be pleasant, if it were practicable, to mention particular names in connection with the labors of each of the sub-committees, and to give special credit to individuals whose energy and judgment largely helped to make the Reunion a grand success. We have not done this, as a rule, but we make an exception in the case of this committee, to say that the very tasteful and pleasing results of its efforts were especially due to the efficiency and good taste of Major S. B. Eaton and Col. H. S. Brown.

Geo. H. Thomas
Maj' Genl. U.S.A.

PRESIDENT, SOCIETY ARMY OF CUMBERLAND

REPORT

[Furnished by the Recording Secretary]

OF THE

PROCEEDINGS OF THE ANNUAL MEETING

OF THE

SOCIETY OF THE ARMY OF THE CUMBERLAND,

HELD AT CHICAGO, ILLINOIS,

DECEMBER 15TH, 1868.

OFFICERS OF THE SOCIETY OF THE ARMY OF THE CUMBERLAND.

President:

Major-General GEORGE H. THOMAS, U. S. A.

Vice-Presidents.

Major-General P. H. SHERIDAN, U. S. A.
Brevet Colonel WILLIAM McMICHAEL, Pennsylvania.
Brigadier-General W. J. SMITH, Tennessee.
Brevet Major-General J. T. CROXTON, Kentucky.
Brevet Major-General J. M. BRANNAN, District of Columbia.
Brevet Brigadier-General W. J. PALMER, Missouri.
Brevet Brigadier-General WM. COGSWELL, Massachusetts.
Colonel GEORGE B. BINGHAM, Wisconsin.
Brevet Brigadier-General J. W. BISHOP, Minnesota.
Brevet Brigadier-General B. F. SCRIBNER, Indiana.
Brevet Brigadier-General W. L. STOUGHTON, Michigan.
Brevet Major-General H. A. BARNUM, New York.
Brevet Major-General W. W. LOWE, Iowa.
Brevet Major-General AUGUST WILLICH, Ohio.
Major-General JOHN M. PALMER, Illinois.
Brevet Brigadier-General J. W. BURKE, Alabama.
Brevet Major-General G. W. MINDEL, New Jersey.
Major S. L. COULTER, Kansas.

Corresponding Secretary:

Brevet Major-General W. D. WHIPPLE, U. S. A.

Recording Secretary:

Brevet Lieutenant-Colonel GEORGE I. WATERMAN.

Treasurer:

Brevet Brigadier-General J. S. FULLERTON.

CONSTITUTION.

ARTICLE I.

The name and title of this Association shall be the " SOCIETY OF THE ARMY OF THE CUMBERLAND," and said Society shall include every officer and soldier who has at any time served with honor in that army.

Honorary members may be elected from those officers who may have become distinguished in any of the armies of the United States.

ARTICLE II.

The object of the Society shall be to perpetuate the memory of the fortunes and achievements of the Army of the Cumberland : to preserve that unanimity of loyal sentiment, and that kind and cordial feeling which has been an eminent characteristic of this army, and the main element of the power and success of its efforts in behalf of the cause of the Union. The history and glory of the officers and soldiers belonging to this army, who have fallen either on the field of battle, or otherwise in the line of their duty, shall be a permanent and sacred trust to this society, and every effort shall be made to collect and preserve the proper memorials of their services, to inscribe their names upon the roll of honor, and transmit their fame to posterity. It shall also be the object and bounden duty of this Society to relieve, as far as possible, the families of such deceased officers and soldiers when in indigent circumstances, either by the voluntary contributions of the members, or in such other manner as they may determine when the cases are brought to their attention. This provision shall also hereafter apply to the suffering families of those members of the Society who may, in the future, be called hence, and the welfare of the soldier's widow and orphan shall forever be a holy trust in the hands of his surviving comrades.

ARTICLE III.

For the purpose of effecting these objects, the Society shall be organized by the annual election of a President, and a Vice-President from each state having soldiers in the Army of the Cumberland, to be nominated by members from the several states, a Corresponding Secretary, a Recording Secretary, and a Treasurer.

The Society shall meet once in every year; the time and place of the next meeting to be selected by ballot at each meeting. All members of the Society who are prevented by any cause from personally attending are expected to notify the Corresponding Secretary, and to impart such information in regard to themselves as they may think proper, and as may be of interest to their brethren of the Society.

Having a fraternal feeling for, and honoring the glorious efforts of, our brothers in arms belonging to other armies who have shared with us the service of saving our Government, the President, and either of the Vice-Presidents shall be authorized to invite the attendance of any officer of the United States armies at any of our annual meetings.

BY-LAWS.

I. All meetings of this Society shall be opened by prayer to Almighty God by a former chaplain of the army, or by a minister of the gospel, to be selected for the occasion by the President of the Society.

II. Every officer and soldier desiring to become a member of this Society shall, upon signing the Constitution, pay to the Treasurer the sum of five dollars as an initiation fee, and thereafter the like sum of five dollars per annum as yearly dues; and shall thereupon be entitled to a copy of the proceedings of the Society, when published, free of charge.

III. Any member who shall be in arrears for dues for a period of two years, shall have his name dropped from the rolls.

IV. All moneys paid out by the Treasurer shall be upon the written order of the Recording Secretary, approved by the written consent of the President; and at each annual meeting of the Society, the Treasurer shall make a full report of his receipts and disbursements.

V. When the place of the next annual meeting of the Society shall be decided upon, the President shall appoint an Executive Committee of three (3) members, resident at such place, or contiguous thereto, whose duty it shall be to make all needful preparations and arrangements for such meeting.

VI. That prior to the final adjournment of the Society, at such annual meeting thereof, the President shall appoint a committee of three members, resident in the city in which such meeting shall be, and not officers of the Society, as a committee on bills and claims, and to such committee all claims against the Society of whatsoever character, should be referred for investigation and allowance before being paid.

VII. No member of the Society shall speak more than once on any question of business, and no longer than five minutes, without the consent of the Society first obtained.

VIII. At each annual meeting there shall be selected, in such manner as the Society shall determine, from the members of the Society, a person to deliver an address upon the history of the Army of the Cumberland, and the objects of the Society at the next annual meeting.

IX. *Cushing's Manual of Parliamentary Law* shall be authority for the government and regulation of all meetings of this Society.

14

ARMY OF THE CUMBERLAND.

THE Society of the Army of the Cumberland met at their headquarters, in the Sherman House, on Tuesday, December 15, 1868, and, at two o'clock P.M., mustering about six hundred members, formed in procession and marched to McVicker's Theatre, which had been kindly and freely offered for the business meetings of the Society. The President, Vice-Presidents, and other officers of the Society, occupied the stage, at the back of which was suspended a life-size portrait of General Rosecrans, painted for, and presented to, the Society by the artist Brevet Brigadier-General S. W. Price. The members of the Society comfortably filled the lower part of the audience room, and many visitors the upper part.

McVICKER'S THEATRE, CITY OF CHICAGO, ILLINOIS, }
December 15, 1868. }

Pursuant to its adjournment at the city of Cincinnati, Ohio, on the 7th day of January, 1868, the Society of the Army of the Cumberland met at two o'clock P.M., at McVicker's Theatre, in the city of Chicago, Illinois.

The Society was called to order by Major-General George H. Thomas, President, and Chaplain Thomas B. VanHorn invoked the blessing of Almighty God.

The President then briefly presented his congratulations upon the prospect of a happy reunion, and suggested that, owing to the unavoidable absence of Brevet Brigadier-General Henry

M. Cist, the Society was without the service of a Recording Secretary.

It was moved and seconded that General William D. Whipple be requested to act as Recording Secretary.

General Whipple suggested that he was now acting as Corresponding Secretary, and thought it well that some other member should fill the position now temporarily vacant; and General Charles F. Manderson was chosen Recording Secretary, *pro tempore.*

It was moved and carried that the minutes of the proceedings of the Society, at its meeting at Cincinnati, Ohio, on February 6th and 7th, 1868, be adopted as published.

The President called for the report of the Local Committee, and General F. T. Sherman, of that committee, stated that no formal report on local organization had been prepared, but he could say that the committee had united its efforts with those of the committees of other societies assembled here, in making preparations for the present reunion, and hoped their arrangement, of which an outline had been published, would be successfully carried out, and be satisfactory to the Society.

Major-General Thomas J. Woods moved that the Society act upon the suggestions made by the committee, and that they be granted further time to report, which motion prevailed.

General S. W. Price, Chairman of the Committee on Memorials, reported the absence of an important member of his committee, and asked further time to report, which, on motion, was granted.

General Whipple, Corresponding Secretary, made a report as to the distribution of the printed report of the first Reunion of the Society, which was accepted and adopted.

The President then appointed the following Committee on Officers of the Society for the ensuing year, and instructed that they should report Wednesday morning:

Lieutenant-Colonel Hunter Brooke, Colonel Lyman Bridges, General Newel Gleason, General J. G. Parkhurst, Colonel J. E. Jacobs, General Thomas F. Knipe, Lieutenant-Colonel G. C. Wharton, Major F. W. Sparling, Colonel George Ginty, Adjutant A. M. Hefbower.

The President also appointed Chaplain James H. Bristow to act as Chaplain of the Society for the ensuing year.

General William Grose reported the condition of the treasury, not including the financial transactions of the present meeting, and this report was accepted and adopted.

The following committee was appointed by the President to report immediately the names of three places from which the Society should select the place for holding its next annual reunion, and the time for holding such reunion:

Colonel G. C. Wharton, Colonel Henry Stone, and General Stanley.

The report of the Committee to Audit Claims being called for, General S. J. McGroarty stated that he was a member of that committee; that their labors appeared to be over, so far as claims against the Society were concerned, and that the committee had audited and ordered paid all proper claims that had been presented to them.

Chaplain Bristow moved that a warrant on the Treasurer issue in favor of General Whipple for an amount that appeared to be due him on the distribution of the published report of the Society, and the motion was seconded.

General J. P. Jackson suggested that the proper course to pursue would be to present the account to the Committee on Claims for its action.

General Durbin Ward moved to lay the motion on the table, whereupon Chaplain Bristow withdrew his motion.

The President called for the report of the Committee on Printing, when it appeared that both members of the Committee,

General Henry M. Cist and Colonel L. Harris, were absent, and therefore no report could be had.

Colonel G. C. Wharton, Chairman of the committee to select three places from which to select, by ballot, the place for the next meeting, reported Louisville, Indianapolis and Cleveland, as such places, and December 15 and 16, 1869, as the time.

On motion, the report of the committee was accepted.

Chaplain Granville Moody moved that the matter be made the special order for to-morrow morning.

A motion was made to amend, and that a ballot be immediately taken.

A motion was made, and carried, to lay the original motion on the table.

It was moved that the rules be suspended, and that the President of the Society select the time and place.

Considerable debate ensued upon this motion, members advocating the advantages of different localities.

The President declined to act as proposed in the motion, and declared it in conflict with the Constitution of the Society, and therefore out of order.

Colonel Robinson and General Barnum advocated the holding of the next reunion at some point in the East, and suggested the city of New York.

After considerable discussion of this proposition, the President ruled that it was not in order to suggest any other places but those reported by the committee.

It was moved, but not carried, that the Secretary be instructed to cast the ballot of the Society for Indianapolis.

It was moved, and carried, that the President appoint twelve tellers to collect ballots, and that the Society proceed to vote.

The chair appointed as tellers General N. Anderson, Colonel Wharton, General Schneider, General Barnum, General Streight, General Ward, Colonel McMichael, Colonel Wood,

Colonel Stone, Colonel Taylor, Colonel Northrop, and General Parkhurst. These gentlemen proceeded to collect and count the ballots.

Chaplain Bristow asked and received permission to present a matter foreign to the business of the Society; and proceeded to present the needs of a Church, and to ask aid for the same.

General Anson Stager tendered the use of the telegraph lines to the Society and its members.

The thanks of the Society were voted to General Stager and the Western Union Telegraph Company, and the Secretary instructed to present the same in writing, on behalf of the Society.

The tellers reported the following as the result of the ballot: Total votes, 449. Indianapolis, 182; Cleveland, 131; Louisville, 136.

It was moved, and carried, that Indianapolis be unanimously selected as the place of the next Reunion, and the 15th and 16th of December, 1869, as the time.

Major-General Butterfield moved that the President appoint a committee of three, whose duty it shall be to cause to be published the Report of this Reunion.

The motion prevailed; and the President appointed Major L. H. Drury, General A. C. McClurg, and General William Grose, as such Committee.

It was voted that this publication be under the instruction and general direction of the President of the Society.

It was voted that a committee of five be appointed by the chair, to nominate to this Convention an orator and alternate for the Annual Reunion of 1869; said committee to report to-morrow morning.

The President appointed General Barnum, Chaplain VanHorn, General Moody, General Burke, and General Elliott.

A motion to reconsider the vote selecting time and place was made and lost.

On motion of Colonel Robinson, it was resolved that the President appoint a committee of three to confer with Associations of the Armies of the Tennessee, Ohio and Georgia, for the purpose of uniting with us at Indianapolis, on the occasion of the Reunion of December 15th and 16th, 1869.

After a spirited debate the resolution prevailed, and the President appointed General J. S. Robinson, General Nicholas Anderson, and Colonel Quinn Morton.

Invitations were read by the Secretary from the Chicago Historical Society to visit its rooms on Wednesday morning, at eleven o'clock; and from the Union Catholic Library Association of Chicago, to visit its Bazaar.

On motion, thanks were tendered for these invitations.

On motion of Colonel T. J. Pickett, the thanks of the Society were tendered to J. H. McVicker, Esq., for the use of his theatre.

It was unanimously voted that the thanks of this Society be tendered to General S. W. Price for his present to the Society of the portrait of General W. S. Rosecrans, painted by him for the Society, and that the portrait be put under the care of the Treasurer.

On motion, the Society adjourned to meet Wednesday morning, at ten o'clock.

CHARLES F. MANDERSON,
Secretary pro tem.

McVicker's Theatre, Chicago, *December* 16, 1868.

The Society met, pursuant to adjournment, General Thomas, the President, in the chair.

The proceedings opened with patriotic selections by the band, after which the President announced that Colonel Whitman had prepared a paper relating to his efforts in looking up the dead of the Army of the Cumberland, and the other armies associated with it, and would read a brief abstract of the paper pending the arrival of the Secretary. The latter, however, came in at this juncture, and Colonel Whitman declined reading his paper at present. The question being submitted to the meeting, it was decided to have the paper read.

The regular proceedings of the Society were then opened with prayer by Chaplain Bristow, after which the Secretary *pro tem.*, General Manderson, read the minutes of the preceding meeting, which, on motion, were approved.

Colonel Whitman then addressed the meeting in relation to the dead of the Army of the Cumberland, saying that he hoped the interest in the great work would be increased, and that some action would be taken. It was eminently fit and proper that we should not forget that noble army of officers and privates who fell so nobly, and whose bodies dot the soil of the wide extent of country traversed by the four armies now represented in this city. The Government, through its agents, has been ardently but efficiently at work in removing the remains of soldiers to regular inclosures, but the people know little or nothing of the extent or completeness of the work. The speaker had been engaged in this matter for about three years, and proceeded to give an outline of its progress since his connection therewith. The paper was ordered published, and a resolution of thanks was tendered to Colonel Whitman.

The committee appointed to select an orator and alternate for the next annual reunion reported, through the Chairman, General Elliott, the selection of Major-General Daniel Butterfield, Twentieth Army Corps, and for alternate, Major-General Negley, of the Fourteenth Army Corps.

General Price, of the Committee on Memorials, reported that the project of procuring biographical sketches of the distinguished members of the Society who have died, has been abandoned as impracticable. The only death which has occurred during the year past has been that of Lieutenant William L. Porter, of the Sixth United States Cavalry, of whom a memorial has been prepared.

The Secretary read a telegram from Secretary McCulloch, at Washington, congratulating the organization upon its happy reunion; also a communication from the Army of the Ohio, containing the resolutions passed by that society.

On motion of Colonel Nicholas Anderson, the President and Vice-Presidents of the Army of the Cumberland were appointed a committee to confer with the proper officials of the Army of the Ohio, with reference to a consolidation of the societies, and with power to act.

Colonel Hunter Brook, Chairman of the Committee on Permanent Nomination of Officers for the ensuing year, reported as follows:

For President—Major-General George H. Thomas.

Vice-Presidents—Pennsylvania, Brevet Colonel William McMichael; Tennessee, Brigadier-General W. J. Smith; Kentucky, Brevet Major-General J. T. Croxton; District of Columbia, Brevet Major-General J. M. Brannan; Missouri, Brevet Brigadier-General W. J. Palmer; Massachusetts, Brevet Brigadier-General William Cogswell; Wisconsin, Colonel George B. Bingham; Minnesota, Brevet Brigadier-General J. W. Bishop; Indiana, Brevet Brigadier-General B. F. Scribner; Michigan, Brigadier-General W. L. Stoughton; New York, Brevet Major-General H.

A. Barnum; Iowa, Brevet Major-General W. W. Lowe; Ohio, Major-General P. H. Sheridan; Illinois, Major-General John M. Palmer; Alabama, Brevet Brigadier-General J. W. Burke; New Jersey, Brevet Major-General G. W. Mindel; Kansas, Major S. L. Coulter; Ohio, Brevet Major-General August Willich.

Corresponding Secretary— Major-General W. G. Whipple.

Recording Secretary—Brevet Lieutenant-Colonel George I. Waterman.

Treasurer— Brevet Brigadier-General J. S. Fullerton.

The report was adopted, and the officers named were declared elected.

On motion of Colonel Hunter Brooke, the thanks of the Society were tendered to the retiring Recording Secretary, General Henry M. Cist, and retiring Treasurer, General William Grose, for the faithful and efficient manner in which they had performed the duties of their office.

General Whipple offered and the Society adopted the following preamble and resolution:

WHEREAS, it is understood that there are now stored in the depot of camp and garrison equipage, at Jeffersonville, Indiana, certain flags, the property of the United States, wearing the devices described in General Orders, dated Headquarters Army of the Cumberland,

Resolved, That the Treasurer be and is hereby directed to purchase the said flags, provided the Government will sell them, and there is money sufficient in the treasury to pay for them after all the other necessary expenses of the Society have been liquidated; that he address the War Department with a view of effecting the purchase; that if, for any reason, the flags can not be obtained, the Treasurer report such reason at the next annual meeting.

Resolved, That, in case the flags become the property of the Society, they shall remain in custody of the Treasurer of the

Society, for the time being, and that they be used for the purposes of decoration at the meetings of the Society.

General Willich offered the following preamble and resolution, which were adopted:

WHEREAS, it is generally known that strange contradictions exist in the different official reports of the war on the same subjects;

Resolved, That the Society of the Army of the Cumberland proceed to the organization of a *Board of Trustees of the War Record*, to be composed of two members from each state represented, to be designated by the President of the Society. It shall be the duty of this Board of Trustees to preserve and watch the official war records. Examine the same carefully, and investigate all apparent mistakes, and correct the same wherever injustice has been done to any particular command or individual.

The President of the Society designated the following officers to constitute such Board of Trustees:

Brevet Brigadier-General J. S. Fullerton, Missouri; Brevet Brigadier-General F. Laibold, Missouri; Brevet Major-General William Grose, Indiana; Brevet Major-General Charles Cruft, Indiana; Brevet Major-General John M. Palmer, Illinois; Major John M. Farquhar, Illinois; Brevet Brigadier-General Charles F. Manderson, Ohio; Brevet Lieutenant-Colonel Hunter Brooke, Ohio; Brevet Brigadier-General John A. Martin, Kansas; Major T. L. Coulter, Kansas; Brevet Brigadier-General John G. Parkhurst, Michigan; Brevet Brigadier-General William L. Stoughton, Michigan; Colonel George B. Bingham, Wisconsin; Colonel O. C. Johnson, Wisconsin; Major William H. Young, Iowa; Colonel William P. Heplum, Iowa; Colonel W. F. Prosser, Tennessee; Captain H. H. Thomas, Tennessee; Colonel M. C. Taylor, Kentucky; Colonel J. P. Jackson, Kentucky; Brevet Brigadier-General William Cogswell, Massachusetts; Lieutenant-

Colonel Horace N. Fisher, Massachusetts; Brevet Major-General H. A. Barnum, New York; Lieutenant-Colonel S. B. Lawrence, New York; Brevet Colonel William McMichael, Pennsylvania; Major-General James S. Negley, Pennsylvania; Major Daniel Heaney, Minnesota; Major-General H. P. Van-clean, Minnesota; Brevet Major-General George W. Mindel, New Jersey; Colonel H. W. Jackson, New Jersey; Brevet Brigadier General George E. Spencer, Alabama.

On motion of General Streight, Major S. L. Coulter, of Kansas, was added to the list of Vice-Presidents of the Society.

Colonel Sims, with an eloquent introduction, moved that three grand cheers be given for General P. H. Sheridan, which were given by the Society standing, amid the waving of hats and handkerchiefs.

At the request of General A. C. McClurg, he was excused from serving on the Committee on Printing, and General A. C. Ducat was appointed to fill his place.

General Willich presented the following preamble and resolution:

WHEREAS, It is honor enough for generations to come to have been a private soldier in the Cumberland Army; and,

WHEREAS, It is the general tendency to return to specie basis; and,

WHEREAS, It appears that the coin of our national military honor is in danger of being swamped by the over-issue of brevet currency, therefore,

Resolved, That the members of this Society resign cheerfully their brevet ranks.

After an animated discussion by Generals Whitaker, J. D. Morgan and Willich, a motion to lay the preamble and resolution on the table prevailed.

On motion, the Society adjourned until two o'clock P.M.

The President called the Society to order, and stated that in accordance with Article V. of the By-Laws he would appoint the following Local Committee:

Major-General Nathan Kimball, Brigadier-General A. D. Streight, Brigadier-General Fred. Knefler.

General Whipple offered the following resolution, which was adopted:

Resolved, That the thanks of the Society be and are hereby tendered to the Local Committee of Arrangements for the meeting of this Society, and to the joint committees of arrangements for the reunion of the four army societies, for the ample and beautiful preparations which have contributed so much to the comfort of our members, and the grand success which has attended this reunion.

The following was also submitted and adopted:

Resolved, That this Society return thanks, most sincere and heartfelt, to the citizens of Chicago, for their hospitality, and to the proprietors of the Sherman House for the ample manner in which they provided accommodations for the headquarters of this Society.

Colonel Henry Stone presented the following resolution, which was adopted:

Resolved, As the sense of this Society, that a national monument should be erected, at some appropriate place, to commemorate the names and deeds of the heroes who gave up their lives in the late war for the suppression of the Rebellion — and to aid in carrying out the objects expressed in the above resolution, be it further,

Resolved, That a committee of five be appointed by the President of this Society to confer and co-operate with a similar committee from our sister Societies of the Armies of the Tennessee,

amended that the first order of business at the annual meeting of the Society, shall be the Election of Officers.

The following resolution was offered and adopted :

Resolved, That the thanks of this Society be presented to the Chicago Board of Trade for the continued evidence of patriotism and respect for the soldier by the tender of their room for our banquet.

General G. W. Elliott offered the following resolution, which was adopted :

Resolved, That members of the staff of Lieutenant-General Sherman, not members of any organization of the Army of the Cumberland, be elected honorary members of the Society of the Army of the Cumberland, with the privilege of becoming members upon subscribing to its Constitution and requirements.

Colonel Archibald Blakeley presented the following resolution :

Resolved, That the Committee on Publication of the Proceedings of this meeting of the Society be requested to procure and publish the orations of Major-General J. D. Cox, Brigadier-General William K. Belknap, and Brigadier-General William Cogswell, delivered last evening before the Societies of the Armies of the Cumberland, Tennessee, Ohio, and Georgia, in the Opera House.

On motion the Society adjourned, to meet at Indianapolis, Indiana, on the 15th of December, 1869.

TREASURER'S OFFICE,
SOCIETY OF THE ARMY OF THE CUMBERLAND.

MR. PRESIDENT, *and Members of the Society of the Cumberland:*

I have the honor to report that since our organization at Cincinnati, in February last, there has been paid into the treasury of said Society money as follows:

		Dr.			Cr.
1868.			1868.		
To Dec. 15.	To 356 members at $5 each,......	$1,780 00	Feb. 13.	By Draft No. 4,074,.........	$825 53
" "	To 2 members' payment of annual dues, $5 each,.........	10 00	Feb. 27.	By Stationery of Robert Clark & Co.,	9 75
" "	To sale of books reported, and accounted for by Secretary,......	75 75	April 1.	By Printing Circulars—Caleb Clark,.	5 00
			June 24.	By Printing Report of Society—Robert Clark & Co.,......	945 37
			June 24.	By am't paid H. M. Cist, Sec'y, above am't included in draft of Feb'y 13. { Amount Paid...... $52 25 } { Included in Draft...... 50 00 }	2 25
			Dec. 10.	By am't paid for book-record of names alphabetically,.........	2 50
			Dec. 10.	By Printing Circulars—E. Pleas,.....	8 00
			Dec. 10.	By Stationery and Postage, use of Treasurer,.........	5 00
			Dec. 15.	By Balance in Treasury.........	62 35
		$1,865 75			$1,865 75

Respectfully,   WM. GROSE, *Treasurer.*

REMARKS ON NATIONAL CEMETERIES.—ORIGINAL MILITARY DIVISION OF THE TENNESSEE.

BY BREVET LIEUT.-COL. E. B. WHITMAN, LATE CAPT. AND A. Q. M. VOLS.

In the midst of personal congratulations, and the social interchange of those thoughts and feelings which the reminiscences of the past are calculated to suggest on an occasion like the present, it is eminently fit and proper that we should not forget — you *do* not forget — that noble army of martyrs, *officers* and *privates*, who laid down their lives a willing sacrifice upon the fields of your renown; whose remains were left by the stern necessities of war far away from home, where kindred and friends could drop no tears over their graves, or protect the hallowed spots from intrusion and desecration; scattered broadcast over remote and now deserted battle-fields; dotting every hill and grove; lining the road-side; along the banks of our rivers; upon the routes of all our railroads; upon deserted camping-grounds, or gathered in the crowded hospital grave-yard — every where over the widely extended country traversed or fought over by the four gallant armies represented here to-day.

So they were. After the lapse of *three* short years, what do we now behold! The *Nation*, the Government, has come, and, in grateful remembrance of its fallen heroes, has gathered up their scattered and shattered remains, and with the careful tenderness of bereaved friends, laid them down in spots consecrated forever to the memory of their deeds.

Greece, in the days of her splendor, laid under contribution the eloquence of her most gifted orators to pronounce eulogiums over the ashes of her fallen sons; and France, in her triumphant period, made a feeble and partial effort to gather up for honorable burial the bones of her citizens who fell in battle; but it remained to be the honorable distinction of free America to have searched the country through with the careful and scrutinizing eye of the most devoted friend, and to gather in the mortal remains of her slain soldiers, and assume forever, as her high privilege, the task of keeping sacred vigils over their graves.

Such a consecration of a nation's power and resources to a *sentiment*, the world had never witnessed. And, when the work shall have been fully carried out; when, by some proper participation, the individual states represented shall have inscribed their record of grateful remembrance within the consecrated inclosures, this movement, as has been said by another, "will deserve to take its place in the annals of all

15

coming time by the side of that wonderful sanitary work which ministered so tenderly to the wants of the living."

Yet, this is no more than we should have expected. In the past history of nations, with perhaps the approach to an exception, the soldier in the ranks has been looked upon as a pawn upon the world's chessboard, with which kings and emperors might play for a time, and, when their work was done, and they had fallen, to be abandoned forever; no longer of use; no longer remembered.

But, in this war, the armies which went forth to do battle for their country were, essentially, in the rank and file, as well as in their commanding officers, an integral and constituent part of the *Government* itself; and we have the grand and sublime spectacle of a *part* of a government devoting itself to voluntary death to save the *rest*.

Fitting, indeed it was, that the surviving portion should rise up in grateful homage to that which had fallen, and by some worthy national act, record, in ineffaceable characters, its holiest, noblest sentiment. Such records, among others, are these points of common sepulture of the dead. Established, ornamented, and forever the objects of national care and protection, they will become so many ineffaceable historical records; illustrated pages, to be seen and read of all men.

To a considerable extent in Southern soil, and in the very presence where bold Treason reared its ungrateful head, they shall teach the children, whose fathers sought to dismember and destroy the Republic, to cherish its institutions, and to seek its honors and rewards. *That Nation which respects and honors its dead, shall ever be respected and honored itself.*

While the Government, by its agents, has been silently, though steadily, pressing this great work to completion, the people generally have a very imperfect conception of its scope and magnitude.

The official reports furnish, indeed, a comprehensive view, in statistics and tabular statements, of its character and progress, but these, even, come under the notice of but few, and fail entirely to satisfy the emotions of deep personal interest felt in the subject by the surviving officers and soldiers of the Army, and by the friends and relatives of the dead.

It has been suggested, and the suggestion has met with approval, that this reunion of the four great armies of the South and South-west would afford a convenient and suitable opportunity for submitting some statements more in detail respecting the disposition which has been made of their dead in the original Military Division of the Tennessee.

Having had the honor of being assigned to special duty in this connection in December, 1865, and having now spent literally *three years* among your dead, I am here before you to present some leading facts pertaining to the origin of the work, and showing the manner, extent, and completeness of its execution.

The earliest evidence of the purpose of the Government to make special provision for the honorable care of those who should die in its service during the war, is found in an act of Congress, approved July 17, 1862, which provides: "That the President of the United States shall have power, whenever in his opinion it shall be expedient, to purchase cemetery grounds, and cause them to be securely inclosed, to be used as a *National Cemetery* for the soldiers who shall die in the service of their country." But no provision was made, either in the act or otherwise, for the payment of any such purchases, and I am not aware that any official action was ever had under it by the President.

Encouraged, perhaps, by this intimation on the part of the Government of what it purposed to do, or more probably influenced by sentiments of humanity, and by a thoughtful sense of the obligation of a great nation to its fallen defenders, the following Order was issued at Chattanooga, December 25, 1863:

"It is ordered that a *National Cemetery* be founded at this place, in commemoration of the battle of Chattanooga, fought November 23rd, 24th, 25th, 26th, and 27th, and to provide a proper resting place for the remains of such as may hereafter give up their lives in this region in defending their country against treason and rebellion.

"[SIGNED]   "By order of MAJOR-GENERAL GEO. II. THOMAS.

"WILLIAM D. WHIPPLE,

"*Brevet Brig.-Gen. and A. A. General, Army of the Cumberland.*"

In the following spring a similar order was issued by General Thomas, establishing another National Cemetery on the *battle-field* of Stone's River. Under these orders appropriate grounds were selected at Chattanooga, by General Thomas himself, and at Stone's River by Brigadier-General H. P. Van Cleve; and the work was commenced at Chattanooga under the charge of Chaplain Thomas B. VanHorn, and at Stone's River, at first, under Captain J. A. Means, of the one hundred and fifteenth Ohio Volunteers Infantry, and subsequently continued under Chaplain William B. Earnshaw. This work was, however, confined to the burial of the dead from the neighboring hospitals, and the collection of those interred upon the battle fields in the immediate vicinity. The work upon both of these cemeteries was performed entirely by detailed men from the volunteer service.

Thus far the movement remained comparatively local in its character, until October, 1865, when Major-General Meigs, Quartermaster General of the Army, issued Order No. 65, directing officers of the Quartermaster's Department to make a special report to his office of the *localities* and *condition* of *cemeteries*, with reference, especially, to their exact *location*, condition, place of deposit, and condition of records, with recommendations of the means necessary to provide for the preservation of the remains from desecration; and whether the *site* should be continued, and the land purchased, or whether the bodies should be removed to some permanent cemetery near.

The attempt to comply with this order in spirit as well as in letter, in a thoroughly satisfactory manner, soon rendered it manifest that a more complete and systematic exploration must be resorted to than was provided for in the ordinary routine of the Quartermaster's Department. To meet this difficulty, it was at once determined to make this work a *specialty* in the Military Division of the Tennessee, at that time commanded by General George H. Thomas.

On the 26th of December, 1865, an order was accordingly issued by General Thomas directing an exploration to be made of the battle fields, cemeteries, and places where Union dead were interred in that Division, and reports thereon be submitted.

The extent and magnitude of such duty none can appreciate more fully than the officers of the armies, and even they can have but an imperfect conception of the practical difficulties that lay in the way of its efficient execution. To be of practical value, for the purpose designed, it would require not only a minute examination of every battle and skirmish ground, but a thorough, systematic exploration of all the various routes of our armies, their places of rendezvous, and of encampment; the locations of hospitals, public and private burial places, door yards, gardens, orchards, fields, and woods, from the Mississippi river to the Atlantic, and from the Ohio to the Gulf.

No efforts were spared to provide for the successful accomplishment of this duty. In all the preliminary arrangements, and during the progress of the work, it is due to the officers in every department of the service to say, that every aid and assistance was most cheerfully rendered. To ask, was to receive.

While the explorations were at once commenced and carried on in those parts of Eastern and Middle Tennessee, from which the dead had not been already removed, diligent preparation was made for extending the researches throughout the entire Division at the earliest opening of spring. Without delay, a circular was prepared, headed, "*Important Information Wanted!*" in which surgeons, chaplains, agents of sanitary and Christian commissions, quartermasters, ex-officers, and soldiers, who had at any time served within the limits of the Division, having knowledge of the places of burial of any Union soldiers, were requested to furnish information to aid in the search, or in identifying the unknown dead. It was added, in explanation, that this exploration was preliminary to the collection of the Union dead every where into National Cemeteries, on the plan of those already in process of completion at Chattanooga and Stone's River. It is proper, however, to say, that this statement was without authority from Washington, and in no way sanctioned by the terms of the Order No. 65, of October 30, from the Quartermaster-General's office. Though, perhaps, premature, as the announcement of a plan, yet, viewed as the expression of a desire, and a faith which has now been fully realized, and taken in connection with other measures afterwards adopted, to which I shall hereafter allude, the utterance will not be thought strange.

These circulars signed by Major-General Donaldson, Chief Quarter-master were widely distributed through the medium of the post office, and published in all the prominent newspapers in the United States.

As the replies came in from every source, the character of the information imparted new and additional interest to the enterprise. It revealed the existence of numerous records of the localities of graves, in forms more or less complete, with the names of the dead, which would not only prove of great value as guides in the search for graves, but, with proper precaution in the disinterments, would lead to the identification of many an unknown body. Further, as preliminary aid, official reports and campaign maps were carefully consulted, and, finally, the Southern people, themselves, resident in the neighborhood where Union dead were supposed to be buried, were appealed to, and not without effect.

On the 1st day of March, 1866, the exploring party, consisting of ten persons, afterwards increased to twenty, mounted, and provided with pack mules to transport camp equipage and provisions, left Nashville, Tennessee, with the battle field of Fort Donelson as its first objective point. From this time until the following Christmas the search was diligently prosecuted with but little interruption. It embraced the prominent points on the Mississippi, Tennessee, and Cumberland rivers; the various lines of railroads in the states comprising the Division; the main routes of the armies, to the front and to the rear; the fields of operation in the Corinth, Vicksburg and Atlanta campaigns, and the several lines of the "grand march to the sea," including battle-fields, skirmish-grounds, hospitals, and the prison pens of Andersonville and Millen or Lawton.

A brief description of the methods pursued in the exploration of those battle-fields on which the dead were buried as they fell, over a large area, may not be without interest. Take the battle-field of Shiloh, for instance, repeated in other similar cases. The entire party formed in manner of skirmish line, at short distances from each other, passed and repassed in line over the entire extent of the field, sweeping it in belts or swaths, pausing at every appearance of a grave, to notice its location, and to copy the inscription, if any. Seven days were thus occupied by the whole party on this field alone. No less than four hundred miles of travel for one man were accomplished, resulting in the discovery of one thousand eight hundred and seventy-four graves, of which six hundred and twenty were identified at the time. These graves were distributed in one hundred and seventy-eight localities, of which twenty-nine were regimental groups.

On the routes of the armies, no less care was taken. As a rule, no residence or person was to be passed without the inquiry, "Do you know, or have you heard of any graves of Union soldiers in this neighborhood?"

and all information, or hints even, was followed up with a careful exploration. In all cases, a minute and circumstantial record was made of all
the facts necessary to serve as a guide for officers, or parties who might
subsequently be employed to make the disinterments and removals.

Frequent reports, showing the results thus obtained, accompanied by
tabular statements, were from time to time forwarded from the field to
headquarters, and to the Quartermaster-General, at Washington.

Although this exploration was designed only as a preliminary work,
a sort of outline, to be filled up afterwards by the more thorough and
minute search of disinterring parties, yet the results were by no means
insignificant. Not less than three hundred different places where battles
or skirmishes had been fought, or troops stationed, or hospitals established, were visited. The existence and exact location of more than forty
thousand scattered graves were determined, occupying more than two
thousand distinct localities; over ten thousand names were copied from
rude head-boards, or from inscriptions on the bark of trees, or obtained
from the inhabitants, of which there probably existed *no record*, outside
of the regimental returns, and, in many cases, not even there, *graves of
missing men.* Between twenty-five and thirty thousand miles of army
routes were passed over, including rivers and railroads. This enumera-
tion does not embrace some twenty-eight thousand burials made from
the larger general hospitals, of which there existed records more or less
complete; or the twelve thousand upwards of prisoners of war buried
at Andersonville, which had been previously reported, and a Roll of
Honor published, by Colonel Moore, under the direction of the Quartermaster-General.

However imperfect and desultory the manner in which our work may
have been performed, it served to furnish at least an outline of what
was required to be done, and a guide in the commencement of the work
of removals. It revealed the sad fact, and brought it to notice, that the
entire country over which the war had extended its ravages, was one
interminable grave-yard, and it early deepened and extended the conviction already felt by many, that it was the duty of Government to
assume, without delay, the place of friends and relatives, and with
tender care collect together and afford proper protection to the remains
of those who had fallen in so noble a service, beyond the reach or care
of friends. It also oftentimes revealed another fact, which added still
greater force to these convictions. I refer to the marked distinctions
shown, as the armies passed away, between the care and protection
of Union and Confederate graves by many of the Southern people themselves, not, it may be, culpable, but natural. The one class were buried
among their friends, and on friendly soil; the other, for the time at
least, in an enemy's country, and beyond the reach of friends.

Gradually, by a natural process, the work of the future took mental
form and shape. Battle-fields, localities of hospitals, routes of armies,

stations of troops, scattered graves, resolved themselves into definite cemeterial districts, ranged around some central spot, convenient and appropriate to receive the dead from all its limits.

Suggestions and recommendations regarding the removal of the dead were in every case embodied in the original field reports.

While this work was being prosecuted in the field, others were not idle. The record of the location of graves, the selection of sites for cemeteries, and plans for the removal of the dead, would prove of no ultimate avail, without the authority of law to execute the work.

The visit of the Congressional Committee to Memphis, in the spring of 1866, to investigate the cause of the riot at that place, afforded a favorable opportunity to bring the subject to the attention of Congress. An informal delegation, consisting of Brevet-Major G. W. Marshall, Assistant Quartermaster, and Chaplain Wm. B. Earnshaw, of the Stone's River Cemetery, accordingly went to Memphis to consult with the gentlemen of that committee. An interview was obtained; copies of the reports already made upon the battle-fields, detailing the condition of the dead, were submitted to their perusal. The facts thus made known to them, together with the personal representations made by these gentlemen, enlisted the deep interest of the Board, especially of Hon. E. B. Washburne, chairman of the committee.

The result was that a bill for the establishment and protection of National Cemeteries was then and there drawn up, or all of the leading points agreed upon. On the return of the committee to Washington, it was introduced into the House and passed; in the Senate, however, by some oversight, it failed to be called up for a third reading, and Congress adjourned without its becoming a law.

Although the bill failed at this term of a passage, the favor with which it had been received, gave assurance that the work would ultimately be sanctioned, and the Quartermaster's Department at Washington proceeded to act upon it.

General Donaldson, Chief Quartermaster of the Military Division of the Tennessee, took a deep interest in the work, and his suggestions and recommendations for that Division were listened to and cordially approved by General Meigs at Washington.

On the 13th of June, 1866, another order in the series was issued by General Thomas, directing " the location, purchase and establishment of National Cemeteries and the preparation of Mortuary Records for the Military Division of the Tennessee."

In some parts of the Division, as at Chattanooga and Stone's River, the work had never been entirely intermitted, and the collection of the dead in Alabama into the city grave-yards, at Montgomery and Mobile, had been commenced under the direction of the Quartermaster-General; but now the work assumed a general character. During the summer extensive preparations were made by General Donaldson, under the direction of the Quartermaster-General, for a vigorous commencement of the work, early in the fall, throughout the entire division.

Contracts were made for furnishing coffins and inclosing the grounds. And here let me remark, to correct erroneous statements that have sometimes been made, *that no contracts were ever let in the Military Division of the Tennessee for the disinterment and reburial of the dead in the National Cemeteries.* It was, indeed, proposed and urged as a matter of economy. On the other hand, it was plead that in this work the Government having assumed to stand in the place of the relatives of the deceased, it should do nothing which, under similar circumstances, they would not themselves do. When bereaved friends should advertise and let by contract, to the lowest bidder, the performance of the last sad rites claimed by the sacred ties of love and affection, then it would be time for the Government to attempt to do such a thing in their behalf.

To return to a description of our work: Sites were selected and approved, and steps taken for their purchase; the country was districted, and officers detailed or assigned to conduct the work in the several districts; agents were employed from among the discharged officers and soldiers of the army; and discharged colored soldiers employed, in most cases, as laborers.

In some portions of the Division the work was necessarily commenced in advance of the explorations. This was especially the case in Northern and Western Georgia, and in Central and Southern Alabama; but in all cases where explorations had been made, and as fast as they were extended over other portions, the several officers in charge were furnished with a carefully prepared list and description of the localities of graves, as far as discovered. and with such names as had been copied, and with copies of all communications of friends giving information, or making inquiries concerning their dead.

On the 9th day of August, 1866, an *order*, known as Order No. 8, describing in detail the method to be pursued in disinterring the dead and keeping the record, was issued from the office of the chief Quartermaster. It says: "The Government, in assuming to perform a work which belongs, as a special right, only to the kindred and friends of the deceased, demands of its agents to discharge the duty with the delicacy and tenderness of near and dear friends." And it closes with the remark "That all officers and men engaged in this delicate and responsible work, will take such personal interest in its faithful execution, and exercise such diligence and care in preserving a clear and distinct trace of every body removed, that no friend or relation of the dead may have any just cause of complaint."

Forms of burial sheets or records were devised and furnished, by the aid of which any intelligent and careful person would be able to keep an intelligible record of every body found, showing, in the case of single graves, the *precise locality* where they were found : and in case of a group or collection of graves, or of trenches, in addition, the *precise order* and method of burial.

Each body, known and unknown, was placed in a separate coffin, and marked to correspond with the entry upon the record sheet; and when transported to the new cemetery, a duplicate copy of this disinterment record was forwarded *as a bill of lading*. When the several coffins were consigned to their new graves, the designation of the *section* and number of grave into which each had been put, was entered on the bill in its proper place. A duplicate copy of these sheets thus completed were then to be forwarded to the office of the mortuary records for use in preparing the catalogues and rolls of honor.

The design of this minute and careful record is so important that I shall be pardoned for entering into an explanation here.

In the course of my investigations, the fact had been developed, — I quote from a report upon this subject forwarded to the Quartermaster-General, February 13, 1867, — "That in very many cases careful records of the *place, names*, and *order of burial*, had been made, and that *these documents* were in existence, either in the hands of those who had prepared them, or of friends and relatives of the deceased, to whom they had been sent, and by whom they had been most carefully preserved. I ASSUMED, THEREFORE, AS THE BASIS OF A PLAN, *that a knowledge and a record of every grave, both of its locality and of its occupant, was in the possession of some living person, and that these means might be made available to restore the name, rank and regiment, and even the date of death, to the occupants of all those graves which, in the lapse of time, and by various casualties and accidents, had lost their external marks.*

"Could these records have been collected for use in advance of the disinterments, the work of recognition and identification would have been simple and easy in all cases. But, in the mean time, the Government had decided to gather up and remove the dead from these scattered graves and groups, both known and unknown alike, to national cemeteries, and were even entering upon their work.

"The question then presented itself for immediate decision, *whether the bodies from all graves found without marks, should be transferred as* ABSOLUTELY UNKNOWN, *and no clue be left by which to trace them from an unknown grave in the new cemetery to their original resting-place, of which there might, and doubtless did, exist a full and complete record in the hand of some person, and which at some future time would be produced?*

"*Manifestly*, under the circumstances, this would of itself be a desecration, and with a knowledge of the facts, a culpable violation of the rights of the friends and relatives.

"In order, therefore, that the work of disinterment and removal might proceed without delay, and yet all the opportunities and means to make the information I have alluded to *permanently available*, a very simple expedient was adopted, in the form of a *tabular sheet of record*, to be used in all cases of disinterment, and by means of which not only could each particular body reinterred in a national cemetery be traced to its original resting-place, but in case of groups, rows and trenches, the precise order and relative position of each body, as originally buried, could be easily known. * * * * *

· "The work once done on this plan by intelligent and careful men, and the application of the principle is very simple and easy.

"These original burial sheets are all carefully preserved and filed in the office of the mortuary records, where the complete records of the division are kept, and the catalogue of each cemetery prepared."

In its practical application I can now say that this system generally proved most satisfactory, and has already led to the identification of a large number who were disinterred and removed as *unknown;* and in the future it promises to be valuable, so long as there remain in existence any records by which a body *might have been* identified before removal, and so long as proper facilities are afforded for the investigation.

This plan, with full illustration and explanation, thus communicated to the Quartermaster-General, was subsequently adopted and made applicable throughout the United States, in General Orders No. 26, Quartermaster-General's Office, March 25, 1867; not, however, until disinterments and removals had been extensively made in other departments. In this order the Quartermaster-General very concisely and clearly expresses the idea by saying: "That the record of the disinterring officer is imperfect unless it will enable a stranger to take the bodies from their new resting-place and replace them in their original graves, in their original order."

These remarks, submitted in passing, showing the possibility of identifying many of the unknown dead in the future, will naturally suggest the duty of the Government to provide facilities, for some time to come, for carrying out and realizing the benefits of the system. It indeed seems a right which the friends of the dead should demand. They may say, with the emphasis of deep feeling: "Ye have taken away *our dead,* and *where* have ye laid them?" Not that they may remove the body, but restore the name at the grave or on the record, in place of the sad inscription, *unknown;* and satisfy the claims of affection by dropping a tear upon the grave.

Furnished with copies of the field notes and records of the *original explorations* as a general guide, the officers and agents in charge of the work were directed to push their researches into all parts of their respective *districts*, where they could hear of any dead, or had any reason to suppose that any were to be found. As a general thing, both officers and men showed a commendable zeal in the work, and deserve great credit for their faithfulness. The thorough minuteness of the search affords positive assurance that but few have been overlooked in this great sepulture. All cases of accidental omission have been provided for, and any hereafter discovered will be removed by the keepers of the cemeteries.

On the breaking up of the original Military Division of the Tennessee, and the formation of the Third and Fourth Military Districts, the supervision of the construction of the cemeteries in Georgia, Alabama and Mississippi, with the exception of that at Corinth, was transferred to the chief Quartermaster of those districts. In order, however, to preserve a unity of plan in the preparation of the record, and to insure the successful application of the original principles which had governed in their preparation, the Secretary of War, by a special order, dated March 23, 1867, directed that all records of disinterments and reinterments should be continued to be forwarded from these districts to the headquarters of the Department of the Cumberland, for use in the preparation of the permanent records and rolls of honor for the entire original Military Division.

In February, 1867, the attention of the chairman of the military committee of the Senate was specially called to the failure to pass the Cemeterial Bill at the previous session. Some modifications were suggested and adopted, the appropriation for the commencement of the work was increased from *fifty* to *seven hundred and fifty* thousand dollars, and the bill for the establishment and protection of national cemeteries passed Congress, and was approved by the President February 22, 1867.

The movement had now become indeed a national work. Under the impulse thus given it was prosecuted with renewed energy; and now, in less than *two* years from the passage of the bill, and in *three* years from the time the first preliminary steps were really taken in this great work, we are able to announce that the work of removing the dead has been completed in the original Military Division of the Tennessee, with the exception of a few at Vicksburg and Natchez. More than one hundred thousand bodies of the scattered dead, who died and were buried within its limits, including those who fell upon the west bank of the Mississippi river, and in the borders of Virginia and North Carolina, in connection with military operations originating in or carried on within the division itself, have been carefully exhumed and reburied, *each* in a *separate* coffin, in some one of the beautiful national cemeteries established mostly within the limits of the division.

Disabled soldiers have been selected by the Secretary of War, under the provisions of the act, and one now resides at each of the cemeteries, to watch over and protect the graves, and to wait upon visitors.

The following is a list of the cemeteries, with a few brief statistics illustrating some points of special interest:

Running number.	Name of Cemetery.	Location.	State.	Number of Acres Enclosed.	Total.	Known.	Unknown.	Number of distinct localities from which the dead have been gathered.	Number of regiments represented.	Number of States represented.
						Number of Dead Interred.				
1	New Albany	New Albany	Indiana	6	2,807	2,025	782	50		19
2	Cave Hill	Louisville	Kentucky		3,905	3,144	761	67	597	19
3	Lexington	Lexington	"		944	797	147	23	147	15
4	Camp Nelson	Near Nicholasville	"	8	3,638	2,252	1,386	228	301	18
5	Danville	Danville	"	2-3	355	344	11	3	94	10
6	Lebanon	Lebanon	"	3	865	832	333	41	136	11
7	Mill Springs	Logan's Cross Roads	Tennessee	10	707	261	446	96	73	11
8	Knoxville	Knoxville	"	75	3,153	1,903	1,250	174	257	18
9	Chattanooga	Chattanooga	"	20	12,843	7,676	5,167	309	655	23
10	Stone's River	Murfreesboro	"	64.48	6,121	3,647	2,474	58	382	17
11	Nashville	Nashville	"	15.34	16,486	11,511	4,975	251	741	22
12	Cumberland River	Fort Donelson	"	10.5	670	120	550	153	38	8
13	Shiloh	Pittsburg Landing	"	38.16	3,583	1,074	2,509	565	203	15
14	Mississippi River	Memphis	"	20	13,961	4,932	9,029	341	574	28
15	Union	Corinth	Mississippi	40	5,671	1,572	4,099	766	272	15
16	Vicksburg	Vicksburg	"		12,644	3,252	9,412	638	382	24
17	Natchez	Natchez	"		2,018	211	1,807	58	49	15
18	Mobile	Mobile	Alabama		560	456	104		127	18
19	Marietta and Atlanta	Marietta	Georgia	30	9,992	6,777	3,215	1,970	546	23
20	Andersonville	Andersonville	"	50	13,704	....	....	146	....	..

The dead from Eastern Georgia, including those from Lawton Prison-pen, have been removed to the national cemetery at Beaufort, South Carolina; and those from Columbus, Paducah, and Fort Holt, Kentucky, to Mound City, Illinois; and those from extreme Eastern Kentucky, and country adjacent to the Ohio River, below Louisville, to New Albany, Indiana — in all about six thousand. All others are buried within the limits of the original division.

The land upon which most of these cemeteries are located has been purchased and paid for, and the jurisdiction has been ceded to the United States by the several States in which they are situated. Permanent stone walls, or temporary wooden fences, sufficient for their present protection, have been constructed around them all.

Under direction of the Quartermaster-General, complete lists of these dead are being corrected and systematically arranged by cemeteries: One copy, together with a complete set of the original burial-sheets, for deposit at each cemetery, and another, in the form of a roll of honor, to be forwarded to the Quartermaster-General for publication. In addition to this, plats of the cemeteries have been prepared, showing the internal arrangement of sections; and enlarged sectional maps showing the exact location and number of each grave.

A general cemeterial map of the entire country from which the dead have been removed, is in process of preparation. Upon this map will be shown the exact location of the cemeteries; the limits of the several districts from which the dead have been removed to each; the location of battle-fields and skirmishes; the lines of march of the armies; the routes of raiders, and all the prominent places where dead have been found.

This, I understand, is to be extended by the Quartermaster-General to include the entire country embraced in the cemeterial operations East and West.

In closing the brief sketch of this great national work within the limits of the original Military Division of the Tennessee, I feel impelled to say that he who thinks to provide for our *slain* more *honorable graves* than those in which they were originally interred, *dying* at the *post of duty*, and *sleeping where they fell*, has but a faint conception of the glory of their deeds, or the significance of this work.

Stand, as I have done, by the grave of Rankin, of the Eighty-First Ohio, killed at the battle of Corinth, and buried at the front, on the spot where he poured out his blood, and read the simple but suggestive inscription upon the rude tablet: "He died doing his whole duty;" or by that of Color Sergeant McCall, of the same regiment, and interpret upon his tombstone the *classic* inscription, made ever sacred to Americans by its utterance from the lips of the lamented Warren as he fell on the heights of Bunker Hill — "*Dulce et decorum est, pro patria mori*"—; or in the midst of the forest solitudes of Shiloh, on the deserted and now silent battle-field, at the common grave of the Color

Sergeant of the sixteenth Wisconsin, and guard, who fell to a man, while gallantly defending the flag of their country, and read their names and youthful ages recorded on a common tablet, and say what act of grateful recognition, by their countrymen, of the priceless value of the services they, and thousands of others as brave and pure, have rendered, in their deeds and in their examples, can add one single ray to the halo of glory that now surrounds them?

All that a grateful country can do, is by honoring the memories, and protecting the sacred remains of those who laid down their lives for its salvation, to show its appreciation of the heroic sacrifice, and teach to succeeding generations lessons of undying patriotism.

"MEMOIR."

LIEUTENANT WILLIAM L. PORTER, FIFTH U. S. CAVALRY.

DIED, April 23, 1868, at Gallatin, Tennessee, William L. Porter, Fifth United States Cavalry, from the effects of an amputation, rendered necessary by injuries received while firing a salute on the 22nd of February, 1868.

The subject of this memoir was born at Lodonia, Northern India, February 9, 1842. He was the oldest child of the Reverend Joseph Porter and Harriet Athern Porter, missionaries of the American Board of Foreign Missions. He was brought to this country by his father, on the occasion of his mother's death, in the year 1849, to receive the education that could not be obtained in the far distant field of labor where his parents spent their lives. His father, returning to India, survived but a year or two, leaving Porter an orphan at the early age of eight or nine years. Being placed at school at South Hanover, Indiana, he remained there until 1857, when he entered Miami University, at Oxford, Ohio, where the breaking out of the Rebellion, in 1861, found him.

On the 19th day of April, 1861, Mr. Porter enlisted at Oxford, as a private, in Company B, Twentieth Ohio Volunteers Infantry, for the period of three months. At the expiration of this term of service, he re-enlisted, in Western Virginia, as a private, in Company B, Twenty-fourth Ohio Volunteers Infantry, for the period of three years. At this date he was detailed as a clerk in the Assistant Adjutant-General's office, at General Rosecrans' Headquarters, under Captain George L. Hartsuff, and there received the training that rendered his services so valuable at a later date, in an enlarged sphere of duty. Remaining there until July 25, 1862, he was transferred to Baltimore, and was assigned to duty in the Assistant Adjutant-General's office, at General Wool's Headquarters.

In the fall of 1862, General Rosecrans, after brilliant services in the armies of the West and South, was ordered to assume command of the army then operating under General Buell, and was ordered to Kentucky, where he assumed command of the Army of the Cumberland. In October of this year, Mr. Porter was ordered to report to Governor Tod, of Ohio, who commissioned him first lieutenant, in Company D, Fifty-sixth Ohio Volunteer Infantry, November 10, and ordered him to report to General Rosecrans, which he did, at Bowling Green, Kentucky. During the stay of the army at Murfreesboro, and while the army was engaged in campaigning in the field, up to the time General Rosecrans was relieved from the command of the Army of the Cumberland, Lieutenant Porter served on General Rosecrans' Staff, as Acting Aid-de-Camp, and was assigned to the responsible branch office of Reports and Returns, together with having supervision of the printing of the General Orders of the Department.

General Thomas, on assuming command of the Department of the Cumberland, continued Lieutenant Porter in charge of the same duties he previously performed. On November 10, 1864, he was mustered out as first lieutenant, but remaining at Department Headquarters, he served without pay until April 9, 1865. On application of General Thomas, he was appointed captain and Assistant Adjutant-General, volunteers, May 16, to date April 9, 1865. In the fall of this year, he was ordered to report to General Stoneman, as Assistant Adjutant-General, and, while on duty at Memphis, was breveted major for efficient services rendered during the war. He was mustered out of the volunteer service November 1, 1866. Returning North, he engaged for a short period in insurance business. His taste for army life returning, he made application for a position in the regular army, which, on the recommendation of the general officers under whom he had served, he secured. On the 13th day of August, 1867, he was appointed second lieutenant Fifth United States Cavalry. He served at Nashville as Assistant Adjutant-General, District of Tennessee, until January, 1868, when he was ordered on duty as Post Commissary and Quartermaster at Gallatin, Tennessee. On the 22nd of February of that year, he was engaged, with others, in firing a salute in honor of Washington's birth day. After firing all but the last salute, he gave directions to fire "one extra one, as the last." The anvil they were using on the occasion exploded, and a fragment striking the leg of Lieutenant Porter, crushed and mangled it terribly. He refused for over two months to allow amputation, as it would render him useless as a cavalry officer; but, finding that he was sinking in his mangled condition, he reluctantly consented to have his leg amputated, and the operation was performed. But, too late! His constitution, naturally vigorous, was prostrated by the two months confinement and intense pain, and it had not sufficient vitality to rally from the effects of the operation. and seven hours after the operation was performed, he passed away. Thus, at the early age of twenty-six, the mortal career of Lieutenant Porter was ended, and his spirit found rest.

Born in that far distant land of wondrous tale and fabled story, he was deprived of the tender care of his parents, at the time the opening mind of the child most needs a father's precept, and a mother's watchful, prayerful care. Becoming an orphan at an early date in his life, he missed these essential guides in the formation of his character.

This gave him a spirit of self-reliance, almost of hardihood, which enabled him to push his way, and make friends, where a more timid mind would have failed.

Lieutenant Porter was of a frank, cheerful nature; active and energetic in all he undertook; lively and warm hearted. He made many friends during his career in the army, who mourn his untimely end. Brave in battle, and cool under fire, he was the admiration of the general officers under whom he served. The three important engagements he participated in were, *Stone River*, *Chickamauga*, and *Mission Ridge*. There is One higher than man, whose ways are past finding out. Lieutenant Porter went through these engagements, frequently under heavy fire, and escaped untouched, to lose his life, at last, in the festal commemoration of the 22nd of February.

Only one year ago, and no one so bright and happy at our first meeting as Lieutenant Porter. Welcoming old friends he had not met since peace sent army friends to the four corners of our land, to their old homes and avocations, exchanging the hearty grasp of fellowship in our new organization, his very presence, with his cheery voice and kindly eye, made it a pleasure to see him, and a happiness to have him with us.

Let us cherish his memory, and guard well the heart memories we hold of him. In his far off Southern resting-place, may his grave have brighter, fresher tints, and the air about it a sunnier hue, and the birds a sweeter tone, by reason of the loving hearts who hold his memory precious, and who turn with warm, loving thoughts to that low resting place in the valley.

[SIGNED]

GENERAL S. W. PRICE,
Chairman Committee on Memorial.

16

LETTERS.

EXTRACT *from letter of Major-General W. S. Rosecrans to Major-General George H. Thomas, expressing regret at his inability to be present at the Reunion.*

" If the memories of the places and plays of childhood touch our hearts, what emotions must be aroused by the scenes and events of the bivouac and the battle! If the sports of youth, and the adventures of young manhood bind hearts in companionship, and create memories and friendships which follow us through life, what hallowed memories, what enduring companionships, what manly friendships must unite those who have cherished the love of country in hearts warmed by the same patriotic fires — who have shared the same privations, faced the same dangers, and felt, under the same canopy of battle, the lofty emotions that thrill the souls of men fighting for such a nation and such a land as ours.

"Is it any wonder that a bond of brotherhood should unite the officers and soldiers of the Union army? a bond admitting the extremest individuality, and variety of character, and yet strong enough to draw to each other men who have been reared in the remotest sections of the Union, and who have served their country in armies on the most distant lines of operations.

"Long may this bond survive those by whose united valor, under God's good providence, we have been preserved from becoming a byword in history, and now stand glorious among the nations of the earth. May it unite our children's children in brave, self-sacrificing devotion to our country through long coming years."

———

NASHVILLE, TENN., *December 10,* 1868.

MY DEAR GENERAL; — I deeply regret that imperative professional engagements render it impossible for me to attend the Chicago Reunion, and I must content myself for this year with sending, through you, my warmest greetings, and best wishes, to our old comrades of the Army of the Cumberland.

Truly and fraternally yours,

G. P. THRUSTON,
Late Brevet Brigadier-General U. S. V.

GENERAL WM. D. WHIPPLE,
Corresponding Secretary Society Army Cumberland.

HEADQUARTERS GENERAL SERVICE DEPOT, }
FORT COLUMBUS, N. Y. HARBOR, }
December 11, 1868. }

MAJOR-GENERAL D. BUTTERFIELD,

V. P. for the New York Society of the Army of the Cumberland:

GENERAL; — I regret exceedingly that my military duties will prevent me from availing myself of your kind invitation to be present in Chicago at the festival reunion of the Society of the Armies of the Cumberland, Ohio and Tennessee.

Nothing could afford me greater satisfaction than to be allowed to participate in the exercises, and partake of the courtesies, of that interesting occasion. To be brought face to face in familiar intercourse, and associated with such high, heroic natures as the gallant countrymen who constitute the membership of that Association, is indeed a rare privilege; and, except for the reason already given, I should as certainly be present in person, as that assuredly I shall be with you in spirit.

Honor to them all! to the famed and noble living, to the enshrined and sacred dead. "The mystic chords of memory," stretching over many battle-fields, binding you together with the strong brotherhood of common memories, common sacrifices, and common fellowships, will, indeed, notably illustrate the immortal beauty of our martyred president's invocation; and most sincerely do I trust that among the observances connected with that liberty beloved and rescued by himself and by you all, may be found the annual gathering of your "Association," to keep, amid the drouths of commerce and of peace, the heart green with remembrances of the close comradeship born out of sorrow and of war.

I am, General, very truly your obedient servant,

H. D. WALLEN,

Brevet Brigadier-General U. S. Army, Commanding.

ARMY BUILDING, NEW YORK, *December* 12, 1868.

GENERAL; — Intimately associated, as I have been, with the armies of the West, it would give me the greatest pleasure to renew my old associations with their representation, at Chicago, on the anniversary of that decisive victory at Nashville; but I regret that it will not be in my power to be present at this very interesting assemblage of officers, among whom are so many of my most attached friends.

I am, General, yours most respectfully,

GEORGE W. CULLUM,

Brevet Major-General U. S. Army.

BREVET MAJOR-GENERAL D. BUTTERFIELD,

V. P. for New York Society of Army of Cumberland.

FORT COLUMBUS, NEW YORK HARBOR, }
December 11, 1868, }

MY DEAR GENERAL;—In reply to your kind invitation of yesterday
to accompany you to Chicago, permit me to say that I know of nothing which would give me greater pleasure, but, on account of a very
severe cold which has kept me down sick for three or four days, I do
not think it would be prudent for me to attempt the journey. I shall
look with anxiety for the order placing me on duty in your office, and
will do my best to give you satisfaction.

Thanking you for your kindness, and wishing you a most pleasant
journey, I remain,

Very truly yours,

CHARLES G. BARTLETT.

BREVET MAJOR-GENERAL BUTTERFIELD.

———

NEW YORK, *December* 11, 1868.

GENERAL;—I have the honor to acknowledge the receipt of your kind
invitation to attend the annual Reunion at Chicago, on the 15th inst.,
and to express my thanks, with regret that I am unable to attend the
meeting.

I am, General, very respectfully,

Your obedient servant,

R. S. SATTERLEE.

MAJOR-GENERAL DANIEL BUTTERFIELD,
U. S. Army.

———

COURT ROOMS, NEW YORK, *December* 11, 1868.

GENERAL;—I have the honor to acknowledge the receipt of your note
inviting me to attend the annual Reunion at Chicago, of the Society of
the Army of the Cumberland, on the 15th inst. Nothing would afford
me more pleasure. My duties, however, as a member of a General
Court Martial will deprive me of that pleasure.

Very truly yours, etc.,

J. J. ABERCROMBIE,
Colonel and Brevet Brigadier-General U. S. Volunteers.

GENERAL DANIEL BUTTERFIELD,
U. S. Volunteers, Vice-President for New York.

OFFICE OF THE BOARD OF ENGINEERS,
FOR PERMANENT FORTIFICATIONS,
NEW YORK, *December* 11, 1868.

GENERAL; — I have the honor to acknowledge the receipt of your note of the 9th inst., inviting me to attend the annual Reunion of the Army of the Cumberland at Chicago, on the 15th inst.

Honoring the glorious services of the Army of the Cumberland, and of the associated Armies of the Ohio and of the Tennessee, which, under their great leaders, Grant, Sherman, Thomas, and Schofield, achieved such mighty results, it would give me much satisfaction to be able to accept the invitation, and to meet in fraternal union so many brave soldiers and esteemed friends, but my immediate duties, and my private affairs forbid, at the present moment, the journey which it requires.

I am, with great respect, your most obedient,

I. G. BARNARD,
Colonel and Brevet Major-General.

BREVET MAJOR-GENERAL D. BUTTERFIELD,
V. P. for New York, Society of Army of Cumberland.

———

COLEMAN HOUSE, NEW YORK, *December* 11, 1868.

DEAR GENERAL; — I return my cordial thanks for your kind invitation to attend the celebration, or annual Reunion, of the Army of the Cumberland on the 15th inst., and regret that I cannot be present on that occasion.

Yours, very truly,

ABNER DOUBLEDAY,
Brevet Major-General.

To BREVET MAJOR-GENERAL D. BUTTERFIELD,
U. S. Army.

———

HEADQUARTERS DISTRICT OF VIRGINIA,
BU. R. F. N. L.,
RICHMOND, VA., *December* 7, 1868.

To MAJOR-GENERAL WILLIAM D. WHIPPLE,
U. S. Army, Cor. Sec. Society Army of the Cumberland:

GENERAL; — I write to express many regrets at my inability to be present at the second meeting of our Society, on the 15th inst. With the memory of our first most auspicious reunion fresh in my mind, it is with inexpressible reluctance I relinquish the design to participate in the second.

Hoping our grand "Society of the Army of the Cumberland" may not be marked " with vivacity of inception, apathy of progress, and prematureness of decay;" but, like that venerable relic of the revolution, " the Society of the Cincinnati," its glories and its memories may be made inheritable by the descendants of its heroes.

I have the honor to remain, with many desires for its perpetuity, and sincere wishes for the prosperity of each individual comrade,

Your most obedient servant,

WILL. A. COULTER,
U. S. Army.

CINCINNATI, *December* 12, 1868.

AT a regular meeting of the Fourth Ohio Cavalry Association, held December 11, 1868, it was ordered that Colonel John Kennett, and Captains H. A. Hamilton, and H. A. Osborn be and are hereby constituted delegates to represent this Association at the meetings of the armies in Chicago, and bear our greetings to the comrades there assembled.

H. H. HAMILTON,
Vice-President, and President pro tem.

LUCIEN WILSON,
    Secretary

REPORT

[Furnished by the Recording Secretary]

OF THE

Proceedings of the Annual Meeting

OF THE

SOCIETY OF THE ARMY OF THE ·TENNESSEE,

HELD AT CHICAGO, ILLINOIS,

DECEMBER 15TH, 1868.

Wm. A. Rawlins
Bvt. Maj. Genl. U.S.A. Ch. of Staff

OFFICERS OF THE SOCIETY OF THE ARMY OF THE TENNESSEE.

President:

MAJOR-GENERAL JOHN A. RAWLINS.

Vice-Presidents:

MAJOR-GENERAL JOHN A. LOGAN,
MAJOR-GENERAL G. M. DODGE,
MAJOR-GENERAL B. F. POTTS,
MAJOR-GENERAL W. Q. GRESHAM,
BRIGADIER-GENERAL T. C. FLETCHER.
BRIGADIER-GENERAL N. RUSK.

Recording Secretary:

LIEUTENANT-COLONEL L. M. DAYTON.

Corresponding Secretary:

BRIGADIER-GENERAL A. HICKENLOOPER.

Treasurer:

MAJOR-GENERAL M. F. FORCE.

CONSTITUTION.

ARTICLE I.

The Association shall be known as "THE SOCIETY OF THE ARMY OF THE TENNESSEE," and shall include every officer who has served with honor in that army.

Honorary members may be elected from those who have served with honor and distinction in any of the armies of the United States.

ARTICLE II.

The object of the Society shall be to keep alive and preserve that kindly and cordial feeling which has been one of the characteristics of this army during its career in the service, and which has given it such harmony of action, and contributed in no small degree to its glorious achievements in our country's cause.

The fame and glory of all the officers belonging to this army, who have fallen either on the field of battle, or in the line of their duty, shall be a sacred trust to this Society, which shall cause proper memorials of their services to be collected and preserved, and thus transmit their names with honor to posterity.

The families of all such officers who shall be in indigent circumstances, will have a claim upon the generosity of the Society, and will be relieved by the voluntary contributions of its members whenever brought to their attention. In like manner, the fame and suffering families of those officers who may hereafter be stricken down by death, shall be a trust in the hands of their survivors.

ARTICLE III.

For the purpose of accomplishing these objects, the Society shall be organized by the annual election of a President and Vice-Presidents. The Vice-Presidents to be chosen, one from each Army Corps of the old Army of the Tennessee, and a Corresponding and a Recording Secretary.

The Society shall meet once in every year, and those officers who, for any cause, are unable to attend its meetings, will be expected to write to the Corresponding Secretary of the Society, and impart such information in regard to themselves as they may desire, and which may be of interest to their brother officers. Honoring the glorious achievements of our brothers-in-arms belonging to other armies, whose services have contributed, in an equal degree, in the re-establishment of our Government, and desiring to draw closer to them in the bonds of social feeling, the President, or either of the Vice-Presidents of this Society, shall be authorized to invite the attendance of any officer of the United States Army at any of our annual meetings.

AMENDMENTS TO THE CONSTITUTION.

FIRST. That the first sentence of the third article of the Constitution be amended so as to read as follows:

"The Society shall be organized by the annual election of a President and six Vice-Presidents, a Recording Secretary, a Corresponding Secretary, and a Treasurer."

BY-LAWS.

ARTICLE I.

That one dollar per annum be paid by each member to the Recording Secretary, the money so raised to be paid by him to the Treasurer.

ARTICLE II.

Money for ordinary expenses of the Society may be expended by the Treasurer upon the warrant of the President. All other expenditures, only in pursuance of a vote of the Society.

ARTICLE III.

The Treasurer shall make a report to the annual meeting of all receipts and expenditures with vouchers.

The Recording Secretary shall report to the annual meeting all money received by him, and all transferred by him to the Treasurer.

The Corresponding Secretary shall report to every meeting all correspondence of general interest.

ARTICLE IV.

All questions and resolutions shall be decided by a majority of the members present. But amendments, proposed to the Constitution, shall be acted upon only at the annual meeting subsequent to the one at which they may be proposed, unless the postponement be dispensed with by a vote of two-thirds of the members present.

ARTICLE V.

The order of business shall be as follows:

1. Reading of the journal of the previous meeting.
2. Appointments of committees on business and for nomination of officers.
3. Receiving reports.
4. Current business.
5. Election of officers
6. Adjournment.

ARTICLE VI.

If the Society shall, at any meeting, omit to designate the time and place of the next meeting, the President shall, by due public notice, fix the time and place.

ARMY OF THE TENNESSEE.

SOCIETY OF THE ARMY OF THE TENNESSEE, }
CHICAGO, ILL., *December* 15, 1868. }

To accomplish its Third Annual Reunion in accordance with its adjournment at St. Louis, and to join in a reunion with the Societies of the Armies of the Cumberland, the Ohio, and the Georgia, the Society of the Army of the Tennessee was called to assemble in the city by the following notices:

WASHINGTON CITY, D. C., *October* 15, 1868.

Officers of the Army of the Tennessee:

You are respectfully notified that in accordance with your last adjournment, and the following call issued by Lieutenant-General W. T. Sherman, the third annual meeting of the Society of the Army of the Tennessee will be held in the city of Chicago, on the 15th day of December, 1868, at 10 o'clock, A.M.

Every officer who has at any time served in the Army or Department of the Tennessee, is entitled to membership, and to all such an earnest invitation is extended to be present, to unite with our brother officers of the Armies of the Cumberland, Ohio, and Georgia, in perpetuating that kindly, cordial and social feeling, which, amidst scenes and events now historical, ever marked our intercourse with the soldiers of these armies, whose hearts still beat in friendly unison when touched by the memories of the past.

All necessary arrangements for the meeting will be made by the following local committee, residents in Chicago:

General William E. Strong, General J. M. Corse, Colonel Harry Gile, General John McArthur, General Joseph Stockton, and Colonel John M. Loomis, to whom letters of inquiry may be addressed.

MAJOR-GENERAL JOHN A. RAWLINS,
President.

BRIGADIER-GENERAL A. HICKENLOOPER,
Corresponding Secretary, Cincinnati, Ohio.
LIEUTENANT-COLONEL L. M. DAYTON,
Recording Secretary, St. Louis, Missouri.

WASHINGTON, D. C., *April* 20, 1868.

Notice is hereby given, that the Societies representing the Armies of the Tennessee, Cumberland, Ohio and Georgia, will meet on the 15th and 16th days of December, 1868, at Chicago, Illinois. The object is purely social, and designed to preserve the memories of the war, and to cherish the friendships formed during that period of our national history. All are cheerfully invited to be present and participate.

An orator has been appointed for each army, and addresses will be delivered on the night of the 15th of December, and a grand banquet will be held on the night of the 16th.

Letters of inquiry may be addressed to General William E. Strong, Chicago, Illinois, who will attend to all preliminary business, until a joint committee of arrangements has been appointed to carry into effect the above plan.

> W. T. SHERMAN,
> *Lieutenant-General U. S. Army.*

Crosby's Music Hall had been selected by the local committee of arrangements, in which to hold the meeting of the Society, and at two o'clock it organized. The President, Major-General Rawlins, and the Senior Vice-President, Major-General Howard, not being present, the second in order of Vice-Presidents, Major-General Giles A. Smith, assumed the chair, and announced the Society ready for the transaction of business.

On motion of Colonel Coleman,

Resolved, That in consequence of the temporary absence of the Secretary, Colonel Dayton, who is engaged in important business of the Society, Colonel T. S. Mather act as Secretary, *pro tem.*

On motion of Colonel Joel,

Resolved, That all general officers present be invited to seats with the President. The President extended the invitation.

On motion of General Leggett,

Resolved, That a committee of seven be appointed to nominate officers for the ensuing year.

The President announced the committee as follows:

Major-General M. D. Leggett, Major-General J. M. Corse, Colonel D. C. Coleman, Brevet Brigadier-General Benjamin Spooner, Colonel J. M. Hedrick, Colonel Thomas Reynolds, and Colonel George G. Pride.

On motion of D. P. Grier,

Resolved, That a committee of seven be appointed to select the place for holding the next annual meeting.

The President announced the committee as follows:

General D. P. Grier, General B. F. Potts, General E. W. Rice, Major-General W. Q. Gresham, Colonel L. M. Dayton, U. S. A., and Colonel K. Knox, U. S. A.

Major-General S. A. Hurlbut offered a resolution that a committee of thirteen be appointed to attend the inauguration of the President elect.

Colonel Fort moved, as an amendment to the resolution of General Hurlbut, that a committee of thirteen be appointed to draft an address of congratulation, to be presented to General Grant, the President elect. Amendment accepted.

General Fletcher offered, as an amendment, that the motion as amended, be postponed for consideration at ten o'clock, December 16, and it was so resolved.

On motion of General Eldridge,

Resolved, That a committee of three be appointed to call upon General Grant, Lieutenant-General Sherman, Major-General Thomas, Major-General Schofield, Major-General Slocum, and General Cox, and invite them to meet the Society of the Army of the Tennessee, at its place of meeting, on December 16, at such hour as they may designate.

The President announced General Eldridge, General Webster, and General Starring as such committee, and requested them to also act as escort.

General Grier offered as a motion,

Resolved, That the Adjutant Generals, Quartermaster-Generals, Commissary-Generals, and their assistants, and all other staff officers of the Governors of the respective states that furnished troops for the Army of the Tennessee during the war, be admitted to membership, and all privileges of this organization, upon their complying with existing regulations.

This motion elicited discussion by different members, and upon the question being brought to vote, was rejected, because it conflicted with the Constitution of the Society.

There being no further business for the present consideration of the Society, on motion of Colonel Wood,

Resolved, That the Society stand adjourned until ten o'clock A.M., December 16, 1868.

SOCIETY OF THE ARMY OF THE TENNESSEE,
CHICAGO, ILLINOIS, *December* 16, 1868.

The Society met in Crosby's Music Hall at ten o'clock A.M., pursuant to adjournment of December 15, and was called to order by Vice-President General Giles A. Smith, who occupied the chair. By his invitation, General Fallows, formerly chaplain of the Thirty-Second Wisconsin, and afterward Colonel of the Forty-Ninth Wisconsin Volunteers, opened the meeting with a prayer appropriate to the occasion, invoking Divine blessings upon the saviors of the nation, asking God to assist them in their counsels, and to make it a happy Reunion.

The President announced the meeting ready for the transaction of business. The first in order being the reading of the journal of the previous meeting.

The Recording Secretary of the Society, Colonel Dayton, then read the proceedings of the last annual meeting, held at St. Louis, Missouri, and, on motion of Colonel Coleman, it was

Resolved, That the records of the last annual meeting, as just read by the Secretary, be adopted, and so entered in the records of the Society.

Next, in the order of business, being appointment of committees on business, Colonel Thomas Reynolds arose to a question of privilege, and desired to formally announce to the Society the death of General Cassius Fairchild, Fifth Vice-President of the Society, one of its most distinguished and beloved members. Permission was granted, when he said that it was designed that General Howe should make the announcement to the meeting, but, owing to the unavoidable absence of that distinguished soldier, the duty devolved upon him. For upward of twenty years he had known General Fairchild. They had been friends and neighbors. For four years they had served side by side in the army. He knew him as a citizen, as a soldier on the march, at the bivouac, and in the bloody field of battle. Knowing and appreciating his character so well as he did, the speaker could not help feeling profound sorrow when he looked upon his vacant chair, and feeling that some token of regard should be offered to their departed comrade.

And, on motion of Colonel Reynolds,

Resolved, That a committee of five be appointed to draft resolutions for the action of the Society, and commemorative of the deceased patriot and soldier, Brigadier-General Cassius Fairchild.

The President announced the committee to consist of Colonel Reynolds, Generals Belknap, M. F. Force, Scribner, and McArthur.

General Rogers desired to announce the death of Lieutenant-Colonel J. J. Jones, Forty-Sixth Illinois Infantry.

And, on motion of General Rogers,

Resolved, That a committee of three be appointed to draft resolutions for the consideration of the Society, as expressive of

17

its feelings upon learning of the death of the lamented Lieutenant-Colonel John J. Jones, Forty-Sixth Infantry.

The President announced the committee to consist of the following gentlemen :

Generals Rogers, Gersham, and Corse.

Colonel Stone announced the death of General Charles Mathies, and on his motion it was

Resolved, That a committee of three be appointed to draft, for the action of the Society, resolutions of condolence for the friends of General Mathies.

The President announced the committee to be as follows : Colonel J. C. Stone, Colonel J. M. Hedrick, and General E. W. Rice.

There being no other committees to appoint, the President announced that in accordance with the by-laws of the Society, the next in order of business was the " receiving of reports." The Secretary desired to file his annual report, and was requested by the President to read it. The report is as follows :

SECRETARY'S REPORT.

St. Louis, Missouri, *December* 1, 1868.

Major-General John A. Rawlins,
  President Society Army of the Tennessee:

General ; — Article third of the by-laws of the Society of the Army of the Tennessee, requires of me, as Recording Secretary of the Society, to render at this annual meeting of the Society a report. Before entering upon that report, I wish to state that article first of the by-laws of the Society fixes the annual dues of the members at one ($1) dollar each.

By resolution of the Society, passed at its annual meeting held in Cincinnati in 1866, it devolved upon the Corresponding Secretary to request of each member a contribution of five ($5) dollars for the purpose of creating a permanent fund for the use of the Society.

In accordance with these provisions for raising money, I now present the following : Since my last annual report there has been paid me by members, in compliance with article first, namely : For dues, two hundred and seventy-six ($276) dollars; and in response to the resolution cited, as passed at the annual meeting of 1866, and received since my last annual report, five hundred and fifty-five ($555) dollars, making paid me for dues and permanent fund, a total of eight hundred and thirty-one ($831) dollars, which I have, in compliance with the by-laws, passed over to the Treasurer, General Force, and herewith inclose his receipts.

This money was nearly all received during the session of the last annual meeting, and after my report for the previous year had been made.

I wish further to state that the Corresponding Secretary has notified the officers who served in the Army of the Tennessee, of this provision of the Society, for raising funds needed to carry out its intentions, by circulating the annual report of the proceedings of the Society, at its annual meeting of 1866, prepared by the Secretary, and ordered published by the Society, fifteen hundred (1,500) copies of which were sent by mail to the known address of members.

Further notification was given the members as follows: I arranged the proceedings of the last annual meeting for publication, and had a thousand copies struck off. These were forwarded to the members by the Corresponding Secretary.

All money for the Society is payable to the Recording Secretary, which necessitates his keeping an individual account with each member. Considering it my duty, both to the Society and to members, to keep them informed of their financial standing with the Society, I prepared a circular, making a statement of their accounts in accordance with the provisions of the Society, and which reads as follows:

SOCIETY OF THE ARMY OF THE TENNESSEE, }
ST. LOUIS, MO., *June* 1, 1868. }

SIR:

Your attention is invited to those parts of the constitution and by-laws that fix the membership, and specify the authorized assessments and dues of the Society.

The Secretary's books show that you are indebted to the Society in conformity thereto:

For assessment, - - - - - - - $
For dues, - - - - - - - - $

Please make an early remittance to the Secretary, to whom all moneys for the Society are payable.

L. M. DAYTON, *Secretary.*

These circulars were also forwarded to members by the Corresponding Secretary at the same time that he sent the report.

I have been thus particular in making my report, in order that you and the members of the Society may know that no effort has been spared to give the proper information to them, that they might know the requirements of the Society.

The circulars mentioned were sent to members in June last, but up to this time only twelve (12) persons have responded. This will show to you all that it is evident the action of the Society thus far to provide its treasury, has not been adequate, and that some further action is absolutely needed, which fact is more specially shown by the Treasurer in his report. I therefore respectfully recommend this subject to the consideration of the finance committee, and the Society, at this meeting.

At our last annual meeting, held in St. Louis, no resolution was passed by the Society to provide for the publication and distribution of the proceedings, but at the suggestion of some of the members, that it was an oversight, I undertook the task, and succeeded as you know. The expenses were paid by funds secured by the local committee of arrangements of that meeting, and the treasury of the Society was not called on for any money.

I would further suggest that some definite action of the Society be taken in regard to the carrying out of a provision of the constitution that contemplates the preservation of the record of its members, especially of those who are lost to us by death. Though it has not been regularly so reported, it is known that several have died since our Society has been organized. Time is fast obliterating from our memories many interesting features of their service and character, and we ought, without further delay, to give this subject our attention. I am, with respect,

Your obedient servant,
L. M. DAYTON,
Lieutenant-Colonel U. S. A.,
Secretary Society of the Army of the Tennessee.

On motion of Colonel Reynolds—

Resolved, That the annual report of the Secretary, as just read, be accepted.

The Treasurer asked permission to file his annual report, in accordance with the by-laws, and by request of the President, read it to the Society. The report is as follows:

TREASURER'S REPORT.

CHICAGO, ILLINOIS, *December 15, 1868.*

At the last annual report the balance remaining in the permanent fund was one hundred and sixty-four dollars ($164.) Since then the Recording Secretary has paid in five hundred and fifty-five dollars ($555), and one coupon on a Government bond has been collected, making, with its premium on gold, twenty dollars and ninety-seven cents ($20.97.) The expenditure has been five hundred and forty dollars ($540), paid in purchase of a Government bond for five hundred dollars ($500), on which another coupon will be due January 1, 1869. *There remains,* with the permanent fund, *this Government bond,* and *one hundred and ninety-nine dollars and ninety-seven cents* ($199.97) in cash.

At the last meeting the balance in the general fund was twenty-one dollars ($21). Since that time two hundred and seventy-seven dollars ($277) have been received. From this fund has been paid out, on the warrant of the President of the Society, two hundred and twenty dollars and seventy-six cents ($220.76), *leaving a balance of seventy-seven dollars and twenty-four cents* ($77.24) remaining.

In 1866, by resolution of the Society, three hundred and forty dollars were appropriated from the permanent fund toward payment of the current expenses of the Society. I respectfully recommend that the balance now in the general fund, and future receipts therein, till the amount equals three hundred and forty dollars ($340,) be transferred to the permanent fund.

I took the responsibility of investing the money of the permanent fund, as soon as enough was received, in a Government bond. I respectfully recommend that the Treasurer be authorized from time to time to make such investments when there is sufficient money on hand.

It was determined, on the organization of the Society, to create a permanent fund, the interest of which would be enough to meet the incidental expenses, other than the supper, of the annual meetings. For this purpose at least ten thousand dollars should be raised. We can not always look to generous citizens to meet these expenses for us. Enthusiasm is a sentiment of too high pressure to be permanent. I respectfully suggest that some immediate steps be taken to carry out this important policy of the Society.

M. F. FORCE,
Treasurer of the Society of the Army of the Tennessee.

On motion of General B. F. Potts,

Resolved, That the report of the Treasurer, as just read by himself, be accepted.

Colonel Reynolds, chairman of the committee appointed to draft resolutions expressive of the feelings of the Society on learning of the death of General Fairchild, asked leave, which was granted, to file their report, which is as follows:

Resolved, That in the death of General Cassius Fairchild, of the Army of the Tennessee, of wounds received in battle, his wife has lost a tender husband, his family an affectionate brother, his country an earnest patriot and gallant soldier, and we, his fellows, a noble and generous comrade.

Resolved, That we tender to his stricken bride and bereaved relatives, a soldier's sympathy, asking them to accept with us the consolation we find in this sorrow, in the knowledge that his name is on the roll of those who were not born to die.

Resolved, That a copy of these resolutions be sent to the widow, and each of the brothers and sisters of the deceased.

[Signed by the Committee.]

On motion of General Force,

Resolved, That the report as filed by the above committee be adopted.

General Leggett, chairman of the committee appointed for the nomination of officers for the Society, asked leave to file their report, which was granted, and reads as follows:

CHICAGO, ILL., *December 15*, 1868.

The committee appointed to nominate officers for the Society of the Army of the Tennessee for the ensuing year, submit, as their report, the following nominations:

For President:

Major-General John A. Rawlins, U. S. A.

For Vice-Presidents:

Major-General John A. Logan,
Major-General G. M. Dodge,
Brevet Major-General B. F. Potts,
Brevet Major-General W. Q. Gresham,
Brigadier-General T. C. Fletcher,
Brigadier-General N. Rusk.

For Recording Secretary:
Lieutenant-Colonel L. M. Dayton, U. S. A.

For Corresponding Secretary:
Brevet Brigadier-General A. Hickenlooper.

For Treasurer:
Brevet Major-General M. F. Force.

[Signed by the Committee.]

On motion of General Fuller,

Resolved, That the report, as read, be adopted.

On motion of General Leggett,

Resolved, That the rules of business proceeding be suspended, for the purpose of taking up the election of officers for the Society for the ensuing year.

On motion of General W. W. Belknap,

Resolved, That the persons presented by the Committee on Nomination of Officers are unanimously elected to the positions recommended, and are duly authorized to act respectively and accordingly as officers of the Society.

The President *pro tem.* announced, that by the resolution just passed, the officers elected for the ensuing year, to be

Major-General John A. Rawlins, U. S. A., President.
Major-General John A. Logan, First Vice-President.
Major-General G. M. Dodge, Second Vice-President.
Brevet Major-General B. F. Potts, Third Vice-President.
Brevet Major-General W. Q. Gresham, Fourth Vice-President.
Brigadier-General T. C. Fletcher, Fifth Vice-President.
Brigadier-General N. Rusk, Sixth Vice-President.
Lieutenant-Colonel L. M. Dayton, U. S. A., Rec. Secretary.
Brevet Brigadier-General A. Hickenlooper, Cor. Secretary.
Brevet Major-General M. F. Force, Treasurer.

The presiding officer, General Smith, asked leave to vacate the chair, in the absence of the President elect, in favor of the First Vice-President elect, General Logan, who assumed the chair as presiding officer, amidst applause, and addressed the Society in these words:

"FELLOW-COMRADES OF THE ARMY OF THE TENNESSEE: I presume that not one of the men whose names are regisstered as your officials for the year, in the report just read, but feels a just pride in your selection, and toward you grateful for the compliment bestowed. Upon assuming the responsibility of your presiding officer, it may be proper for me to say something in regard to those officers of the army who are not present with us here to-day. In selecting General John A. Rawlins as your President, you have made a noble choice. He is a man of intellect and courage — one whose nobility is unquestioned, and whose generosity is as boundless, in expanse, as the ocean.

"Alas! there are others absent from our midst with whom we have fought side by side upon many a bloody field — McPherson, than whom the war produced no greater commander save one, our President elect. There are many others whom I think of now. They died that we might live. Then let us so live that we may emulate them in a noble death. I hope that while presiding I shall secure all due aid and assistance in the performance of my duties from the Army of the Tennessee."

The committee appointed to draft resolutions commemorative of General Mathies, asked leave and presented, as their report, resolutions as follows:

Resolved, That the Society of the Army of the Tennessee learns, with the deepest regret, of the death of the late General Charles S. Mathies, of Iowa, an adopted citizen of the United States, who, in the late war for the Union, first served as captain in the distinguished First Iowa Volunteers, then as Lieutenant-Colonel of the Fifth Iowa, then as Colonel of that noted command, from which, for the most intrepid gallantry and efficient conduct at the battle of Iuka, he was promoted to the rank of Brigadier-General, in that capacity maintaining the reputation he had justly earned, and greatly adding to it throughout all the campaigns and operations of General Sherman to the victory of Missionary Ridge, where he was severely wounded.

Resolved, That the pure personal character, strict individual and political integrity, valor, and military services of General Mathies, most justly won for him general respect while he was living, and entitle his memory to be cherished in the hearts of all good and patriotic citizens, now that he is dead.

[Signed by the Committee].

On motion of General Dodge,

Resolved, That the report of the committee appointed to draft resolutions of respect to the late General Charles S. Mathies, be adopted.

The committee appointed to report resolutions respecting Colonel John J. Jones, presented the following report:

WHEREAS, It has pleased Him above to take from us our brave and honored comrade, Colonel John J. Jones, late Colonel of the Forty-sixth Illinois, therefore, be it

Resolved, That we revere his memory, and remember with pride his brave and daring deeds at Fort Donelson, Shiloh, and other fields throughout the late war.

Resolved, That we tender to his bereaved wife and friends the consolations of this organization.

Resolved, That a copy of these resolutions be furnished to the widow and parents of the deceased.

[Signed by the Committee].

On motion of General Giles A. Smith,

Resolved, That the report of the committee appointed to draft resolutions of respect to Colonel John J. Jones be adopted.

Colonel Coleman, chairman of the committee appointed at the last annual meeting, to report a design of seal and certificate of membership of the Society, reported that it had been impossible to get a meeting or conference of the committee, and that nothing had been done; and, on his own motion,

Resolved, That the committee appointed to report a design for seal and certificate of membership be discharged.

On motion of General Potts,

Resolved, That Generals Force, Hickenlooper, and Yorke be authorized as a committee to report to the Society a design for seal and certificate of membership.

General Sanborn moved that, before the resolution should be put to vote, it be amended so as to read, " That the committee be authorized to *adopt* a design for seal and certificate of membership for the Society."

General Potts accepted the amendment, and the resolution, so amended, was adopted.

General Grier, chairman of the committee appointed to select the place for the next annual meeting of the Society, reported that the committee had not reached any conclusion, and desired an extension of time for considering the matter, and that the committee might confer with resident officers of different cities in which it would be desirable to hold the meeting.

On motion,

Resolved, That the report of the committee appointed to select the locality for holding the next annual meeting be accepted, and the committee is granted further time, according to the necessities of the faithful performance of their duties in making such selection; and, when made, will report the same at once to the President, General John A. Rawlins.

The committee appointed to report a design for a Society badge was called on for a report.

The chairman of the committee, Colonel Joel, not being present, and not having made any report, Colonel Dayton, next in order of the committee, stated, that so far as he knew, the committee had never been called together for deliberation, and he had been unable to learn that any thing had been done, and presumed there had not; and, therefore, asked, by reason of there being no probability that the committtee appointed would do any thing, that the committee be discharged.

By resolution of the Society the committee was discharged.

On motion of General Dodge,

Resolved, That Generals Force, Hickenlooper, and Yorke, the committee appointed to select and adopt a device for seal and certificate of membership, shall constitute a committee to adopt and report a device for badge of the Society, and are instructed to incorporate in such device a representation of the corps badge of each corps that served in the Army of the Tennessee.

General Hickenlooper, upon behalf of the McPherson Monument Committee, was granted leave to read and file his report of transactions for the past year, as follows:

CHICAGO, *December* 15, 1868.

GENERAL JOHN A. RAWLINS,
President Society of the Army of the Tennessee:

SIR; — On behalf of the Committee on McPherson Monument, I have the honor to submit for the information of the Society the following report:

The balance remaining in my hands November 14, 1867, as per report submitted at our last annual meeting -	$3,121 11
Amount reported to General Leggett, - - - -	1,934 32
Amount reported by McPherson Monument Association, of Clyde, Ohio, exclusive of $3,000 expended for grounds and improvements, - - - - - - - -	2,000 00
Total reported on hand November 14, 1867, -	$7,055 43

Since that date I have received the following subscriptions:

November 18, 1867, Lieut. Charles E. Griffin,	-	$25 25
November 21, 1867, Dr. S. P. Bonner	- -	5 00
January 6, 1868, Captain J. S. Foster,	- -	5 00
January 18, 1868, Francis Skiddy,	- - -	1,000 00
January 20, 1868, Colonel T. Reynolds,	- -	56 00
January 28, 1868, General W. E. Strong,	- -	300 00
March 9, 1868, Colonel L. M. Dayton,	- -	100 00
June 27, 1868, Colonel James Peckham,	-	35 00
September 23, 1868, Colonel E. F. Winslow,	-	18 00
December 12, 1868, Captain John Ried,	-	33 00
Received from Interest account,	- - - -	276 74—$1,853 99

$8,909 42

There having been no expenditures from this fund during the year, leaves balance in my hand at this time, of   - $4,975 10

I have received no information either from General Leggett, or the McPherson Monument Association, at Clyde, Ohio, which will enable me to give any definite information in regard to the funds in their hands. Supposing it has increased by accumulating interest only, (six per cent), it will amount to not less than, in the hands of General Leggett,   -   2,060 04

And in the hands of McPherson Monument Association, of Clyde, Ohio,   -   -   -   -   -   -   -   -   2,130 00

Making the aggregate of   -   -   -   -   -   - $9,165 14

At our last meeting considerable enthusiasm was manifested by our members upon the subject of raising a sufficient sum to enable the committee to proceed with the erection of the monument. Various sums were pledged, and subscription blanks were given to twenty-two persons making such pledges, but only *three* of them have reported collections, viz.: General W. E. Strong, Colonel Thomas Reynolds, and Colonel L. M. Dayton.

In reply to my letters requesting information as to progress made in this matter, *five* of those persons answer, assigning various reasons for having neglected to carry out the good intentions expressed at St. Louis; the remainder are unheard from.

In conclusion, I can not too earnestly urge upon you the necessity of further and more energetic exertion, and remind you that we, as a Society, have pledged ourselves to the erection of this monument.

As the Army of the Tennessee has never yet failed in any thing it has undertaken, let us not do so in this, but put forth renewed efforts, and the result will add one more to the many achievements which we are proud to look back upon.

A. HICKENLOOPER, *Secretary.*

At the conclusion of reading the report of General Hickenlooper, he desired General Logan to express his views in regard
to this subject, which he did, in the most interesting and feeling
manner, eliciting the commendation of the members present.
The mention of McPherson's name, and that the Society proposed to assist in the erection of a monument over his grave, was
sufficient to claim the earnest attention of all.   Colonel McMillan also made some remarks, approving the efforts of the Society,
and thought if a committee were appointed to solicit subscriptions in New York City, money might be obtained there.

On motion of General Hickenlooper,

Resolved, That Colonel Charles R. McMillan, Colonel S. M.
Bowman, and Colonel G. G. Pride, be appointed a special
committee to solicit subscriptions in the city of New York, on
behalf of the Society of the Army of the Tennessee, in aid
of the McPherson Monument Association.

On motion of General Noyes,

Resolved, That the most earnest thanks of the Society of
the Army of the Tennessee are accorded to Mr. Francis Skiddy,
of New York, for his liberal contribution of one thousand dollars in aid of the McPherson Monument fund.

At this point Lieutenant-General Sherman entered the hall,
and was received, on presentation, with many cheers and rapturous applause.   Learning what the point of business was that
the Society was discussing, he stated that he had something
referring to it, and which he would at once engage in, if in
order.

Specially stating to the reporters present, that he had to speak
of private affairs of General McPherson and a young lady to
whom he was engaged to be married, when killed, he requested
the reporters to omit this subject in their report, he said :

FELLOW-SOLDIERS ;—I understand that the subject now commanding your attention is that of the McPherson Monument.

You recollect that at the time McPherson was killed, he was engaged to a young lady whom he met at the house of Mr. Louis McLean. It was my good fortune to become acquainted with Mr. McLean, in California, in 1846, and we both remained in that country until we became the respective heads of banking houses. Mr. McLean was a good Union man. The lady was very accomplished, and now considered herself the widow of McPherson, and was generally so recognized by Mr. McLean, with whom she lived in California. The other day, at St. Louis, I was called upon by Mr. McLean, who had come there on a visit, and, during the course of our conversation, he told me that he had collected four thousand three hundred and fifty dollars ($4,350) in California, as contribution to the McPherson Monument fund, but that his widow wished that the monument should be erected at West Point. Nevertheless, that if I could procure her consent, the amount should be forwarded for the Clyde Monument. I immediately wrote the young lady a long letter, in which I stated the claims that Clyde, where the hero was born, had in the premises, and I have since received her consent that the money collected by Mr. McLean shall go toward the monument now erecting over the grave of McPherson. Mr. McLean has signified this fact to me in a telegram which I received on Saturday last, and will now read to you:

New York, *December* 8, 1868.

General W. T. Sherman,
      St. Louis, Missouri:
  You can rely on the California subscription in my hands for monument to General J. B. McPherson, amounting to some four thousand three hundred and fifty dollars ($4,350.)

Louis McLean.

I now pledge to your Association, for the use as named, that sum of money, and in doing so I will suggest that the selection of the monument, and its erection, be accomplished as speedily as possible. I need not tell you of McPherson's claims upon us, or how much I honored him, and appreciated his nobleness as a gentleman, a soldier, and your commander, but I do think if a modest memorial is erected over his grave now, with the money we have, it will do him more honor than if we defer until years hence and erect one more costly.

General Sherman desired further to say a few words in connection with letters he had, though not regarding the matter under immediate consideration, he asked it as a privilege, because he had some engagements that would prevent his remaining during the regular course of business. He spoke of the lamented General Ransom in the strongest terms of approbation as a soldier and gentleman, and also read a letter from a Mr. Bridgeman, of New York, in which he hopes the matter of erecting a monument to General Ransom will be looked to at this meeting. He submitted the letters for consideration of the Society, and asked its members to do what they could in furtherance of the object. The letter reads:

New York, *December 12, 1868.*

LIEUTENANT-GENERAL SHERMAN:

DEAR SIR;—The remains of my friend, General Ransom, who died at Rome, Georgia, more than four years ago, were taken to Chicago, for interment, by his request. The city that he loved, honored him as one so gallant should be honored at his burial, but, if I mistake not, there is not a stone to mark the spot where he sleeps, and no movement on foot to place one there. It has occurred to me that some word might be said by some of the speakers at the reunion next week, that would incite to action the generous people of Chicago, who are going ahead so fast that they forget the past, and need to have their memory jogged. Certainly that city should build a monument to one so brave and noble, who has laid down his life in their service.

I am sure you will sympathize with what I have written. I hope you will excuse the liberty a stranger takes. I will only add, I am a friend of Mr. Healy, the artist.

Very respectfully,

W. H. BRIDGEMAN.

General Sherman here spoke of Admiral Farragut, and Vice-Admiral D. D. Porter, presenting letters from them explaining why they could not accept his invitations and attend this reunion. Admiral Porter was at one time in command of the Mississippi Squadron, and worked in perfect harmony with the commanders of the Army of the Tennessee. His letter was wholly private, and but few extracts could be read from it; these, however, elicited much applause from the hearers.

Admiral Farragut's letter was read in full, as follows:

DEAR GENERAL; — Your very kind letter of the 2nd inst., inviting me to join your reunion of the Western armies, at their regular annual meeting, has just been received. To be present upon such an occasion, for the most excellent purpose of keeping alive and cementing more strongly the bonds of friendship formed in trials of fire and blood, and, in fact, every hardship incident to a war of the most desperate character that ever afflicted a nation, and through which their gallant leaders conducted them with such unparalleled success, from the mountains of the West to the ocean beach on the East, would, I can assure you, give me the greatest possible gratification, if it was only to experience the pleasure of hearing the soldiers of that grand army fight their many battles over again, and make their criticisms on the acts of their comrades, whilst I could — in my time I could — occasionally tell them how these affairs were looked upon by the different nations of Europe; how they had, by their deeds, astonished and aroused the admiration of the most distinguished military men throughout the countries I have so recently visited; but I regret that it will not be in my power to visit the West this winter. I beg you to believe me, however, when I say that I fully appreciate your desire to receive me with yards manned, and the kind expressions of friendship, which, I can assure you, I cordially reciprocate. I sincerely hope I may have the pleasure of meeting you during next spring, but my time is so much occupied at present that I am not able to make any engagements ahead.

I am, General, very sincerely yours,

D. G. FARRAGUT.

LIEUTENANT-GENERAL SHERMAN,
United States Army.
NEW YORK, *December* 8, 1868.

General Sherman now made one more appeal to the members to hasten the movement toward erecting a monument to General

McPherson, giving it as his opinion that we should secure all subscriptions, and complete the whole, during the coming year. He was now done, and kindly thanking his listeners for the patience with which they heard him, he withdrew, the members giving him rapturous applause and three cheers.

Resuming the business under consideration, General Hickenlooper, on behalf of the committee, explained at some length, the impracticability of fixing upon any particular date upon which to close the subscriptions. As the monument is to be erected not alone for the present, but for future generations, the committee do not deem it advisable to be too hasty in concluding a long and laborious task. Their past efforts must be taken as an earnest of what will be done in the future; while there is no doubt that the subscriptions pledged will be promptly paid, the committee could not consent to go on and contract for the monument until the money necessary to pay for it is actually in their possession, or under their immediate control. The fund is steadily increasing, and in the opinion of the committee, it would be better to wait until the desired sum, fifteen thousand dollars ($15,000), can be obtained, rather than erect a monument with the comparatively small sum now on hand. As soon as the California fund, and the Clyde Association subscriptions are paid in, the committees will be in a condition to act; but even then ample time must be given them to advertise for plans, make their selection, and contract for the work. After which, he reported the subscriptions received during the present meeting, as follows:

Colonel Ad. Sanders,	$5 00
Major O. D. Kinsman, -	5 00
Colonel F. H. Madenburg, -	10 00
General J. B. Sanborn,	25 00
Captain L. F. Ross,	10 00
General H. T. Reid	100 00
Captain A. Barto, -	5 00
General G. M. Dodge, -	50 00

18

Surgeon Plummer,	$5 00
Lieutenant Francis Rutger,	5 00
Captain Ed. Spear,	25 00
Colonel John H. Howe,	5 00
Surgeon A. E. Heighway,	10 00
Cash,	2 00
General W. E. Strong,	50 00
Captain E. W. Lucas,	5 00
Colonel L. H. Whittlesey,	5 00
General C. E. Lippencot,	5 00
Colonel H. Scofield,	5 00
General E. F. Noyes,	10 00
General J. W. Sprague,	10 00
Colonel John P. Hall,	5 00
Major-General John A. Logan,	150 00
Colonel S. A. Stockdale,	20 00
Colonel John Logan,	50 00
Colonel Richard Rowett,	10 00
General Giles A. Smith,	50 00
General L. E. Yorke,	25 00
Colonel A. Sabine,	50 00

And his statement was greeted with cheers.

On motion of Colonel Dayton,

Resolved, That the thanks of the Society are hereby accorded to Mr. Louis McLean, formerly of San Francisco, now of Baltimore, for the assistance he has given us through aiding Lieutenant-General Sherman in securing the California subscription, to be used by our Society, with its association fund, to place the McPherson Monument over his remains, at Clyde, Ohio.

On motion of General Smith,

Resolved, That the report of the committee on McPherson Monument, as given by General Hickenlooper, be accepted.

The proceedings of the Society were again interrupted by the arrival of Major-General George H. Thomas, U.S.A., and President of the Society of the Army of the Cumberland, who was greeted in a most kindly manner by rounds of cheers. It seemed to be a very gratifying incident to our Society to be visited by the President of a kindred Society — by one who had, during long campaigns, so ably co-operated with their own efforts in the one common object. General Logan formally presented him to the Society, when he said:

SOLDIERS;—As I belonged to the Army of the Tennessee for a short time, I hope you will permit me to make a few remarks. I am gratified to be so courteously received. Now, at the present time, there is a very interesting meeting of the Army of the Cumberland, to which I especially belong, and I must be there to keep them in order.

Three cheers were proposed for General Thomas, and given with a will.

The subject of a monument for General Ransom was then brought up by General Dodge, who urged the matter, and expressed the hope that some definite action would be taken.

General Wallace referred to the letter of Mr. Bridgeman, that had been read to the Society, and said that the remains of General Ransom are now deposited in Rose Hill Cemetery, the point selected for them, and that an association of the friends of General Ransom, and citizens of Chicago, were endeavoring to erect a monument to his memory, and desired the assistance of the Society.

On motion of General Dodge,

Resolved, That a committee of five be appointed to confer with the citizen association of Chicago intending to erect a monument commemorating General T. E. G. Ransom; said committee to be Generals W. E. Strong, F. A. Starring, Ezra Taylor, Joseph Stockton, and Colonel L. H. Whittlesey.

On motion of General Giles A. Smith,

Resolved, That the thanks of the Society are accorded as follows: To the local committees who have had in charge the arrangement of this reunion, for their untiring exertions, judgment and skill displayed in contributing so largely to the success and pleasure of this meeting. To the Glee Club that has done so much to enliven the occasion by their excellent singing. To the various railway companies who have carried our members to and from this meeting at reduced rates. To the citizens of this city, ladies and gentlemen, for their uniform kindness and courtesy, and their personal presence, on appropriate occasions, to encourage and add to the interest of our meetings.

On motion of General Wallace,

Resolved, That the thanks of the Society be conveyed to General Giles A. Smith, for the able, gentlemanly and devoted manner in which he has presided at this meeting while a Vice-President of the Society.

On motion,

Resolved, That the thanks of the Society are tendered " The Chicago Board of Trade " for the great respect and deference that has been shown by it toward those gathered here to participate in this reunion, in giving the free use of their unequaled trade room to hold our banquet in, and for adjourning their regular trade session this day, that the room might be prepared for us, and that this recognition of the same be communicated in writing.

On motion of General M. R. M. Wallace, it was

Resolved, That the thanks of the Society be tendered our distinguished comrade, General W. W. Belknap, for his able and eloquent address, delivered at the Reunion of the Societies of the Armies of the Tennessee, Cumberland, Georgia and Ohio, at Crosby's Opera House, last evening, in behalf of this Society, and that the Corresponding Secretary be instructed to notify him in writing.

General Grant visited the Society at this time, escorted by the committee selected for that purpose. His entrance to the hall was the signal, and was followed by the most emphatic enthusiasm and bursts of cheers. The Society and spectators entire, arose and stood to receive their old and first commander, under whose guidance they had won so many victories, and preserved the nation to peace. In introducing him the President said:

GENTLEMEN;—I have the pleasure of presenting to you the President elect, who has proved his faith by his works.

He was received with long and loud cheers, and in response said:

GENTLEMEN OF THE ARMY OF THE TENNESSEE;—My first associations in the beginning of the rebellion through which we have so happily passed, were with you. I am heartily glad to be with you and with the other officers of the armies who fought so gallantly with you. I thank you heartily for this reception, and the country thanks you for your deeds. I am now suffering from one of those neuralgic headaches with which I am periodically afflicted, and which prevents me, even were I so inclined, from saying any thing further on this occasion.

On motion of General Force,

Resolved, That it is the opinion of the members present, that officers who served in such parts of the Army of the Mississippi prior to its being consolidated with the Army of the Tennessee, but who were compelled to abandon the service by reason of wounds or disabling sickness, are entitled to membership in this Society.

In the mean time, Generals Schofield and Cox, and Governors Oglesby and Marshall had arrived to visit the Society. In response to loud calls, General Schofield was presented and received with repeated cheers. He made a few remarks, devoted principally to a description of the joint movements of the grand army under General Sherman from Atlanta to the sea, and of the other parts in the battles of Franklin and Nashville. At the conclusion, cheers were again given him.

General Sherman was loudly called on for a speech, and in response said :

GENTLEMEN ; — I have spoken to you already, and I will probably be engaged for eight hours to-night presiding at the banquet. I have manifested, and always will manifest, a spirit of submission to the desires of my old army comrades, and will do so now. I wish, however, to preserve my voice and keep it as clear as possible for use this evening. For these reasons, I hope you will excuse me from making further remarks at present.

Governor Oglesby was called for, and on being introduced by the President said : That he was a living specimen of the gratitude of the people to the soldiers. It was because he was a soldier that the people of the great State of Illinois had made him Governor. He was but a new member of the Society, but was glad to meet his associates. They came here for pleasant talk and associations. He thanked God that all political excitement was banished from the reunion, and no political talk was attempted to be indulged in. This was a reunion of good and patriotic men, who met to talk of past misfortunes, and of a future bright with promise. The people feel proud of the soldiers, and the soldiers of the people. From their distinguished Commander-in-Chief to the lowest in the ranks, all were worthy of honor. This State was fortunate, far more fortunate than her sister States, in being the scene of this gathering. The officers must feel they have received gratitude enough. Grant, Sherman, Schofield, Pope and Logan were sufficiently complimented by the generous expressions of delight received from the people. [Turning to General Sherman :] Noble, good man, you have saved your country and the cause of human liberty, and all honor to you. He was not much of a soldier himself. He served one year, and was wounded at the battle of Corinth, and believed it was that wound that gave him his commission as Major-General of Volunteers, and the governorship of this great State. He received a mortal wound, but did not die. With his brother Governors, Cox, Fletcher and Marshall, he was assigned his duty, and would receive his rations at the banquet to-night. The war did one good thing, as it would give them a grand, good, fat supper. Generals Grant, Sherman, Thomas, and the balance of them, would be at the upper end of the tables, and the Governors take the butt end. He hoped to meet them all at seven o'clock, or before, hungry as bears, with empty knapsacks, empty haversacks, and empty stomachs.

Governor Fletcher of Missouri responded to calls, saying that he was proud of having been a member of the Army of the Tennessee. Though he had left the army before the close of the rebellion, it was only to assume the position of Governor of his State, to which he had been called, and where he had performed duty in the same cause that others had in the field.

General J. D. Cox and Governor Marshall were called upon for speeches, but both declined upon the ground that they did not wish to occupy the time of the Society that should be used in doing business.

The regular proceedings of current business being again resumed, on motion of Lieutenant-Colonel Dayton,

Resolved, That the sincere regrets of the Society are hereby expressed at the absence from this reunion of our worthy, accomplished, and much-esteemed President, Brevet Major-General John A. Rawlins, and that this resolution be communicated to him in writing by the Secretary.

On motion of Colonel Pride,

Resolved, That the Secretary and Corresponding Secretary act as a committee to publish the proceedings of this meeting for the members of the Society, one thousand copies to be printed and by them distributed.

On motion of Colonel Pride,

Resolved, That the thanks of the Society are accorded Colonel Dayton, the Recording Secretary, General Hickenlooper, the Corresponding Secretary, and General Force, the Treasurer, for the able manner in which they have performed the duties of their offices.

The Secretary informed the President that, under the present head of business, he had a communication from the Society of the Army of the Ohio, which should be acted upon before the Society adjourned. He was directed to read the communication referred to, which is as follows:

ARMY REUNION, ROOMS ARMY OF THE OHIO, }
December 15, 1868. }

SIR;—I have the honor to transmit, herewith, copies of resolutions this day passed by the Society of the Army of the Ohio.

I am, with much respect,

Your obedient servant,

JULIUS WHITE,
Secretary of the Army of the Ohio.
To Secretary of Society Army of the Tennessee.

The resolutions were, as transmitted, as follows:

Resolved, That a committee, to consist of the President and the Vice-Presidents of this Society, present in Chicago, be appointed to confer with the Societies of the Cumberland, the Tennessee, and the Georgia, relative to a union or consolidation of the whole into one Society.

Resolved, That a committee be appointed to confer with the several Societies of the Western Armies, relative to the time and place for holding the next joint reunion.

Colonel Hartsuff, Colonel Graves, and Colonel Wheeler appointed as such committee.

On motion of General Leggett,

Resolved, That a committee of three, consisting of Generals Leggett, Force and Hickenlooper, be appointed to confer with any committees of other Army Societies relative to a consolidation of the various Societies of the Armies of the West into one Society; also in regard to the time and place where these Societies shall hold their next joint reunion; but that said committee is instructed to inform such other committees with whom they may confer, that this Society is opposed to any consolidation.

The President now announced that there was no more business to claim further attention from the Society, but that it was ready for the usual form of adjournment. He, however, hoped that when they separated they would do so as they met, with the best feeling toward one another. They were now citizens who once were soldiers. Much they have done has gone to adorn history, but there is much they can do to make as bright a record in the future. He then dwelt feelingly and eloquently on the fallen brave, urging his hearers never to forget the widows and the orphans of their dead comrades. The nation can pay its debt, but there is one debt it can never pay — the debt of gratitude it owes to the men who fell in her behalf. They should never be forgotten, but they and their children should be held in fond remembrance, and willing hands be extended to aid and relieve the widows and orphans.

Music—"*Star Spangled Banner.*"

On motion,
Resolved, That the Society now stand adjourned.

L. M. DAYTON,
Recording Secretary.

The following telegram was received after the Society had adjourned, and is here given to show the interest manifested in the Society by our President:

DANBURY, CT., *December* 16, 1868.

GENERAL A. HICKENLOOPER,

  Cor. Sec'y Society of the Army of the Tennessee:

Please say to those of the Army of the Tennessee, and of its comrade armies, that while my health is such as to prevent my being with them, I congratulate them upon their grand reunion, and hope their happiness may be as great as the names present make the occasion distinguished.

JNO. A. RAWLINS,

President Society Army of the Tennessee.

IN MEMORIAM.

Death of General Cassius Fairchild.

It is with feelings of deep regret we announce the death of General Cassius Fairchild, one of our Vice-Presidents, and United States Marshal of Wisconsin, which took place at the residence of his father-in-law, Robert Haney, at seven o'clock A.M., October 24, 1868, after a lingering illness, resulting from a wound received in defence of the flag of his country.

General Fairchild was born on the 16th of December, 1829, at Franklin Mills (now Earlville), Portage County, Ohio. He was a brother of General Lucius Fairchild, Governor of Wisconsin, and Charles Fairchild of Boston, a son of Hon. Jairus C. Fairchild, first Treasurer of the State of Wisconsin, first Mayor of the city of Madison, and a gentleman of fine ability, high character and great prominence in the early history of the State. Cassius came to Milwaukee in the year 1843, with his uncle, Mr. F. J. Blair. Soon after, his parents moved to the same place, and resided there till the spring of 1848, when they removed to Madison. He was Deputy Treasurer under his father, and was connected with him, for years, in the mercantile business in that city. He was, for several terms, an Alderman, and for one year President of the Common Council. In 1859 he was the Democratic candidate for the Legislature, and was elected by a considerable majority.

Cassius Fairchild was appointed Major of the sixteenth Regiment of Infantry, during the late war, promoted to Lieutenant-Colonel on the 10th of October, 1861, and made Colonel of his regiment on the 17th of March, 1864. In the battle of Shiloh, while in command of a line of skirmishers, he was seriously wounded in the hip; but, as soon as his wound would permit, was with his regiment, and remained with it until the end of the war, doing gallant service for the flag he loved so well. When the war closed, he was remembered among the deserving and gallant men, and breveted Brigadier-General.

In 1866, General Fairchild was appointed United States Marshal for the District of Wisconsin, and removed from Madison to Milwaukee. It was believed that he had nearly, if not quite, recovered from the effects of his wound; but some months ago a slight injury again developed it, and in a few days brought him to his bed, from which he has never risen. At times, he has rallied, so that his friends have felt strong hopes for his recovery; but these hopes have been dissipated, and on the morning of the 24th of October, he sank gently to rest forever.

There are few men whose death could create more painful feelings in the minds of the community than that of General Fairchild. As a gallant officer, as a high-minded and conscientious official, and as a noble-hearted social friend, he was universally known and respected, and his death will be sincerely mourned by all.

There is — connected with the death of General Fairchild — a touching incident. When stricken down upon his bed of sickness, he was engaged to a young lady of Milwaukee, and the day for the marriage was set. When the day arrived, he who expected to be a bridegroom was prostrate, and the solemn faces of physicians told, in plain words, that there was little hope for his recovery; that death had put forth a stronger claim than the altar; but in this chamber of death, the two hearts which had loved so tenderly, and had looked forward to so much of happiness on earth, were united. It was not the happy bridal scene which had been hoped for, and there were tears instead of smiles, but the hearts which had loved so well, were united. Now death has put forth its claim, and the household is left with a vacant chair, and with sad and aching hearts.

The funeral services took place at St. Paul's Church, Milwaukee, Tuesday morning, October 27, 1868. The remains were taken to Madison by the morning train, the St. Paul Railroad Company having provided a special car for the funeral party. A number of citizens accompanied the funeral from there. A large crowd was in waiting at the depot, and a procession of a mile of carriages followed the hearse — to which the Milwaukee Light Guard acted as a guard of honor — to Forest Hill Cemetery. There the body was laid, beside his father and mother, to its last repose, with the beautiful and impressive service of the Episcopal Church, performed by Rev. Mr. Spalding, of Grace Church, and Rev. Mr. Ashley, of St. Paul's Church, Milwaukee. The burial casket was covered with many beautiful floral offerings, in emblematic designs.

J M Schofield
Maj Genl

REPORT

[Furnished by the Recording Secretary]

OF THE

PROCEEDINGS OF THE ANNUAL MEETING

OF THE

SOCIETY OF THE ARMY OF THE OHIO,

HELD AT CHICAGO, ILLINOIS,

DECEMBER 15TH, 1868.

ARMY OF THE OHIO.

AT a meeting of officers of the Army of the Ohio, held at the Briggs House, in Chicago, on the 15th day of December, 1868, on motion, General J. D. Cox was elected temporary chairman, and Julius White, Secretary, *pro tem.*

On motion of General Stiles, books were opened for registration of names of those who desire to become members of the proposed Society of the Army of the Ohio.

General J. H. Ledlie moved that a committee of three be appointed to draft a Constitution and By-Laws. Motion carried; and General J. H. Ledlie, General R. W. Smith, and Colonel W. M. Wherry were appointed such committee.

On motion of General R. W. Smith, the following committee were appointed to report names for officers of the permanent organization:

General R. W. Smith, Colonel H. Capron, General Casement, General T. J. Henderson, and Colonel G. W. Schofield.

On motion, the meeting adjourned to meet December 16th, at Caledonian Hall, at nine oclock, A.M.

DECEMBER 16, 1868.

Meeting convened at the hour designated, General J. D. Cox, President, *pro tem.*, in the chair.

On motion it was resolved to proceed to the organization of the Society of the Army of the Ohio.

General Robert W. Smith, on behalf of the members resident in Chicago, delivered an address of welcome.

ADDRESS OF WELCOME, BY GENERAL R. W. SMITH.

My Fellow-comrades of the Army of the Ohio: We have assembled here to-day in obedience to the command of the distinguished leader of the armies of the West, Lieutenant-General Sherman. We have come from the East, and from the West, from the North, and from the South; we have come from the office, and from the farm, from the exchange, and the marts of merchandise: thrown aside our briefs and Blackstones, left our offices of state, and our seats in the halls of legislation. We have left behind us the cares and duties of the hour, and assembled here on a common level, for a common purpose — the reunion of our army.

When we all last met, the scenes and circumstances then surrounding us were very different from what we witness now. Our meeting then was in the camp, and on the field, beset with threatening danger, in the face of a hostile and determined foe, far from pleasure, friends and home. We met then in the midst of war.

We meet now in peace, not to plan campaigns, or mingle in the bitter strife, but to join joyfully in this grand reunion, and welcome each other with a soldier's greeting. It is well that we thus come together to review the past, and to be enlivened by the inspiration which this occasion will furnish.

In all ages of the world, associations of men, who have been engaged in the prosecution of great enterprises, when their labors have been well done, have met together to congratulate each other upon their achievements, and to join in mutual pleasures. Families often, after long and wide separations, meet at stated intervals to renew the scenes of long ago, and to repeat the stories of distant years.

While this is true in the civil and peaceful relations of life, how much the more should the sunny comrades of a long and terrible war, whose friendships are those begotten amid danger, whose attachments were formed and strengthened by mutual privations and mutual perils, when their work has been accomplished, their duty done, and history proclaims it *well done*, come together to look back upon their victories and their triumphs, and renew their vows of friendship and fidelity for the future! As soldiers of a common cause, we owe this to ourselves, and to each other. We owe it to the patriotism of the heroic dead, that we may pay just tribute to their memory. We owe it to the widowed and orphaned living, that we may assure them of our sympathy, and give them kind promise of our remembrance and our aid. We owe it to our country, that while we remember her struggles and her perils, we can recount her victories, admire her greatness and power, and kindle anew our devotion to her flag.

We say, then, comrades of the Army of the Ohio, welcome!

But, while we most cordially bid *you* welcome, we are but too sadly reminded that your thoughts, and ours, are not all joyous. Memory true to herself and to us, brings to this scene recollections of sadness. *All are not here.* Many brave and true, who went forth when their country and duty called, who went as hopeful and willing as we, as gallant and brave as any, are not here to join with us in the pleasures and greetings of this pleasant gathering.

> " The brave have gone to rest,
> The brothers of combats on the breast
> Of the red field they reaped."

Their lips are silent, and no friendly word of cheer will be heard from them to-day.

19

"On fame's eternal camping ground
  Their silent tents are spread,
And glory guards with solemn sound
  The bivouac of the dead."

They died that their country and liberty might live. And, though no towering shaft or storied urn marks well their last resting-place, a grateful republic, in sacredness, will cherish their memory, and the nation's fame and greatness will be their monument. May the remembrance of their heroism, and their willing sacrifice of life to duty, enlarge and hallow the patriotism of the living. But we leave them in silence and in sadness, to welcome you, their survivors, to the reunion.

We welcome you to Chicago — that sent forth thousands of her sons to battle for their country and for freedom; whose earnest, loyal women followed the soldier to the camp, and to the field, with their blessings and their prayers; and who gave so largely of their labor and their means to provide for his wants and relieve his sufferings.

We welcome you to our courtesies, and our hospitalities; to our homes and our hearts. In the name and behalf of your fellow-comrades of Chicago, we say again to the officers of the gallant Army of Ohio, welcome, comrades, thrice welcome.

The Committee on Permanent Organization reported the following nominations:

President:

General J. M. Schofield.

, Vice-Presidents:

General A. E. Burnside, of Rhode Island;
General A. H. Terry, of Connecticut;
General George Stoneman, of New York;
General J. D. Cox, of Ohio;

General M. S. Hascall, of Indiana;
General T. J. Henderson, of Illinois;
General George L. Hartsuff, of Michigan;
General T. H. Ruger, of Wisconsin;
General Thomas, of Minnesota;
Colonel W. E. Hobson, of Kentucky;
Colonel Stewart, of New Jersey.

Recording Secretary:
General Julius White, of Illinois.

Corresponding Secretary:
Colonel J. A. Campbell, D. C,

Treasurer:
Colonel W. W. Wheeler, of Illinois.

The report was accepted, and the election declared to be unanimous.

General Schofield, on taking the chair, said:

FELLOW-SOLDIERS:—I take great pleasure in meeting you in this reunion. In your name, I extend to the local committee of Chicago, our heartfelt thanks for the abundant preparations they have made to make our stay here as pleasant as possible.

The Committee on Constitution and By-Laws reported the following, which were adopted:

CONSTITUTION.

ARTICLE I.

This Society shall be called and known as "THE SOCIETY OF THE ARMY OF THE OHIO," and shall embrace all such officers and soldiers as have at any time served in this army, and who have been honorably discharged from such service; or who remain in service in the regular army — who shall have subscribed to the Constitution and By-Laws of the Society, and paid their initiation fee.

Honorary members may from time to time be elected from among the officers of other armies of the United States who have served with distinction in their armies.

ARTICLE II.

The object of the association shall be to preserve and perpetuate the history of the Army of the Ohio; to preserve and unite those patriotic sentiments, and to maintain and strengthen that courteous and friendly intercourse for which the members of this army have always been distinguished. To preserve the name and fame of the members of this army who have fallen in the field, or otherwise perished in the service of their country, shall be one of the sacred duties of this association, and no efforts shall be spared to collect and preserve, in the archives of the Society, the testimonials of their deeds and services.

This Society tenders to the widows and orphans of our fallen comrades its warmest sympathy, and sacredly pledges itself to provide for the wants and relieve the sufferings of all such as are destitute, by the voluntary contributions of the members, or in such other way as may from time to time be determined. It further pledges itself to use all proper effort, and procure for all such disabled soldiers and their families as are entitled thereto, the pensions now provided by law. The welfare of the soldier's widow, the good name and education of his children, shall always be regarded as a sacred trust of the association.

ARTICLE III.

The officers of this Society shall consist of a President, and one Vice-President from each State that furnished troops for the "Army of the Ohio," a Corresponding Secretary, and Recording Secretary and Treasurer. The Vice-President of each State shall be selected by the members residing in such State. The foregoing officers shall be elected at the regular meeting of this Society, and the vote of the majority of the members present shall elect.

ARTICLE IV.

The meetings of the Society shall be held annually, at such time and place as a majority of the members present at any regular meeting may determine by ballot. All members of the Society shall use their best endeavors to promote the interests of the association, and maintain kind feelings and unanimity among the members. The members are expected to attend all regular meetings of the Society, and in case of their inability to do so, will report to the Corresponding Secretary the cause of their absence.

ARTICLE V.

This constitution may be altered or amended at any regular meeting of the Society, provided the alteration or amendment proposed is submitted in writing, or filed with the Recording Secretary at least one month before the regular meeting at which it is proposed to present the same; and provided, further, that two-thirds of the members be present at such meeting.

BY-LAWS.

ARTICLE I.

The regular meetings of the Society shall be opened by prayer by some suitable person, to be selected by the presiding officer.

ARTICLE II.

All officers and soldiers who have served in the Army of the Ohio, and have been honorably discharged from service, or may now be in the regular service, are entitled to membership, and upon signing the Constitution and By-Laws of the Society, and paying an initiation fee of $5, shall be entitled to full membership.

ARTICLE III.

The regular dues of members shall be $5 per year for officers, and $3 per year, for enlisted men, and shall be paid annually. Any member permitting his dues to remain unpaid for a period of over two years shall be dismissed from membership, and can only be restored by the payment of all back dues and a vote of two-thirds the members present at a regular meeting.

ARTICLE IV.

All dues shall be paid to the Recording Secretary, and no moneys shall be expended by the Treasurer except upon the written order of the Recording Secretary, countersigned by the President; and at each annual meeting of this Society the Treasurer shall report in detail the amount of money received, and the disbursements made.

ARTICLE V.

When the place of holding the next annual meeting of the Society shall be determined, the President shall appoint an Executive Committee of five members, whose duty it shall be to make all necessary preparations and arrangements for such meeting, but who shall not be authorized, by virtue of such appointment, to contract any debts for which the Society shall be held liable.

ARTICLE VI.

No member of the Society shall speak more than once on any question of business under discussion by the Society, and no longer than five minutes, without the consent of the Society.

ARTICLE VII.

At each annual meeting there shall be selected, in such manner as the Society shall determine, two persons from the members thereof—one to deliver an address of welcome, and the other an oration upon the history of the Army of the Ohio, and the objects of this association, at the next annual meeting.

ARTICLE VIII.

These by-laws may be altered, amended, or additions made thereto, at any regular meeting of the Society, by a vote of two-thirds the members present.

ARTICLE IX.

This Society, at its meetings, shall, in the discussion of matters brought before it, observe the rules governing deliberative bodies.

General Stiles moved that a committee, consisting of the Chairman, Vice-Presidents, and other officers, be appointed to confer with the Army of the Cumberland, and the other armies, with reference to consolidation. The motion prevailed.

General Schofield called General Cox to the chair, and spoke as follows:

It has so happened, during the progress of the war, that we have fallen under the command of distinguished generals, who, on account of their positions, have not become members of our organization. I now propose to invite them to become honorary members of our Society. For that purpose, I move that Generals Grant, Sherman and Thomas, and the staff officers who served under them during the war when in the Army of the Ohio, be elected honorary members of our Society.

The motion was carried amid great applause.

On motion of General M. D. Manson, General **D. C. Buell** was elected an honorary member of the Society.

On motion of General Stiles, a committee, consisting of the President and Vice-Presidents present in Chicago, was appointed to confer with the societies of other armies relative to the expediency of consolidating the several societies into one.

General George Stoneman moved that a committee of three be appointed to confer with the other armies as to the time and place of the next annual meeting, and that the Committee on Consolidation report at the same time.

The Chairman appointed the following gentlemen as the Committee on Conference: General George L. Hartsuff, General Graves, and Colonel W. W. Wheeler.

Adjourned, to meet at the Briggs House, at twelve M., same day.

The Society reconvened at the above-named hour.

On motion of Colonel J. A. Campbell,

Resolved, That the President and Secretaries be authorized to transact the necessary business of the Society until the next meeting ; also that they be authorized to fill the blank for an additional Corresponding Secretary with the name of a member residing at the place where the next meeting is to be held, when such place has been designated.

On motion of Colonel John Mason Brown, the thanks of the Society were tendered to the resident members, and to the citizens of Chicago generally, for their generous hospitality.

Adjourned *sine die.*

W W Slocum
Maj Genl

REPORT

[Furnished by the Recording Secretary]

OF THE

Proceedings of the Annual Meeting

OF THE

SOCIETY OF THE ARMY OF GEORGIA.

HELD AT CHICAGO, ILLINOIS,

DECEMBER 15TH, 1868.

ARMY OF GEORGIA.

SHERMAN HOUSE, CHICAGO, ILL.,
December 15, 1868.

PURSUANT to call, the officers of the Army of Georgia met at the Sherman House, at ten o'clock.

The call was heartily responded to, and a full attendance present.

On motion, General William Cogswell, of Massachusetts, was called to the chair.

On motion of General Barnum, of New York, Major-General Henry W. Slocum was chosen to preside.

On motion of General Robinson, of Ohio, Captain R. B. Brown, of St. Louis, was chosen Secretary.

General Barnum moved that a separate organization be formed, to be known as " The Society of the Army of Georgia ;" and the motion was carried unanimously.

General Morgan moved that a committee of three be appointed to draft a Constitution and By-Laws; and the motion was carried.

The President appointed Generals Morgan, Barnum, and Walcott, as such committee.

General Cogswell moved that a committee of three be appointed to report officers for permanent organization. Carried.

The President appointed Generals Cogswell, and Robinson, and Captain Taylor.

This committee reported as follows:

For President:

Major-General Henry W. Slocum, of New York.

Vice-Presidents:

Generals Jeff. C. Davis, A. S. Williams, Mower, Ward, Bay·
ard, Jacobs, Carlen, Morgan, Geery, and Walcott.

The report was accepted, and adopted; after which the
following additional officers were chosen:

Recording Secretary:

Captain D. Taylor, jr., of Ohio.

Corresponding Secretary:

Captain R. B. Brown, of St. Louis.

Treasurer:

Brevet Brigadier-General H. M. Whittlesey, Washington, D. C.

Generals Robinson and Barnum, of the Twentieth Corps,
General J. G. Mitchell, and Colonel Tolen Jones, of the Fourteenth Corps, were elected an Executive Committee.

On motion, the meeting adjourned, to meet again Wednesday,
at nine A.M.; when all officers and soldiers of the Fourteenth
and Twentieth Corps were earnestly requested to be present to
act on matters of importance.

MAJOR-GENERAL HENRY W. SLOCUM,
President.

CAPTAIN DAVID TAYLOR, JR.,
Recording Secretary.

HEADQUARTERS SOCIETY ARMY OF GEORGIA, ⎱
SHERMAN HOUSE, CHICAGO, ⎰
December 16, 10 A.M.

Society called to order, General II. W. Slocum, President, in the chair.

Committee on Constitution and By-Laws were called upon for report.

General Barnum, of said committee, reported the Constitution and By-Laws, which were discussed, amended, and adopted as follows:

CONSTITUTION.

ARTICLE I.

This Society shall be called and known as "The Society of the Army of Georgia," and shall embrace all such officers and soldiers as have at any time served in this army, and who have been honorably discharged from such service; or who remain in service in the regular army, who shall have subscribed the Constitution and By-Laws of the Society.

Honorary members may, from time to time, be elected from among the officers of other armies of the United States, who have served with distinction in their armies.

ARTICLE II.

The object of the Association shall be to preserve and perpetuate the history of the Army of Georgia; to preserve and unite those patriotic sentiments, and to maintain and strengthen that courteous and friendly intercourse for which the members of this army have always been distinguished; to preserve the name and fame of the members of this army, who have fallen in the field, or who have otherwise perished in the service of their country, shall be one of the sacred duties of this Association, and no efforts shall be spared to collect and preserve in the archives of the Society, the testimonials of their deeds and services.

This Society tenders to the widows and orphans of our fallen comrades its warmest sympathy, and readily pledges itself to provide for the wants and relieve the suffering of all such of them as are destitute, by the voluntary contribution of its members, or in such other way as from time to time may be determined.

It further pledges itself to use all proper effort to procure for all such disabled soldiers, and their families, as are entitled thereto, the pensions and bounties now provided by law.

The welfare of the soldier's widow; the good name and education of his children, shall always be regarded as a sacred privilege and trust of the Association.

ARTICLE III.

The officers of this Society shall consist of a President, and one Vice-President from each of the ten army organizations, one Corresponding Secretary, one Recording Secretary, and a Treasurer.

The Vice-President from each of the ten organizations, shall be selected by the members belonging to such organization.

The foregoing officers shall be elected at the regular meeting of this Society, and a vote of a majority of the members present shall elect.

ARTICLE IV.

The meeting of the Society shall be held annually, at such time and place as a majority of the members present, at any regular meeting, may determine by ballot. All members of the Society shall use their best endeavors to promote the interests of the Association, and maintain kindly feelings, and unanimity among the members. The members are expected to attend all regular meetings of the Society; and, in case of their inability to do so, will report to the Corresponding Secretary the cause of their absence.

ARTICLE V.

This Constitution may be altered or amended at any regular meeting of the Society, provided the alteration or amendment proposed is submitted in writing, and filed with the Recording Secretary at least one month before the regular meeting at which it is proposed to present the same; and provided further, that two-thirds of the members be present at such meeting.

BY-LAWS.

ARTICLE I.

The regular meetings of the Society shall be opened by prayer, by some suitable person, to be selected by the presiding officer.

ARTICLE II.

All officers and soldiers who have served in the Army of Georgia, and have been honorably discharged from service, or may now be in the regular service, are entitled to membership; and, upon signing the Constitution and By-Laws of the Society, shall be entitled to full membership.

ARTICLE III.

The regular dues of members shall be $—— per year for officers, and $—— per year for enlisted men, and shall be paid annually. Any member permitting his dues to remain unpaid for a period of over two years, shall be dismissed from membership, and can only be restored by the payment of all back dues, and a vote of two-thirds of the members present at a regular meeting.

ARTICLE IV.

All dues shall be paid to the Recording Secretary; and no funds shall be expended by the Treasurer, except upon the written order of the Recording Secretary, and countersigned by the President; and, at each annual meeting of this Society, the Treasurer shall report in detail the amount of funds received, and the disbursements made.

ARTICLE V.

When the place of holding the next annual meeting of the Society shall be determined, the President shall appoint an executive committee of five members, whose duty it shall be to make all necessary preparations and arrangements for such meeting; but who shall not be authorized, by virtue of such appointment, to contract any debts for which the Society shall be held liable.

ARTICLE VI.

No member of the Society shall speak more than once on any question of business under discussion by the Society, and no longer than five minutes, without the consent of the Society.

ARTICLE VII.

. At each annual meeting there shall be selected, in such manner as the Society shall determine, an orator, and alternate, from the members thereof, of whom one shall deliver an address appropriate to such occasion, and on such subject as shall be of especial interest to the members of the Society of the Army of Georgia; said address to be delivered at the next annual meeting.

It shall be the duty of the retiring President to deliver an address of welcome.

ARTICLE VIII.

These By-Laws may be altered, amended, or additions made thereto, at any regular meeting of the Society, by a vote of two-thirds of the members present.

ARTICLE IX.

This Society, at its meetings, shall, in the discussion of matters brought before it, observe the rules governing deliberative bodies.

A communication was received from General Julius White, Secretary Army of the Ohio, accompanied by resolutions from said Society, inviting committees of conference as to the feasibility of consolidating the Societies of the four (4) Western Armies, viz.: The Army of the Tennessee, the Army of the Cumberland, the Army of Georgia, and the Army of the Ohio — into one Society; also as to time and place of holding next reunion.

General Henry M. Whittlesey moved that the communication be received, and that a committee of three be appointed;—carried.

A Committee of Conference, and on time and place of holding the next reunion, were chosen, as follows: Generals Zeulich, Smith and Salomon.

On motion of General Robinson,

Resolved, That the Armies of the Tennessee, of the Cumberland, of the Ohio, and of Georgia, be consolidated into one grand Army Society. Resolution unanimously adopted.

The following were elected honorary members: Generals Grant, Sherman, Thomas, Sheridan, Scofield, Hooker, and Joseph Knight.

General Henry M. Whittlesey offered the following resolutions, which were unanimously adopted:

Resolved, *First*, That the congratulations of this Army Society are tendered to General Cogswell for the eloquent and able address which he delivered before the assembled armies last evening; and the success with which he represented this army at Crosby's Opera House last night.

Resolved, *Second*, That it shall be the duty of the President, and of the Executive Committee (in conjunction), to cause five hundred (500) copies of the Constitution and By-Laws of this Army Society, together with all the proceedings of the meetings in organizing the same, to be published, and that to said committee, together with the President of the Society, be left the fixing of the time and place of the next reunion ;—adopted.

General Cogswell moved that the President appoint a committee of five on History of the Army of Georgia, whose duty it shall be to compile, as soon as possible, a complete history of the Army of Georgia, and submit the same to the President, for his approval, before the same be printed.

General Henry M. Whittlesey moved that General Slocum be made *ex-officio* member of said committee ;—carried.

Captain David Taylor moved that we now adjourn, to meet at the call of the President. Adjourned.

MAJOR-GENERAL HENRY W. SLOCUM,

President.

CAPTAIN DAVID TAYLOR, JR.,
  Recording Secretary Society Army Georgia.

HEADQUARTERS SOCIETY ARMY GEORGIA, ⎱
SHERMAN HOUSE, CHICAGO, ⎰
December 17, 1868 — 10 A.M.

Pursuant to call of the President, Society assembled at Headquarters ; President Major-General Henry W. Slocum in the chair.

The President announced the following Historical Committee : General John G. Mitchell, Fourteenth Corps, Generals H. M. Whittlesey, H. A. Barnum, and William Cogswell, and Captain A. E. Lee.

The Secretary offered the following resolution, which was adopted unanimously :

Resolved, That the members of the Society of the Army of Georgia hereby tender to their comrades of the Armies of the Tennessee, the Ohio and the Cumberland, their unfeigned thanks for the courtesy they have received from each of those respective Societies during the Grand Reunion of the last two days; and that we express to each of those Societies the great pleasure and

20

satisfaction we have enjoyed at this reunion, and that we join in congratulations to the members of the Societies of the Tennessee, of the Ohio, and of the Cumberland, on the complete success of this grand meeting.

General Zeulich offered the following:

Resolved, That this Society return their sincere thanks to the citizens of Chicago, and to the press, and to the members of the local committees having in charge the various matters appertaining to this Grand Reunion;—adopted.

General Zeulich also offered the following:

Resolved, That we return a vote of thanks to the members of the Board of Trade of Chicago for their kindness in tendering the use of their spacious hall for the Grand Banquet;—adopted.

On motion of General Zeulich, it was

Resolved, That at our next meeting all officers and soldiers are requested to appear in full uniform, designating their respective rank;—adopted.

General Barnum moved that we adjourn, subject to the call of the President;—adjourned.

MAJOR-GENERAL HENRY W. SLOCUM,
President.

CAPTAIN DAVID TAYLOR, JR.,
Recording Secretary Army of Georgia.

LIST OF MEMBERS OF THE SOCIETY OF THE ARMY
OF THE CUMBERLAND.

Adae, Carl, A. G., Capt. 4th Ohio Cav., Cincinnati, Ohio.

Atwater, M. B., Capt. 51st Ill. V. I., Newton, Iowa.

Allen, Theo. F., Brev.-Col. U. S. V., Cincinnati, O.

Anderson, Ed. L., Capt. 52nd O. V. I., Cincinnati, O.

Anderson, E. G., Co. C., 74th Ind. V. I.

Anderson, Geo. T., Capt. Co. D, 51st Ind. V. I.

Anderson, N. L., Col. 6th O. V. I., Cincinnati, O.

Ammen, Jacob, Brig.-Gen. U. S. V., Lockland, O.

Ashbrook, A. P., Lieut. 17th O. V. I., Lancaster, O.

Armstrong, William F., Capt. 74th O. V. I., Cincinnati, O.

Abbott, Will. A., Capt. 79th Ind. V. I., Indianapolis, Ind.

Atkins, Smith D., Col. 92nd Ill. V., Brev. Major-Gen., Freeport, Ill.

Andrews, N. S., Col. 12th U. S. Cav., Detroit, Mich.

Audalbu, Ed. L., Capt. 72nd O. V. I.

Bartholomew, W. H., Maj. 34th Inf., Columbus, Miss.

Bailey, O. H. P., Lieut.-Col. 73rd Ind., Plymouth, Ind.

Babcock, S., Lieut. 1st Wis. Inf., Milwaukee. Wis.

Baldwin, A. P., Capt. 6th O. Ind. Light Bat., Ackron, O.

Baker, Edward, Co. B. 3rd Ky. Cav., Princeton, Ind.

Bane, O. F., Capt. 123rd Ill., Chicago. Ill.

Baker, H. N., Capt. 47th Ill.

Blackstone, Jr., J., 15th Penn. Vol. Cav., Pittsburgh, Penn.

Babbitt, A. T., Capt. 93rd O. V. I.

Blanke, Wm., Capt. 24th Ill. V. I., Chicago. Ill.

Barrell, Henry C., Surg. 38th Ill. Vol., Springfield, Ill.

Bauer, O. F., Capt. 123rd Ill., Chicago, Ill.

Barrow, S. S., Capt. 9th Mich. Vol. Inf., Chicago, Ill.

Barnum, H. A., Brev. Maj.-Gen., Syracuse. N. Y.

Ballow, J. T., Capt., Peru, Ind.

Blakesly, Archibald, Lieut.-Col. 78th Penn. Vol. Inf., Pittsburgh, Penn.

Barker, W., Capt. 20th Ohio Bat., Cleveland, O.

Bass, Wm., Sergeant 59th Ill., Chicago, Ill.

Barlow, J. W., Brev. Lieut.-Col. U. S. Engineers, U. S. A.

Bayliss, Lot P., 1st Lieut. and Q. M. 74th Ind. Vol., Ft. Wayne, Ind.

Bradley, L. P., Lieut.-Col., Brev. Brig.-Gen. U. S. A., Omaha, Neb.

Bacon, C. H., Surg. 13th U. S. Cav., Lockport, Ill.

Balding, T. E., Capt. 24th Wis. Inf., and Brev. Maj.-Gen. U. S. A., Milwaukee, Wis.

Babcock, E. E., Hosp. Steward 88th Ill., Freeport Ill.

Baker, John J., Lieut.-Col. 19th Mich. Vol., Sturgis, Mich.

Bannister, D, Brev.-Col. and Paymaster U. S. V., Columbus, O.

Barber, G. M., Brev. Brig.-Gen. U. S. V, Cleveland, O.

Barger, B. F., Maj. 33rd O. V. I., Cincinnati, O.

Barker, John D. Capt. 1st Ohio Cav., Marietta, O.

Barnes, John, Capt. 23rd Ky. Inf., Cincinnati, O.

Barnett, James, Brev. Brig.-Gen. U. S. V., Cleveland, O.

Blake, John W., Col. 40th Ind. Vol. Inf., Indianapolis, Ind.

Barrett, W. W., Brev. Brig.-Gen. U. S. V., Columbus, Miss.

Brandt, O. B., Capt, 17th O. V. I., Lancaster, O.

Brannan, John M., Brev. Maj.-Gen. U. S. A.

Bates, Caleb, Maj. and A. D C., U. S. V., Cincinnati, O.

Beattie, Alex. H., Capt. U. S. V., Helena, M. T.

Bennett, Henry, Chicago Art., Chicago, Ill.

Bestow, Marcus P., Brev.-Col. and A. A. G. Vol., N. Y. City.

Bremner, David F., Capt. 19th Ill. Vol. Inf., Chicago, Ill.

Bickam, Wm. D., Maj. and A. D. C., U. S. V., Dayton, O

Bird, Ira H., Lieut. and Q. M. 2nd O. V. I., Cincinnati, O.

Bigelow, J. C., Lieut.-Col. 134th Ill. Inf., Chicago, Ill.

Beeber, J. W., 1st Lieut. Co. F, 87th Ind. Vol., Rochester, Ind.

Bingham, George B., Col. 1st Wis., Milwaukee, Wis.

Bishop, J. W., Brevet Brig.-Gen., Mankato, Minn.

Billings, Edwin L., Capt. Co. K., 57th Ind., Goshen, Ind.

Bidwell, T. S., Assistant Surgeon 124th O. Vol. Inf., Chicago, Ill.

Biggs, Jonathan, Brevet Brig.-Gen. U. S. V., Olney, Ill.

Bridges, Lyman, Brevet Colonel U. S. V., Chicago, Ill.

Bristow, Benjamin H., Col. 8th Ky. Cav., Louisville, Ky.

Bristow, James H., Chaplain 5th Ky. Inf., Covington, Ky.

Brooke, Hunter, Brevet Lieut.-Col. U. S. V., Cincinnati, Ohio.

Brookfield, E. V., Brevet Major and C. S. U. S. V., Cincinnati, Ohio.

Brown, J. Morris, Brevet Major U. S. A., through Adj.-General.

Boden, William, Lieut.-Col. 23rd Ky. Vet. Vol. Inf., Newport, Kentucky.

Bohan, John, 1st Lieut. 8th Ind. Vol. Inf., Kokomo, Ind.

Boone, Thomas C., Colonel 115th Ohio Vol. Inf., Salem, O.

Boyden, A. H., Major and A. P. M. U. S. V., Chicago, Ill.

Brown, Thomas, Captain 88th Ill., Chicago, Ill.

Bowles, C. B., Sergeant Co. H 92nd Ill. Vol. Inf., Ashton, Ill.

Broettbeck, S. D., Major 12th Iowa, Highland, Ill.

Boltz, Fred. F., Captain 88th Ind. Vol.

Boydston, Nelson N., Major 30th Ind. Vol. Inf., Warsaw, Ind.

Brooks, Edwin F., 1st Lieut. and Adj. 1st Wis. Cav., Chicago, Ill.

Bogue, Roswell G., Surgeon 19th Ill. Inf., Chicago, Ill.

Brock, Jos. B., Capt. Co. D., 93rd Ohio Vol. Inf., Middletown, O.

Boyd, J. M., Col. 19th Ohio Inf.

Boyd, James S., Col. 51st Ill. Inf., Chicago, Ill.

Brown, A. A., Captain Co. H., 15th Wis. Inf. Vol., Northfield, Minn.

Boal, C. T., 1st Lieut. 88th Ill. Inf., Chicago, Ill.

Brown, Theo. F., Brev. Brig.-Gen., U. S. V., Chicago, Ill.

Brooks, C. B., 89th Ill., Aurora, Ill.

Blodgett, A. Z., 96th Ill. Vol. Inf., Waukegan, Ill.

Bones, William, Capt. 22nd Wis. Vol. Inf., Cresco, Iowa.

Bucke, William H., Major 52nd O. Vol. Inf., Cincinnati, O.

Buford, L. M., A. D. C. to Maj.-Gen. Crittenden, Rock Island, Ill.

Burroughs, George, Brevet Major U. S. A., through Adj.-General.

Butterfield, Daniel, Brevet Major-General U. S. A., N. Y. City.

Bunts, William C., 125th Ohio Vol. Inf., Cleveland, O.

Buttrick, E. L., Lieut.-Col. 24th Wis., Chicago, Ill.

Burt, A. S., Capt. 27th Inf. U. S. A.

Buck, R. M., 1st Sergeant Co. B. 86th Ill. Vol., Henry, Ill.

Burns, R. S., Captain Co. G. 75th Ill., Franklin Grove, Ill.

Burke, Joseph W., Col. 10th Ohio Inf., Brevet Major-Gen., Huntsville, Alabama.

Burness, Samuel L., 1st Lieut. 15th U. S. Inf., Philadelphia, Penn.

Bluthard, F. I., Surgeon 23rd Wis. Vol. Inf., Chicago, Ill.

Bryant C. H., Brevet Colonel U. S. V., Cincinnati, O.

Cable, C. A., Captain 18th O. Vol. Inf., Nelsonville, Ohio.

Calkin, Edward, 1st Lieut., Rochester, Ind.

Carlin, William P., Brevet Major-Gen. U. S. A., Nashville, Tenn.

Carter, G. U., Lieut.-Col. 84th Ind. Vol. Inf., Winchester, Ind.

Chalfant, David, Captain 51st O. Vol. Inf., Ulricksville, O.

Clark, George D., 1st Brig. Band 3rd Ohio Vol., Meriden, Mich.

Clark, Albert, 2nd Lieut. 9th Ill. Cav., Genesee, Ill.

Carpenter, John E., Capt. and Acting Adj.-Gen., Memphis, Tenn.

Chandler, George, 1st Lieut. 88th Ill. Vol. Chicago, Ill.

Crawford, F. C., Brevet Major and A. A. G. 3rd Div. 20th Corps, Terre Haute, Ind.

Chapman, C. W., Col. 74th Ind. Vol., Warsaw, Ind.

Crane, Alex. B., Lieut.-Col. 85th Ind. Vol. Inf.

Chadborne, A. S., Lieut.-Col. 88th Ill., Chicago, Ill.

Carter, W. D., Asst.-Surg. 44th Ill , Nashville, Ill.

Clarkson, Theodore F., Capt. Co. D. 96th Ill. Vol., Waukegan, Ill.

Calef, J. H., 88th Ill. Inf., Chicago, Ill.

Clark, Geo. W., 4th Mich. Cav., Chicago, Ill.

Caron, Henry L., Lieut. and Adj. 13th U. S. C. I., Brev.-Maj., N. Y. City.

Chandler, Wm. P., Lieut.-Col. 35th Ill. Vol., Danville, Ill.

Chamberlain, Orville T., Capt. Co. G 74th Ind. Vol. Inf., Elkhart, Ind.

Crane, Wm. E., Capt. 4th O. V. C., Cincinnati, O.

Carahan, R. H. Brev. Brig.-Gen., Danville, Ill.

Cravath, E. M., Chap. 101st O. V. I., Cincinnati, O.

Campbell, James E., A. M. Mate Miss. Squadron U. S. N., Hamilton, O.

Campbell, T. W., Col. 17th Ky. Cav., Bowling Green, Ky.

Clendenin, Frank, Maj. 147th Ill. Vol., Morrison, Ill.

Clenahan, John M., Lieut.-Col. 15th Ohio Inf., Ottawa, Kan.

Crittenden, J. N., 1st Lieut. Mich. Engineers, Chicago, Ill.

Clifford, W., Capt. 31st Inf., Holly Springs, Miss.

Cist, Henry M., Brev. Brig.-Gen. U. S. V., Cincinnati, O.

Chickering, J. W., Brev.-Capt. U. S. A., Ft. Sully, Dakota Ter.

Childs, John C., Lieut.-Col. 3rd Tenn. Vol. Inf. Wilson, Tenn.

Christopher, A. C., Lieut.-Col. 6th O. V. I., Cincinnati, O.

Christian, Wm. H., Private Co. K 19th Ill., Chicago, Ill.

Coulter, S. L., Maj. 64th O. V. I., Erie, Neosho Co., Kan.

Croxton, John T., Brev. Maj.-Gen. U. S. V., Paris, Bourbon Co., Ky.

Cox, C. B., Maj. 84th Ill. Vol. Inf., Vermont, Fulton Co., Ill.

Connelly, Thos. J., Capt. 9th Mich. Vol. Inf., Jackson, Mich.

Colburn, W. J., Capt. and Act. Q. M., Brev.-Maj. Vol., Chattanooga, Tenn.

Coe. E. S., Lieut.-Col. 124th O., Cleveland, O.

Crosby, Lyman B., Capt. 87th Ind. Inf., Cedar Falls, Iowa.

Connolly, Robert J., 2nd Lieut. 73rd Ind., Logansport, Ind.

Cole, A. S., Brev.-Maj. U. S. V., Kenosha, Wis.

Cosgrove, A. P., Private Co. D 44th Ind., South Bend, Ind.

Cogswell, Wm., Brev. Brig.-Gen. U. S. V., Col. 2nd Mass. Inf., Salem, Mass.

Collins, C. D., 1st Lieut. 124th O. Vol., Cleveland. O.

Cook, David S., Capt. Co. G 78th Penn. Vet. Vol. Inf., Chicago, Ill.

Cotwango, John, 75th Ill., Dixon, Ill.

Copp, James F., Capt. Co. F 89th Ill. Vol., Rock Island, Ill.

Collier, J. H., Capt. 12th U. S. C. I., Antioch, Ill.

Clock, Albert, 2nd Lieut. 9th Ill. Cav., Genesee, Ill.

Collins, H. E., Lieut.-Col. 2nd Ky. Vol. Cav., Cincinnati, O.

Cochnower, J. H., 1st Lieut. 74th O. V. I., Cincinnati, O.

Coulter, William A., Captain U. S. A., Washington, D. C.

Cox, A. P.. Captain M. M. Brigade, Oxford, O.

Cox, Thomas, Captain 1st Ky. Vol. Inf., Cincinnati, Ohio.

Craft, Hiram J., Major 98th O. Vol. Inf., Indianapolis, Ind.

Crofton, R. E. A., Brevet Lieut.-Col. U. S., through Adj.-Gen.

Cruft, Charles, Brevet Major-Gen. U. S. V., Terre Haute, Ind.

Cummings, H. H., Captain 105th O. Vol. Inf., Tidionte, Penn.

Church, L. B., Captain U. S. V., Turner's Junction, Ill.

Cullen, Robert, Captain 74th Ohio Vol. Inf., Hamilton, O.

Curtis, James, Brevet Maj. U. S. A., Mobile, Ala.

Davis, S. W., Captain 1st O. Vol. Inf., Dayton, Ohio.

Davis, Charles W., Col. 51st Ill., Chicago, Ill.

Davis, Hasbrouck, Brig.-Gen., Col. 12th Ill. Cavalry.

Davis, R. W., Colonel 14th Mich. Inf., Pontiac, Mich.

Davis. H. G., Brigadier-General U. S. Vol., Goshen, Indiana.

Deane, Charles H., Brevet Lieut.-Col. and A. Q. M., Peoria, Ill.

Deal, Paul, Captain 3rd Ohio Cav., Lima, Ohio.

Denny, William A., Captain 90th Ohio Inf., Chicago, Illinois.

Deardoff, D. P., Captain 74th Ind. Vol., Goshen, Ind.

Denison, J. C., Hospital Steward 36th Ill., Elgin, Ill.

De Sand, C. V., Captain Co. C 9th Mich. Inf., E. Saginaw, Mich.

Devol, George H., 1st Lieut. 38th Ind. Vet. Vol. Inf., New Albany, Indiana.

Dickinson, E. H., Sergt. 5th Iowa Cav., Dubuque, Iowa.

Dick, George F., Colonel 86th Ind., Bloomington, Ill.

Dox, H. P., Brevet Brigadier-Gen., Chicago, Ill.

Dickey, M. Van, Lieut. 94th Ohio Vol. Inf., Franklin, Ohio.

Dilger, H., Capt. U. S. V., Springfield, Ill.

Donaldson, J. L., Brevet Maj.-Gen. U. S. A., St. Louis, Mo.

Donovan, J. M., Captain 6th Ohio Vol. Inf., Cincinnati, O.

Dornbush, Henry, Captain 10th O. Vol. Inf., Dayton, O.

Doughty, J. A., Colonel 17th Tenn. Vol. Cav., Clinton, Tenn.

Dowdy, R., Captain 1st Tenn. Vol. Mounted Inf., Hales' Mills, Tenn.

Drouillard, J. P., Captain U. S. A., Nashville, Tenn.

Douglas, R. J., 2nd Lieutenant Co. D 96th Ill., Waukegan, Ill.

Dooley, J. H., Captain Co. F 40th Ind., Lebanon, Ind.

Dodge, I. B., Col. 30th Ind. Vol. Inf.. Warsaw, Ind.

Dysart, A. P., Col. 34th Ill. Vol., Nachusa, Lee County, Ill.

Dockstader, J. G., Lieut. 51st Wis. Vol. Inf.

Down, Hylor, A. Q. M. S. 19th Ill. Vol. Inf., Chicago, Ill.

Durand, Calvin, Sergeant Board of Trade Battery, Chicago, Ill.

Dunbar, G. Edwin, Col. and Chief Q.M. Kilpatrick's Cav., Kalamazoo, Mich.

Duffield, Henry M., Lieut. and Adj. 9th Mich. Vol. Inf., Detroit, Mich.

Drury, Lu. H., Major 1st Wis. Vol. Artillery, Chicago, Ill.

Dryden, D. H., Major Pay Department U. S. V., Dayton, O.

Duffield, W. W., Colonel 9th Mich. Vol. Inf., Belmont, Ky.

Ducat, Arthur C., Lieut.-Col. and Brev. Brig.-Gen. Ass't Inspector-Gen. Vol., Chicago, Ill.

Dunlevy, Howard, Captain 79th O. Vol. Inf., Dayton, O.

Duston, Daniel, Brev. Brig.-Gen. U. S. V., Sycamore, Ill.

Evans, M., Maj. 96th Ill. Inf., Waukegan, Ill.

Elam, John W., Capt. Co. D 87th Ind., Valparaiso, Ind.

Ewing, Geo. W., Act. Ord. Sergeant. Ft. Wayne, Ind.

Earle, Charles W., Capt. 96th Ill., Chicago, Ill.

Earhart. G. T., Lieut. 35th O. V. Inf., Hamilton, O.

Earnshaw, J., Capt. U. S. V., Cincinnati, O.

Earnshaw, Wm., Chap. U. S. A., Dayton, O.

Elliott, W. J., Brev. Maj.-Gen. U. S. A., Ft. Boise, Idaho.

Evans, J. D., Maj. 39th Ind. Vol. Inf., Indianapolis, Ind.

Emmett, J. M., Lieut. Co. C 34th Ill. Vol., Franklin Grove, Ill.

Emmons, F. A., Maj. 147th Ill. Inf., Chicago, Ill.

Erbe, Arthur, Capt. Co. II 24th Ill., Chicago, Ill.

Erickson, Christian, Capt. 82nd Ill. Inf., Chicago, Ill.

Ellis, M. D., Capt. 87th Ind., Peru, Ind.

Ellis, E. C., Capt. 93rd O. V. I., Dayton, O.

Emingre, A. J., Capt. 93rd O. V. I., Miamisburg, O.

Falkner, I. K., 7th Vol. Cav.

Farrington, Geo. E., 1st Lieut. 85th Ind. Vol. Inf., Terre Haute, Ind.

Frankebergro, J. C., Lieut.-Col. 188th O. V. I., Cincinnati, O.

Frazer, Isaac, Capt. 88th Ill., Chicago, Ill.

Fake, Fred. L., Q. M. 89th Ill. Chicago, Ill.

Fraser, Thos. K., 1st Lieut. 1st Ky. Vol. Inf., Cincinnati, O.

Farquhar, John M., Maj. 89th Ill. Inf., Chicago, Ill.

Fergusson, Geo., 1st Lieut. 96th Ill. Inf., Waukegan, Ill.

Free, John W., Maj. 31st O. V. I., New Lexington, O.

Pearing. B. D., Brev. Brig.-Gen. U. S. V., Cincinnati, O.

Free, W. H., Brev. Col. U. S. V., New Lexington, O.

Feighly, J. C., Lieut. 31st O. V. I., New Lexington, O.

Fletcher. Robert, Brev. Col. U. S. V., Cincinnati, O.

Findley, R. P., Col. 74th O. V. I., Mattoon, Ill.

Fritsch, Otto, Capt. 68th N. Y. V. I., Chicago, Ill.

Fisher, Horace N., Lieut.-Col. U. S. V., Brookline, Mass.

Finch. A. J., Maj. 12th U. S. C. I., Chicago, Ill.

Fisher, J. A., Capt. 2nd O. V. I., Cincinnati, O.

Fisher, John H., Capt. A, D. C. U. S. V., Brookline, Mass.

Frizzel, J. W., Brig.-Gen., Owenville, O.

Fitch. M. H., Brev. Col. 21st Wis., Milwaukee, Wis.

Finckhouse, John J., Col. 98th Ill. Inf., Effingham, Ill.

Finch, John Wm., Maj. 26th Wis. Vol. Inf., Milwaukee, Wis.

Fitch, T. D., Surgeon 42nd Ill. Inf Chicago, Ill.

Fitzwilliam, Francis J., Capt. 33d O. V. I., Bloomington, Ill.

Fitch, Geo. W., Capt. 12th U. S. C. I., Chicago, Ill.

Flood, Ira A., Capt. 98th Ill. Vol. Inf., Vincennes, Ind.

Ford, Henry, Corporal 36th Ill. Vol. Inf., Crystal Lake, Ill.

Foote, Allen R., Lieut. 21st Mich. Vol. Inf., St. Louis, Mo.

Fox, P. V., Lieut.-Col. 1st U. S. V. V. Engineers, Grand Rapids, Mich.

Ford, Gus., C. Capt. 31st Ind. Vol. Inf., Cincinnati, O.

Foster, Edgar J., 1st Lieut. Co. K. 79th Ind., Indianapolis, Ind.

Forsyth. James W., Brev. Brig.-Gen. U. S. A., Chicago, Ill.

Fullerton, J. S., Brev. Brig.-Gen. U. S. V., St. Louis, Mo.

Fulmer, Jessie, Brev. Maj. U. S. A. Williamsport, Tenn.

Flynn, G. W., Lieut. and Adj. 25th Ill. Inf., Champaign, Ill.

Gratiot, E. A., Brevet Lieut.-Col. P. M. U. S. A., Plattville, Wis.

Gaubert, C. H., Capt. and A. Q.M. Chicago, Ill.

Granger, A. H., Captain 42nd Ill., Chicago, Ill.

Gamble, James E., 1st Lieut. 4th Indiana Battery, Chicago, Ill.

Gantz, J. T., 34th Ill. Vol.

Galbraith, Robert, Col. 5th Tenn. Vol. Cav., Shelbyville, Tenn.

Gallagher, John F., Captain 2nd Ohio Vol. Inf., Franklin, Ohio.

Gary, M. B., Battery C 1st O. Light Artillery, Geneva, O.

Gano, C. L., Lieut.-Col. 69th Ohio Vol. Inf., Sharonville, O.

Garfield, J. A., Maj.-Gen. U. S. V., Hiram, O.

Grayson, J. W. M., Lieut.-Col. 4th East Tenn. Vol. Inf., Taylorsville, Tenn.

Gleason, Newel, Brevet Brig.-Gen. U. S. V., Laporte, Indiana.

Greenwood, W. H., Lieut.-Colonel and A. I. Gen., St. Louis, Mo.

Gentry, George C., Col. 47th Wis. Vol. Inf., Brevet Brigadier-General, Green Bay, Wis.

Getty, William, 2nd Lieut. 12th Ind. Battery, Chicago, Ill.

Gilman, Charles, Captain 6th O. Vol. Inf., Cincinnati, O.

Griffith, D. J., Surgeon 2nd Ky., Louisville, Ky.

Gilbreath, W. C., Lieut. 20th Battery Ind. Vol., Chicago, Ill.

Grose, William, Brevet Maj.-Gen. U. S. V., Newcastle, Ind.

Goodhue, William, Adj. 4th Ky. Inf., Danville, Ky.

Grosvenor, C. H., Brevet Brig.-Gen. U. S. V., Athens, O.

Glover, Amos, Captain 15th Ohio Vol. Inf., Powhattan, O.

Grubbs, R. M., Captain 84th Ind. Vol. Inf., Knightstown, Ind.

Gurlitz, A. T., Lieut. 2nd Ky. Vol. Cav., Cincinnati, O.

Guthrie, John B., 1st Lieut. U. S. A. Through Adj.-Gen.

Guenther, George, 1st Lieut. Co. C 24th Ill., Chicago, Ill.

Guernsey, H. H., 1st Lieut. 14th U. S. C. I., Janesville, Wis.

Hale, Fran. Ed., Capt. 1st Mich. Vol. Artillery.

Hambright, Henry, Brevet Col. U. S. A. Through Adj.-Gen.

Hamilton, Thornt., Adj. 21st Ky. Vet. Vol. Inf., Lexington, Ky.

Hannah, George W., Captain 124th Ind. Vol. Inf., Connersville, Ind.

Hayden, Richard N., 12th Ill. Cav., Chicago, Ill.

Hannan, W., Captain 124th Ohio Vol., Dayton, O.

Harms, Charles A., Capt. 43d Ill. Vet. Vol. Inf.

Harries, George H., Brevet Lieut.-Col. U. S. V., Cincinnati, Ohio.

Harrington, J. W., Capt. 9th Tenn. Vol. Cav., Cincinnati, O.

Haight, Edward, Brev. Lieut.-Col. 16th U. S. Inf., N. Y. City.

Harter, G. D., 1st Lieut. 115th O. Vol. Inf., Canton, O.

Hawthorn, L. A., Brevet Major U. S. V., Newport, Ky.

Hayward, George L., Captain 1st O. Vol. Inf., Cleveland, O.

Hazzard, J. DeV., Brevet Maj. 79th Penn. Vol. Inf., Monongahela City, Penn.

Harris, L. A., Col. 2nd Ohio Vol. Inf., Cincinnati, O.

Hawk, R. A., Capt. 12th Ill. Vol., Monmouth, Ill.

Hammond, Charles M., Col. 100th Ill. Vol. Inf., Joliet, Ill.

Hall, H. W., Captain 59th Ill. Inf., Shelbyville, Ill.

Hart, Samuel S., Capt. 13th Wis., Chicago, Ill.

Hayden, James R., Capt. 19th Ill. Vol. Inf., Chicago, Ill.

Hand, ——. Capt. 24th Ill. Vol., Chicago, Ill.

Hand, Lew. B., Lieut. Chicago Board of Trade Battery, Chicago, Illinois.

Harlaw, Wellington, Capt. Co. A 4th Ky. Inf., Danville, Ky.

Harbottle, Wm. Penn, Sergt.-Maj. 100th Ill. Inf., Wilmington, Ill.

Hamlin, D. W., Capt. Co. E 138th Ind. Vol., Etna Green, Ind.

Harrington, R., Capt. 9th Ill. Cav., Geneseo, Ill.

Hair, J. S., A. B. Q. M., Chicago, Illinois.

Hassler, Dan. K., 1st O. and Adj. 14th U. S. C. I., Dayton, O.

Hapeman, Douglas, Colonel 104th Ill. Inf., Ottawa, Ill.

Harwood, E., Sergt.-Major, Joliet, Illinois.

Harding, A. C., Brig.-Gen., Monmouth, Ill.

Hauson, Henry N., Lieut. Co. H 21st Wis. Vol., Toledo, O.

Hemphill, William S., Captain 4th Ind. Cav., Warsaw, Ind.

Heighway, A. E., Surgeon U. S. V., Cincinnati, O.

Heard, C. D., Lieut.-Col. 30th Ind. Vol., Ft. Wayne, Ind.

Heaney, D., Brevet Maj. U. S. V., Rochester, Minn.

Heard, J. Theodore, Brevet Lieut.-Col. Med. Director 4th Army Corps, Boston, Massachusetts.

Hefelbower, Ad. M., 1st Lieut. 3rd O. Vol. Cav., Nashville, Tenn.

Heilburn, A., 1st Lieut. 9th O. V. Inf., Cincinnati, O.

Hennessey, M. T., 1st Lieut. 23rd Ky. Vol. Inf., Cincinnati, O.

Herrick, H. J., Surgeon 17th O. V. I., Cincinnati, O.

Helm, Clinton, Surgeon 92nd Ill. Inf., Byron, Ogle Co., Ill.

Hernalt, G. F., Maj. 10th Ind. Cav., Franklin, Ind.

Hill, J. H., Lieut. Bat. B. 1st O. V. L. A., Minonk, Woodford Co, Ill.

Hildreth, J. H., Corporal Chicago Bd. of Trade Bat., Chicago, Ill.

Hicks, Geo., Maj. and Brev. Col. 96th Ill. Vol., Mt. Carroll, Ill.

Hinkley, L. D., Lieut. 10th Wis. Inf., Waupun, Wis.

Hill, H. R. Lieut.-Col. 115th O. East Liverpool, O.

Hinman, F. H., U. S. N., Cleveland, O.

Hibbard, Geo. B., Brev. Maj. and Capt. and A. Q. M., Chicago, Ill.

Hills, Charles F. 1st Lieut. 51st Ill. Vol., Chicago, Ill.

Hoffman, William E., 1st Lieut. 31st U. S. Inf.

Hoffman, Southard, Lieut.-Col. and A. A. G. Vol., N. Y. City.

Hooper, William, Vermont, Ill.

Hoyt, F., Capt. Com. Sub., Tremont House, Chicago, Ill.

Hollingsworth, E. T., Lieut.-Col. 19th Ohio, Albion, Mich.

Hover, T. A., 139th Ind. Vol.

Hobbs, A. M., Capt. 36th Ill. Vol., Bristol, Kendall Co., Ill.

Hoar, Charles, 1st Lieut. 21st Ill. Inf., Henry, Ill.

Homer, Wm. J., Lieut. 123rd Ill. Vol. Inf., Charleston, Ill.

Horton, B. J., Lieut. 24th O. V. I., Cincinnati, O.

Hosea, L. M., Brev. Maj. U. S. A., Cincinnati, O.

Hotchkiss, C. T., Brev. Brig.-Gen. U. S. V., Chicago, Ill.

Hough, Alfred L., Brev. Col. U. S. A. Through Adj.-Gen.

Houk, L. C., Col. 3rd Tenn. Vol. Inf., Clinton, Tenn.

Hodges, Henry C., Maj. and A. Q. M., Brev. Lieut.-Col. U. S. A.

Howard, Jos., Brev. Col. U. S. A., Union, West Va.

Holden, L. P., Maj. 88th Ill. Inf., Chicago. Ill.

Howell, Wm. A., Capt. Co. G. 89th Ill. Vol., Altoona, Ill.

Hoblitzell, W. S., Lieut.-Col. 5th Ky. Cav., Cave City, Ky.

Hopkins, Enos, Maj. Mich. Engineers, Nashville, Tenn.

Howland, Henry, Col. Q. M. Dep., Chicago, Ill.

Hudnall, Jas. J., Capt. 4th Ky. Vol. Inf., Falmouth, Ky.

Hunter, Robert, Capt. 74th O. V. I., Cincinnati, O.

Howell, J. P., Capt. Co. B 86th Ill. Inf., Henry, Ill.

Holt, John M. Sergeant 8th Kan., Moline, Ill.

Hull, W. A., Capt. 9th Mich. Inf. Petroleum Centre, Venango Co., Penn.

Hull, G. A., Capt. U. S. A., Jeffersonville, Ind.

Hunt, P. B., Lieut.-Col. 4th Ky. Vol., Lexington, Ky.

Hubbard, Jr., Gurden S., Brev.-Maj. 88th Ill. Vol. Inf., Chicago, Ill.

Hulburd, E. M., Lieut.-Col. 18th Mich. Inf., Hudson, Mich.

Humphreys, Geo., Col. 88th and 139th Ind.

Humphreys, L., Col. and Med. Ins., South Bend, Ind.

Hyde, J. D., Lieut. and Adj.

Inman, Chas., Maj. 2nd Tenn. Vol. Cav., New Garden, Tenn.

Innes, William P., Brev. Brig.-Gen. U. S. V., Nashville, Tenn.

Innes, William, Col. 15th I. S. C. Inf., Chicago, Ill.

Isom, John F., Capt. 25th Ill. Vol. Inf., and A. Q. M., Cleveland, O.

Jackson, Huntington W., Brev. Lieut.-Col. A. D. C., Chicago, Ill.

Jackson, J. P., Lieut.-Col. 23rd Ky. Vol. Inf., Cincinnati, O.

Jasse, John M., Surgeon 32nd Ind. Vol.

Jackson, Thos. J., Col. 6th U. S. A., New Albany, Ind.

Jacobs, J. E., Brev. Col. U. S. V., St. Louis, Mo.

Jacobi, A., 24th Ill., Chicago, Ill.

Jeffers, Stephen, Major.

Johnson, A. M., 77th Ill., Galesburg, Ill.

Johnson, Henry W., Maj. and Q. M., Michigan City, Ind.

Jones, Stephen E., Capt. and A. D. C., Louisville, Ky.

Johns, F. A., Capt. 98th Ill. Vol. Inf., Olney, Ill.

Johnson, George, Capt. 11th O. V. I., Cincinnati, C.

Johnson, George W., 1st Lieut. 19th U. S. Inf., Covington, Ky.

Johnson, James, Capt. 71st O. Vol. Inf., Cincinnati, O.

Johnson, O. C., Colonel 15th Wis. Vol. Inf., Madison, Wis.

Johnson, R. W., Maj.-Gen. U.S.A. Through Adj.-Gen. U. S. A.

Johnson, Thomas, Col. 65th Ind. Vol. Inf., Cincinnati, O.

Johnston, E. W., Adj. 5th Ky. Vol. Inf., Louisville, Ky.

Jones, H. C., Captain 18th O. Vol. Inf., McArthur, O.

Jordan, Thomas J., Brevet Brig.-Gen. U. S. V., Harrisburg, Pa.

Judson, A. M., Private 77th Ill., Galesburg, Ill.

Jukes, C. J., 100th Ill. Vol.

Karill, Wm. M., Surgeon, Princeton, Ill.

Kearney, Thomas H., Surg. 45th Ohio Vol. Inf., Cincinnati, Ohio.

Keifer, J. Warren, Brev. Maj.-Gen. U. S. V., Springfield, O.

Keller, A. R., Captain and A. Q. M. U. S. V., Lancaster, O.

Kelley, W. J., Surgeon 15th Ohio Vol. Inf., Fremont, O.

Kemper, And. C., Capt. U. S. V., Cincinnati, O.

Kennedy, J. F., Captain U. S. V., Cleveland, O.

Kennedy, William N., Major 24th Wis., Milwaukee, Wis.

Kennett, John, Col. 4th Ohio Vol. Cav., Cincinnati, O.

Keene, L. S., Surgeon 29th Ind. Vol.

Kelly, Henry C., Capt., Chicago, Illinois.

Kelly, James, Captain, Columbus, Mississippi.

Kelly, R. M., Col. 4th Ky. Vol., Lexington, Ky.

Keller, A. R., Capt. and A. Q. M., Lancaster, O.

Kellogg, S. C., Brevet Lieut.-Col. U. S. A. Through Adj.-Gen. U. S. A.

Knecht, Adam, Jr., Lieut. 52nd O. Vol. Inf., Dayton, O.

Kercher, D. M., Colonel 10th Regt. Wis. Vol., Ripon, Wis.

Kent, George W., 1st Lieut. Co. B 88th Ill., Greeley, Ill.

Kendall, McCay, Surgeon 3rd O. Vol. Cav., Bucyrus, O.

Kirby, J. M., Col. 101st Ohio Vol. Brevet Brig.-Gen., Upper Sandusky, O.

Kline, Jacob, Capt. 25th Inf., Brev. Maj. U. S. A., Washington, D. C.

King, Rufus, B. C. Maj. and C. S., Chicago, Ill.

Kimmel, Louis, Capt., LaFayette, Indiana.

Kingman, Martin, 1st Lieutenant, Peoria, Illinois.

Knipe, Thomas F., Brig.-General, Harrisburg, Penn.

Kilgour, W. M., Brev. Col. U. S. V., Sterling, Ill.

Kimball, Nathan, Brevet Major-General U. S. V., Indianapolis, Indiana.

King, Robert P., 1st Lieut. U. S. A., Philadelphia, Penn.

Kirk, E. B., Captain and A. Q. M. U. S. A. Through Adj.-Gen.

Kitchell, Edward, Brev. Brigadier-General U. S. V., Olney, Ill.

Kniffin, G. C., Lieut.-Col. U. S. V., Paris, Ky.

Knight, George A., Captain 188th Ohio Vol. Inf., Catletsburg, Ky.

Klokke, E. W. C., Brevet Maj. 24th Ill., Chicago, Ill.

Kyle, James, Capt. 94th Ohio Vol. Inf., Xenia, O.

Lambright, Lewis, 1st Lieut. 35th Ohio Vol. Inf., Middletown, O.

Landis, A. H., Ass't Surg. 35th O. Vol. Inf., Millville, O.

Landis, F. B., Captain U. S. Vol., Hamilton, O.

Landrum, W. J., Brevet Brig.-Gen. U. S. V., Lancaster, Ky.

Lane, P. P., Col. 11th Ohio Vol. Inf., Cincinnati, O.

Lawrence, Samuel B., Lieut.-Col. U. S. A., New York.

Lapham, J. W., Major 115th Ill. Vol. Inf., Evanston, Ill.

Lamborn, Charles B., Lieut.-Col. 15th Penn. Cav., St. Louis, Mo.

Lasalle, Godfrey, Sergeant 9th Ill. Vol. Cav., Geneseo, Ill.

Lacy. II. A., Captain and A. Q.M., Detroit, Mich.

LaFayette, Mulnix, 8th Kansas, Sheridan, Ill.

Langley, J. W., Col. 125th Ill. Vol. Inf., Champaign, Ill.

Leslie, John R., 83d Ill., Chicago, Illinois.

Lytle. R. P., Capt. Co. B 27th Ill. Inf., Decatur, Ill.

Leedy, John R., Surgeon 74th Ind., Warsaw, Indiana.

Leib, Henry F., Adj. 90th Ohio Vol. Inf., Columbia, O.

Le Duc, William G., Brevet Major-Gen. U. S. V., Hastings, Minn.

Lenur, J. B., Capt. 2nd Mich. Vol.

Lemert, George A., Captain 97th Ohio Vol. Inf., Dresden, Ohio.

Leonard, G. P., Captain 1st Ohio Vol. Inf., Dayton, Ohio.

Leonard, J. A., Major 188th Ohio Vol. Inf., Dayton, Ohio.

Lincoln, A. A., Lieut. 3rd Missouri Vol., Chicago, Illinois.

Livermier, D. E., Lieut.-Col. 3rd Ohio Cav., Chicago, Ill.

Little, Samuel J., Brevet Col. U. S. V., Nashville, Tenn.

Linklater, Jerry II., 1st Lieut. Co. D 96th Ill., Waukegan, Ill.

Loomis, James B., Capt. 7th Mich. Cav., Albion, Michigan.

Logan, R. F., Surgeon 15th Ky. Vol. Inf., Louisville, Ky.

Lovell, Ogden, Captain 42nd Ill. Vol., Chicago, Ill.

Loveless, B., Co. A 36th Ill. Vol., Elgin, Illinois.

L'Hommedieu, Samuel, Capt. 35th Ohio Vol. Inf., Hamilton, O.

Long, Charles L., Lieut.-Col. 35th Ohio Vol. Inf., Dayton, O.

Long, Eli, Major-General U. S. A., Cincinnati, O.

Loomis, C. O., Brevet Brig.-Gen. U. S. V , Coldwater, Mich.

Lowe, William R., Brevet Major U. S. A. Through Adj.-Gen.

Lowe, W. W., Brevet Brig.-Gen U. S. A

Loughlin, William M., Capt. U. S. V. V. Engineers, Lake Forest, Illinois.

Lyon, Samuel, Capt. 2nd Ky. Vol. Cav., Gallatin, Tenn. Through Adj.-General.

Ludlow, Israel, Lieut. 5th U. S. Artillery, Cincinnati, Ohio.

Ludlow, William E., 10th Ind. Vol. Inf., Cincinnati, O.

Lybrand, A., Capt. 73rd Ind. Vol. Inf., LaFayette, Tippecanoe Co., Indiana.

Lynd, George M., Capt. 100th Ill. Inf., Lockport, Ill.

McAdams, Wm., Lieut. 59th Ill. Vol. Inf., Kansas, Ill.

McCarthy, J. F., Surgeon 29th Ind. Inf., Valparaiso, Ind.

McArthur, W. W. II., Capt. 31st O. V. I., Springfield, O.

McDermott, C., Surgeon U. S. V., Dayton, O.

McMerchin, W. E., Lieut.-Col, 21st Ill. Salem. Ill.

McNair, James E., 1st Lieut. 6th Tenn. Vol. Cav., Trezevant, Tenn.

McClenahan, John, Lieut.-Col. 15th O. V. I., Ottawa, Kansas.

McWilliams, John, Lieut. and R. Q. M. 129th Ill. Vol., Odell, Ill.

McGroarty, J. S., Brev. Brig.-Gen. U. S. V., Cincinnati, O.

McIlvaine, F. E., Brev. Lieut.-Col. U. S. A., N. Y. City.

McClurg. A. C., Brev. Brig.-Gen. U. S. V., Chicago, Ill.

McMurtry, Alex. O., Capt. 88th Ill., Milwaukee, Wis.

McWiliams, J. G., Maj. 51st Ill. Inf., Chicago, Ill.

McMichael, William, A. A. G., Brev.-Col. U. S. V., Philadelphia, Penn.

McCook, Edward M., Brev. Maj.-Gen. U. S. A., New Mexico.

McCook, John J., Capt. U. S. V., Steubenvi le, O.

McCook, Anson G., Brev. Brig.-Gen. U. S. V., Steubenville, O.

McCoy, Daniel, Brev. Brig.-Gen., Col. 175th O. V. I., Thomson, Carroll Co., Ill.

McCoy, Theodore W., Capt. 39th Ind. Vol. Inf., Jeffersonville, Ind.

McCrory, Wm., 1st Lieut. 7 S. S. Gen. Sherman's guard, Chicago, Ill.

McCullough, J. R., Asst. Surg. 1st Wis. Vol. Inf., Jefferson, Wis.

Manderson, Chas. F., Brev. Brig.-Gen. U. S. V., Canton, O.

Mannen, Thomas H., Maj. 40th Ky. Vol. Inf., Cincinnati, O.

Martin, Alfred, Maj. 6th Ky. Vol. Inf., Covington, Ky.

Martin, W. H., Brev. Brig.-Gen. U. S. V., Dayton, O.

Mason, C. W., Capt. 35th Inf., Brev. Col. U. S. A.

Mathews, Stanley, Col. 51st O. V. I., Cincinnati, O.

Manzy, James H., Capt. 68th Ind. Vol. Inf., Rushville, Ind.

Markeser, P. C., Capt. 8th Iowa Vol. Inf., Dubuque, Iowa.

Maxwell, O. C., Brev. Brig.-Gen. U. S. V., Dayton, O.

Mather, C. J., Capt. Co. F., 15th Penn. Cav.

Marks, S., Surg. 10th Wis. Vol., Wilwaukee, Wis.

Martin, J. O., Col. 17th N. Y. Vol., Indianapolis, Ind.

Maeder, J. T., Capt. 25th U. S. Inf., Keokuk, Iowa.

Marshall, J. M., Maj. 5th U. S. Inf. Vol., Indianapolis, Ind.

Mars, F. H., Maj. 1st Wis. Cav., Chicago, Ill.

Mattson, C. R., 13th Wis.

Marsh, F. E., Capt. and Brev. Maj., Chicago, Ill.

Marsh, Jason, Col. 74th Ill. Vol., Rockford, Ill.

Messer, John, Lieut.-Col. 101st O., Brev. Brig.-Gen., Chicago, Ill.

Merrill, C. H., Signal Corps, U. S. A., Chicago, Ill.

Merrick, C. C., Capt. 51st Ill., Chicago, Ill.

Merrill, Samuel, Lieut.-Col. 70th Ind. Vol. Inf., Indianapolis, Ind.

Megrue, C. G., Maj. 4th O. V. C., Cincinnati, O.

Merrill, Wm. E., Brev. Col. U. S. A., Chicago, Ill.

Metzner, Adolph, Capt. U. S. V., Indianapolis, Ind.

Miller, L. F., Maj. 33rd Ind., Brev. Col. U. S. V., Williamsport, Warren Co., Ind.

Meyers, Vincent, Capt. 1st Tenn. Lt. Art., Claiborne, Tenn.

Mindel, Geo. W., Brev. Maj.-Gen. U. S. V., Philadelphia, Penn.

Miller, Clement F., 1st Lieut. and Adj. 1st Mich. Engineers, Battle Creek, Mich.

Mitchell, Oscar, 2nd Lieut. Co. K 2nd Ky. Inf., Chicago, Ill.

Miller, Ben. C., 1st Lieut. Co. K 11th Ind. Cav., City Hospital, Chicago, Ill.

Minty, Robt. H. G., Brev. Maj.-Gen. U. S. V., Jackson, Mich.

Middleswart, H. F., Capt. 92nd O. V. I., Marietta, O.

Miller, B. F., Surgeon 2nd O. V. I., Cincinnati, O.

Miller, S. J. F., Surgeon 5th Ky. Vol. Inf., Cincinnati, O.

Michaelis, O. E., Brev.-Capt. Ord. Corps, Washington, D. C.

Milward, H. K., Colonel 18th Ky. Vol. Inf., Lexington, Ky.

Merrill, Lewis, Brevet Brig.-Gen. "Merrill's Horse," Brevet Col. U. S. A.

Milward, Will. R., Col. 21st Ky. Vet. Vol. Inf., Lexington, Ky.

Montagnier, Jules J., Captain 6th Ohio Vol. Inf., Cincinnati, O.

Moody, Granville, Brevet Brig.-Gen. U. S. V., Ripley, O.

Moore, O. F., Col. 33rd Ohio Vol. Inf., Portsmouth, O.

Moore, R. M., Lieut.-Col. 10th O. Vol. Inf., Cincinnati, O.

Morgan, O. H., Captain 7th Ind. Vol. Battery, Chicago, Ill.

Morgan, William A., 1st Lieut. 23rd Ky. Vol. Inf., Cincinnati, O.

Moriarty, William C., Adj. 35th Ind. Vol. Inf., Indianapolis, Ind.

Morton, Quin, Lieut.-Colonel 23rd Mo. Vol. Inf., Shelbyville, Ind.

Mosenmeier, B., Ass't Surgeon 33rd Ohio Vol. Inf., Cincinnati, O.

Moxley, J. D., Major 1st Ohio Vol. Cav., Chillicothe, O.

Montague, H. O., Captain 1st Wis. Inf., Whitewater, Wis.

Moore, Absalom B., Col. 104th Ill. Inf., Ottawa, Ill.

Morgan, James D., Brevet Major-General, Quincy, Ill.

Morrison, A., Captain 5th Battery Ind. Light Art., Plymouth, Ind.

Munn, Lewis, Brevet Brig.-Gen. Brevet Colonel U. S. A.

Mullen, John S., 2nd Minn. Vol., Nashville, Tenn.

Mulnix, LaFayette, Private 8th Kansas, Sherin, Ill.

Mullins, M., Lieut.-Col. 40th Ky. Inf., Falmouth, Ky.

Murdock, L. K., Captain 10th Ohio Vol. Inf., Cincinnati, O.

Muscroft, C. S., Surgeon 10th O. Vol. Inf., Cincinnati, O.

Mussey, W. H., Lieut.-Col. U. S. A., Cincinnati, O.

Negley, James S., Maj.-Gen. U. S. V., Pittsburg, Penn.

Nelson, D. M., Captain Co. A 10th Tenn. Cav., Knoxville, Tenn.

Nicar, Edwin, Captain 15th Ind., South Bend, Ind.

Nicholson, George B., Sergt. Co. K 6th O. Vol. Inf., Cincinnati, O.

Nodine, R. H., Col. 25th Ill. Vol. Inf., Champaign, Ill.

Nost, J. M., Col. 19th Ohio Vol., Ohio.

Nuten, H. A., Captain 12th U. S. Colored Inf., Rockford, Ill.

Oldershaw, P. P., Capt. U. S. V., New York City.

Olmstead, Samuel G., Chaplain, Louisville, Ky.

Otis, E. A., Captain U. S. V., Chicago, Ill.

O'Connell, P., Major U. S. V., Dayton, O.

O'Kean, Mortimer, Col. 38th Ill. Inf., Olney, Ill.

O'Donoughue, W., Surg. 1st Mich. Engineers, Albion, Mich.

Opdyke, E., Brevet Major-Gen. U. S. V., New York City.

Orr, George W., 1st Lieut. 15th U. S. Col. Inf., Indianapolis, Ind.

Palmer, Wm. J., Col. 15th Penn. Cav., Brevet Brig.-General, St. Louis, Mo.

Palmer, J. J., C. S. U. S. A., Indianapolis, Ind.

Patten, Robert W., Co. E 3rd Wis. Vol., Brodhead, Wis.

Paine, C. N., Capt. Co. B 21st Wis. Inf., Oshkosh, Wis.

Patrick, N. T., Lieut.-Col. 5th Iowa Cav., Omaha, Nebraska.

Patterson, E. L., Capt. Co. D 79th Ohio Vol. Inf., Cleveland, O.

Park, H. S., Capt. Co. C 2nd Ky. Cav., Henderson, Ky.

Parkhurst, J. G., Brevet Brig.-Gen. U. S. V., Detroit, Mich.

Parrott, E. A., Col. 1st Ohio Vol. Inf., Dayton, O.

Patton, J. T. Capt. 93rd Ohio Inf., Dayton, O.

Prather, Allen W., Col. 120th Ind. Vol. Inf., Columbus, Ind.

Perin, G., Surgeon U. S. A., New port Barracks, Ky.

Pearl, A. M., Capt. 3rd Ohio Vol. Cav., Berlin Heights, O.

Peters, Matthew H., Major 74th Ohio Vol. Inf., Watseka, Ill.

Peak, George B., Capt. Co. A 35th Ill., Decatur, Ill.

Pepoon, G. W., Capt. 96th Ill. Vol. Inf., Warren, Ill.

Pickett, G. P., 2nd Lieut. 34th U. S. Inf., Lauderdale, Miss.

Pickett, Thomas J., Col. 132nd Ill. Inf., Paducah, Ky.

Philips, L. S., 1st Ohio Vol. Art., Cleveland, O.

Pierce, C. W., Brevet Major 85th Ill. Vol., Demopolis, Ala.

Price, S. W., Brevet Brig.-Gen. U. S. V., Lexington, Ky.

Phelps, William, Col., Paymaster U. S. A., Detroit, Mich.

Prosser, Wm. F., Col. 2nd Tenn. Cav., Nashville, Tenn.

Porter, Horace, Col. and Brevet Brig.-Gen. U. S. A., Washington, D. C.

Putnam, Jr., Douglas, Lieut.-Col. 92nd Ohio Inf., Hot Furnace, O.

Pickands, James, Col. 124th Ohio Inf., Cleveland, O.

Pollock, John K., Brevet Maj. 96th Ill. Vol. Inf., Milburn, Ill.

* Porter, William L., Brevet Major U. S. V.

Pugh, J. L., Lieut.-Col. 4th Ohio Vol. Cav., Cincinnati, O.

Putnam, David, Capt. 92nd Ohio Vol. Inf., Athens, O.

Quigley, William F., Lieut. 18th Ohio Vol. Inf., Nelsonville, O.

Quinn, R. L., Capt. 75th Illinois, Franklin Grove, Ill.

Ransom, Edward P., Captain U. S. V., Cincinnati, O.

* Deceased.

Ransom, J. S., Capt. 44th Ill. Vol. Inf., Kalamazoo, Mich.

Ramnells, R. M., 1st Lieut. and R. Q. M., 87th Ind.

Raffin, Alex. W., Lieut.-Col. 19th Ill., Chicago. Ill.

Rathburn, H. B., Lieut. Co. D 2nd Mich. Cav., Chicago, Ill.

Rauch John H., Surgeon U. S. A., Brevet Col., Chicago, Ill.

Raymond, Lewis, Chaplain 51st Ill. Vol. Inf., Chicago, Ill.

Raymond, Samuel B., Lieut.-Col. 51st Ill., Chicago, Ill.

Ransom, W. C., Brevet Lieut.-Col. U. S. A., Louisville, Ky.

Raymond, W. F., Capt. 11th N. Y. Cav., Cedarville, N. Y.

Ramsey, Robert H., Major and A. A. G., Brev. Col. U. S. A., Pottsville, Schuylkill Co., Penn.

Read, E., 11th Ind. Cav., Terre Haute, Ind.

Remington, Thomas, J. L., Major 74th Ill., Rockford, Ill.

Reynolds, J. J., Brevet Maj.-Gen. U. S. A., Austin, Texas.

Reed, N. A., 1st Lieut. U. S. V., Cincinnati, O.

Regan, D., Capt. 18th O. Vol. Inf., Dayton, O.

Reaperman, Douglas, Colonel 104th Illinois.

Reibold, Daniel, Corporal 1st Iowa Cav., Dayton, O.

Richards, Edward S., Brev. Lieut.-Colonel U. S. V., Cincinnati, O.

Rigg, Joseph, Capt. 187th O. Vol. Inf., Champaign, Ill.

Rider, R. G., Major 85th Ill.

Richards. W. T., Major 81st Ind. Vol. Inf., LaFayette, Ind.

Rhines, James, 1st Lieut. Co. E 88th Ill., Toledo, O.

Rice, T. T., 81st Ind., Chicago, Ill.

Rice, J. W., Major 3rd Ill. Cav., Springfield, Ill.

Ringland, George, 79th Ill. Vol., A. A. Surgeon, Kansas, Ill.

Rosecrans, William S., Maj.-Gen. U. S. A.

Robinson, George F., Capt. 89th Ill. Vol. Inf., Chicago, Ill.

Roper, George S., Capt. C. S. U. S. Vol., Alton, Ill.

Robinson, J. S., Brevet Maj.-Gen. U. S. V., Kenton, O.

Royse, D., Adj. 40th Ind. Vol., LaFayette, Ind.

Rose, F. E., Col. 77th Penn. Vol.

Rowan, C. E., Capt. 96th Ill. and Brevet Major U. S. A., Chicago, Illinois.

Rockwood, Frank B., Co. C Board of Trade Battery, Chicago, Ill.

Rose, Rufus, Major 51st Ill., Chicago, Ill.

Runyan, John N., Captain Co. A 74th Ind. Vol. Inf., Warsaw, Ind.

Ruhn, John, 1st Lieut. 15th U. S. C. I., Nashville, Tenn.

Rust. H. A., Major 27th Ill., Chicago, Ill.

Russell. James A., 1st Lieut. and R. Q. M. 84th Ill., Vermont, Fulton Co., Ill.

Runkle, Ben. P., Brevet Maj.-Gen. U. S. V., Louisville, Ky.

Russell, A. O., Major 6th O. Vol. Inf., Cincinnati, O.

Santmeier. J. P., Captain U. S. V., Cincinnati, O.

Sharp, D. N., Adj. 5th Ky. Vol. Inf., Shelbyville, Ky.

Sanford, J. E., Co. C 38th Ohio Vol., Chicago, Ill.

Sparling, Fred. W., Surgeon 10th Mich. Vol. Inf., Nashville, Tenn.

Slade. Samuel, Capt. 51st O. V. I., Port Washington. O.

Sand, C. V. D. R., Capt. 9th Mich. Inf., E. Saginaw. Mich.

Stackhouse, W. P., Captain 19th Ind. Vol. Bat., Greensfork, Ind.

Staunage, Jas. O., Capt. U. S. V., Cincinnati, O.

Stanley, David S., Colonel 22nd U. S. I., Brev. Maj.-Gen. U. S. A., Ft. Sully, Dakota Ter.

Stanton, Byron, Asst.-Surg. U. S. V., Newberg, O.

Sawyer, E. G., Lieut.-Col. 9th Penn. Cav., Lykens, Penn.

Straub, W. F., Capt. U. S. V., Cincinnati, O.

Slaughter, Jas. J., 1st Lieut. Co. H 115th Ill., Delaware, Ill.

Salisbury, Leroy, 1st Lieut. 36th Ill. Vol. Inf., Chicago, Ill.

Shannon, Jas. H., Col. 138th Ind. Vol., Laporte, Ind.

Savage, E. G., Lieut.-Col. 9th Penn. Cav., Lykens, Dauphin Co., Penn.

Spalding, E. G., 1st Lieut. Co. K 22nd Mich., Port Huron, Mich.

Stafford, C. A., Brevet Brigadier-Gen. 1st O. I., Lancaster, O.

Sabin, Oscar C., 1st Lieut. 29th Ind. Vol. Inf., Chicago, Ill.

Swazey, John C., Brev. Maj. C. V. I., Newcastle, Ind.

Salter, F., Surgeon U. S. V., Enterprise, O.

Spaulding, J. J., Captain 88th Ill. Inf., Chicago, Ill.

Stanbaugh, James W. R., Captain 75th Ill. Vol. Inf., Sterling, Ill.

Shaffner, L., Lieut.-Col. 153rd Ill.

Schlaud, J., 16th Ill.

Stanley, T. R., Col. 18th O. Vol., and Brev. Brig.-Gen., Chattanooga, Tenn.

Slaughter, John, Co. F 34th Ill. Vol., Ashton, Ill.

Swallow, George R., Col. 10th Ind. Cav., Jerseyville, Ind.

Sabin, C. E., Hospital Steward 36th Ill., Elgin, Ill.

Schneider, Ed. F., Lieut.-Col. 8th Kan. Vol. Inf., Canton, O.

Seib, Amos D., 1st Lieut. 1st O. Vol. Cav., Marysville, O.

Shepherd, A. C., Capt. and C. S. U. S. V., Rochester, Ind.

Sheridan, Philip H., Lieut.-Gen. U. S. A., Chicago, Ill.

Sherwood, J. R., Brev. Brig.-Gen. U. S. V., Bryan, O.

Steele, John W., Brev. Lieut.-Col. U. S. V., Elyria, O.

Stewart, John, Brev. Maj. U. S. V., Cincinnati, O.

Schweinfurth, Frank, Lieut. 24th Ill. Vol. Inf., Chicago, Ill.

Stewart, Wm. M., Brev. Maj. 100th Ill. Vol., Bloomington, Ill.

Stinson, R. B., Capt. 60th Ill.

Stephens, S. H., Lieut. "Chicago Board of Trade Battery" Ill. Vol., Nashville, Tenn.

Schick, C. U.

Schermerhorn, Jno. M., Capt. 92nd Ill., Lena, Stephenson Co., Ill.

Sheets, B. F., Lieut.-Col. 93rd Ill. Vol., Oregon, Ogle Co., Ill.

Sweet, C., Captain, Chicago, Ill.

Speed, James B., Adj. 27th Ky. Inf., Louisville, Ky.

Speed, John, Capt. and A. A. G. Vol., Louisville, Ky.

Sterling, John, 1st Lieut. Co. A 30th Ind.

Sherman, Geo. D., Maj. 36th Ill. Inf., Elgin, Ill.

Sheldon, H. G., Capt. Co. D 101st O. V. I., Toledo, O.

Sheren, Samuel B., Maj. 15th Ill. Cav., Aurora, Ill.

Sexton, W. H., Lieut. 83rd Ill. Inf., Monmouth, Ill.

Seidman, G. B., Lieut. 12th Mo. Cav. Lena, Ill.

Sherman, F. T., Brev. Brig.-Gen. U. S. V., Chicago, Ill.

Sweet, R. J., Brev. Brig.-Gen., Chicago, Ill.

Sweet, John E., Colonel 151st Ind. Inf., Chicago, Ill.

Sperry, Anson, Brev. Lieut.-Col. Asst.-Paymaster, U. S. A., Chicago, Ill.

Smith, John D., Lieut. Co. K 92nd O. V. I., Altona, Ill.

Smith, Charles B., Lieut. and A. A. Q. M. 5th Iowa Cav., Omaha, Neb.

Smith, Geo. W., Colonel 88th Ill. Inf., and Brev. Brig.-Gen.

Smith, Wm. H., Chaplain 75th Ill., Polo, Ogle Co., Ill.

Smith, Wm. S., Brev. Brig.-Gen., Chicago, Ill.

Smith, J. C., Brev. Brig.-Gen. 96th Ill., Galena, Ill.

Smith, Melvin, 1st Lieut. Co. F 105th Ill. Vol. Inf., Ill.

Smith, Norman M., Lieut.-Col. 19th Penn. Cav., Pittsburgh, Penn.

Smith, C., Captain, Chicago, Ill.

Smith, S. B., Major 93rd O. V. I., Dayton, O.

Smith, W. J., Brev. Brigadier-Gen. U. S. V., Memphis, Tenn.

Smith, Frank G., Capt. 4th Art., Brevet Major U. S. A.

Schmith, Carl, Capt. and A. A. G. U. S. V., Cincinnati, O.

Scribner, B. F., Brev. Brig.-Gen. U. S. V., New Albany, Ind.

Shiner, Henry G., Captain 23rd Ky. Vet. Vol. Inf., Cincinnati, O.

Sidell, Wm. H., Brev. Brig.-Gen. U. S. A., Ft. Abercrombie, Dakota Ter.

Stillwell, J. R., Chaplain 79th O. V. I., Indianapolis, Ind.

Streight, A. D., Col. 51st Ind. Inf., and Brev. Brigadier-Gen., Indianapolis, Ind.

Shipman, S. V., Major 1st Wis. Cav. and Brev. Colonel U. S. V., Madison, Wis.

Stire, F. H., 1st Lieut., Lacon, Ill.

Simpson, J. H., Capt. 4th Mich. Cav., Adrian, Mich.

Stoner, Henry M., Sergeant 30th Ind. Vol., Cedarville, Ind.

Scoville, H. C., Capt. Co. K 92nd Ill. Vol. Inf., Rockford, Ill.

Scott, W. T., 3rd Ky. Vol. Inf.

Stoughton, Wm. L., Colonel 11th Mich. Inf., and Brev. Maj.-Gen. U. S. V.

Spotts, L. M., 87th Indiana Vol., Rochester, Ind.

Song, H. C., Captain 87th Ind., Rochester, Ind.

Sowers, Percy A., Lieut.-Col. 35th O. V. I., Canton, O.

Stoufer, John W., 88th Ill., Gridley, Ill.

Slocum, H. W., Maj.-Gen. Vol., Brooklyn, N. Y.

Scott, N. A., Sergeant, 83rd Ill. Vol., Monmouth, Ill.

Stone, N. E., Lieut. 2nd Ky. Cav., Celina, O.

Stone. B. B., Capt. 92nd O. V. I., Belpre, O.

Stone, Henry, Brevet Colonel U. S. V., Nashville, Tenn.

Spooner, E. D., 1st Lieutenant 5th U. S. Art., Cincinnati, O.

Slocum, J. J., Colonel U. S. V., Cincinnati, O.

Scott, T. W., Major U. S. V., Olney, Ill.

Sturges, E. P., Lieutenant 1st O. Vol. Lt. Art., Mansfield, O.

Sutphen, J. M., Capt. 90th O. V. I., Lancaster, O.

Stuzk, C., U. S. Cav.

Stundart, Wm. E., Capt. Co. B O. V. C., Toledo, O.

Shyrock, R. G., Colonel 87th Ind., Rochester, Ind.

Symes, G G., Colonel 44th Wis., Paducah, Ky.

Tanehill, C. O., Capt. Co. B 65th O. V. I., Perryville, O.

Tasso. John M., Surgeon 32nd Ind.

Taylor, M. C., Col. 15th Ky. Vol. Inf., Shelbyville, Ky.

Taylor, Jr , David, Captain Co. B 113th O. V. I., Taylor's Station, O.

Thatcher, T. R., Capt. 17th Ohio Vol. Inf.

TenEyck, T., Capt. 18th Inf., Brev. Major U. S. A., Ft. Sedgwick, Colorado.

Temple, M. D., 1st Lieut. Bridge's Bat. Ill. Vol., Chicago, Ill.

Treanor, John L., Lieutenant-Col. 5th Ky. Inf., Louisville, Ky.

Ter Bush, Sylvan, Major 10th Mich. Inf., Chicago, Ill.

Teetor, H. B., Brev. Lieut.-Colonel U. S. V., Cincinnati, O.

Tipton, A. F., Lieut. 8th Iowa C., Elkader, Iowa.

Tingle, James, 1st Lieut. 93rd O. V. I., Dayton, O.

Tinney, Henry C., A. A. G. U. S. V., Lafayette, Ind.

Tinker, Henry H., Captain 6th O. V. I., Cincinnati, O.

Tillman, Wm., Brev. Lieut.-Col. Paymaster, Detroit, Mich.

Thomas, George H., Major-Gen. U. S. A., San Francisco, Cal.

Thomas. Jerome B., Asst.-Surg. U. S. V., Dayton, O.

Thomas, Will. R., Capt. U. S. V., Sycamore, Ill.

Throop, E. S., Adj. 6th O. V. I., Cincinnati, O.

Tower, Isaiah F., Capt. 93rd O. V. I., Dayton, O.

Townsend, Robert, Lieut. 23rd Ky. Vol. Inf., Newport, Ky.

Townsend, H., Lieut. 9th Ky. Vol. Inf., Warren, O.

Toll, Charles H., Brev. Major and C. S., Clinton, Iowa.

Todd, E. P., 2nd Lieut. Co. E 96th Ill. Vol., Apple River, Ill.

Townsend, Wm. R., Capt. 42nd Ill. Vol.

Tower, J. B., Brev. Major-General U. S. A., Care Adjutant-Gen.

Thompson, J. E., Captain 30th Ind., Benton, Ind.

Tuttle, Russel M., Brev. Capt. and Topographical Engineer, Hornellsville, N. Y.

Turchin, J. B., Brig.-Gen. U. S. V., Chicago, Ill.

Turnbull, John M., 1st Lieut. 36th Ill., Monmouth, Ill.

True, Clinton J., Colonel 4th Ky. Vol., Lexington, Ky.

Thruston, G. P., Brev. Brig.-Gen. U. S. V., Nashville, Tenn.

Turner, Wm. C., Brevet Colonel U. S. V., Cleveland, O.

Turney, Samuel D., Lieut.-Colonel U. S. V., Circleville, O.

Tindale, Hector, Brig.-Gen. U. S. V., Philadelphia, Penn.

Tryner, George A., Sergeant 21st Ill. Inf., Bloomington, Ill.

Unold, John, Capt. 105th Ill. Vol. Inf., West Lyons, Ill.

Utley, Wm. L., Colonel 22nd Wis. Vol. Inf., Racine, Wis.

Van Antwerp, W. W., Capt. and Brev. Major 4th Mich. Cav.

Vance, W. J., Brevet Captain U. S. V., Findlay, O.

Vandegrift, George, A. A. G., U. S. V., Cincinnati, O.

Vanderveer, F., Brigadier-General U. S. V., Hamilton, O.

Vandeveer, Wm., Brig.-General, Brev. Major-General, Dubuque, Iowa.

Vanderveer, John, Capt. 35th O. V. I., Hamilton, O.

Vanhorne, Thomas T., Chaplain U. S. A., Piqua, O.

Varney, R. W., Asst.-Surg. 31st O. V. I., N. Y. City.

Vail, Nicholas J., Major 14th U. S. C. I., Chicago, Ill.

Van Osdel, John M., Capt. Co. K 59th Ill. Vol. Inf., Chicago, Ill.

Vincent, Wesley, Asst.-Surg. 11th Mich. Vol. Inf., Chicago, Ill.

Vocke, Wm., Capt. 24th Ill. Vol. Inf., Chicago, Ill.

Von Fritsch, Otto, Capt. 68th Reg. N. Y. Vol. Inf., Chicago, Ill.

Votau, M., Capt. 123rd Ill. Vol. Inf., Neoga, Ill.

Wade, D. E., Surgeon 2nd O. V. I., Cincinnati, O.

Ward, Durbin, Brevet Brigadier-General U. S. V., Lebanon, O.

Ward, J. H., Lieut.-Col. 27th Ky. Vol. Inf., Louisville, Ky.

Watkins, W. W., Adjutant 1st Wis. Vol. Inf., Milwaukee, Wis.

Watts, Joseph R., Lieut. U. S. V., Louisville, Ky.

Watkins, J. B., 1st Lieut. 89th Ill. Vol. Inf., Clinton, Iowa.

Wharton, G. C., Lieut.-Col. 10th Ky. Vol. Inf., Louisville, Ky.

Waterman, Luther D., Surgeon 39th Ind. Vol., Indianapolis, Ind.

Watson, J. A., Major 75th Ill., Dixon, Ill.

Waterman, George I., Captain 51st Ill., Brev. Lieut.-Col., Chicago, Ill.

Wade, A. B., Colonel 73rd Ind., South Bend, Ind.

Ward, A. A., Surgeon 43rd Wis. Vol., Madison, Wis.

Warren, John W., Captain 89th Ill. Vol., Chicago, Ill.

Watts, E. S., Col. 2nd Ky. Cav., Evansville, Wis.

Waterman, Alfred, Surgeon 105th Ill. Vol., Wheaton, Ill.

Warnock, James, Capt. 2nd O. V. I., Cincinnati, O.

Wendt, Henry, Q. M. 24th Ill., Chicago, Ill.

Wendt, Henry M., 1st Lieut. 11th Ind. Bat., Ft. Wayne, Ind.

Whedon, A., Capt. Co A 82nd Ind., Jeffersonville, Ind.

Webber, J. R., Capt. C. S., Morris, Ill.

Welch, Horace, 1st Lieut. 125th O., Canton, Texas.

Weeks, J. F., Surgeon 51st Ill. Inf., Chicago, Ill.

Whittlesey, Henry M., Brev. Brig.-General, Washington, D. C.

Wily, H., Capt. Co. A 59th Ill. Vol.

Wilson, M. H., 1st Lieut. and Adj. 11th O. V. I., Chicago, Ill.

White, David H., Captain Co. E 74th Ind., Middlebury, Ind.

Williams, Henry M., 1st Lieut. 11th Ind. Bat., Ft. Wayne, Ind.

Wilson, W. T., Brev. Brigadier-Gen., Upper Sandusky, O.

Williston, John H., Major 41st O. Inf., Cleveland, O.

Williams, George O., Capt. and A. D. C., Omaha, Neb.

Whitman, Q. D., 104th Ill. Vol. Inf.

Wister, Stephen C., Lieut.-Col. 41st Reg. O. V. I.

White, John C., Musician 16th U. S. I., Chicago, Ill.

Wilson, R. L., Paymaster U. S. A., Sterling, Ill.

2 I

Wilson, J. H., Lieut.-Col. 35th Inf'y, Brev. Maj.-Gen. U. S. A., Keokuk, Iowa.

Wickersham, M. D., Colonel, Mobile, Ala.

Wickersham, D., Col. 10th Ill. Vol. Cav., Springfield, Ill.

Whitaker, Walter C., Brevet Maj.-General, Louisville. Ky.

White, L. A., Captain Ill. Light Art., Chicago.

Widmer, John H., Major 104th Ill. Inf., Henry, Ill.

Wright, L., Colonel 1st Mass., Chicago, Ill.

Wilson, J. H., A. Q. M., Laporte, Ind.

Whiting, W. A., Captain 88th Ill. Vol.

Whipple, W. D., Brevet Maj.-Gen. U. S. A., San Francisco, Cal.

White, Norman P., Capt. 4th O. V. C., Cincinnati, O.

White, W. O., Capt. 4th Tenn. Vol. Cav., Cleveland, Tenn.

Whitemore, H. C., Capt. 2nd Ill. Vol. Light Art., Sycamore, Ill.

Wilder, J. T., Brev. Brigadier-Gen. U. S. V., Greensboro, Ind.

Wiley, G. W., Capt. and A. C. S. U. S. V., Indianapolis, Ind.

Willard, John P., Brev. Lieut.-Col. U. S. A. Through Adj.-General.

Williams, Wm. N., 2nd Lieut. U. S. A., Madison, Ind.

Willich, A., Brigadier-General U. S. V., Cincinnati, O.

Wills, A. W., Lieut.-Col. U. S. V., Philadelphia, Penn.

Wilshire, J. W., Capt. 45th O. V. I., Cincinnati, O.

Willett, Jas. R., Major 1st U. S. Vet. Vol. Engineers, Nashville, Tenn.

Wilson, James S., Capt. and A. A. G., U. S. V., Dayton, O.

Wilson, W., Capt. 124th O. V. I., Cleveland, O.

Wilson, W. C.. Col. 40th and 135th Ind. Vol. Inf., Lafayette, Ind.

Wilstach, C. F., R. Q. M. 10th Ind. Vol. Inf., Lafayette, Ind.

Wing, Charles T., Col. U. S. V., Nashville, Tenn.

Wolcott, Frank, Lieut.-Col. 20th Ky. Vol. Inf., Covington, Ky.

Wood, Thomas J, Brev. Major-General U. S. A., Dayton, O.

Worrell, J. P., Captain 86th Ill., Henry, Ill.

Woods, T. E., Captain 123rd Ill. Mounted Vol. Inf., Mattoon, Ill.

Wood, Wm. R., Color-Sergeant 6th O. V. I., Cincinnati, O.

Worheser, P. C., Capt. Co. G 8th Iowa Cav.

Woodcock, Albert, Major 92nd Ill. Vol., Oregon, Ill.

Wolfley, Lewis, Major 3rd Ky. Cav., New Orleans, La.

Wykoff, P. W., Lieut. 86th Ill. Vol., Henry, Ill.

Young, Thomas L., Brev. Brig.-Gen. U. S. V., Cincinnati, O.

Yeoman, S. W., Brevet Colonel U. S. V., Washington, O.

Zahm, Lewis R., 1st Lieut. and Adj. 3rd O. V. C., Chicago, Ill.

Zahm, Lewis, Colonel 3rd O. V. C., Monroeville, Huron Co., O.

Zellweger, Jacob, Private 9th O. V. I., Ft. Lyon, Colorado Ter.

LIST OF MEMBERS OF THE SOCIETY OF THE ARMY OF THE TENNESSEE.

[Furnished by the Secretary of the Society.]

Armstrong, W. F., Captain, Hillsborough, Ill.

Allen, Jr., David, Capt., St. Louis.

Andre, Wm., Capt., St. Louis, Mo.

Abbott, George, Major, St. Louis, Mo.

Audenried, J. C., Lieut.-Col. Gen. Sherman's Staff, Washington City.

Alexander, L. F., Capt., La Salle, Ill.

Andrews, C. C., Gen., St. Cloud, Minn.

Andel, C., Captain, Belleville, Ill.

Adams, A., Surgeon.

Allen, F. S., Lieut., Chicago, Ill.

Adams, C. H., Lieut.-Col., Chicago, Ill.

Arndt, A. F. R., Major, Detroit, Mich.

Arnold, J. A., Major, Joliet, Ill.

Allen, G. M., Captain.

Averill, John T., General.

Andrews, W. D. E., Captain, Rockford, Ill.

Alexander, J. I., Colonel, Terre Haute, Ind.

Bonner, Frank, Lieutenant.

Buckland, R. P., Gen., Fremont, Ohio.

Belknap, W. W., General, Keokuk, Iowa.

Bleitz, John, St. Louis.

Banks, J. C., Lieutenant, Antwerp, Ohio.

Baldwin, W. H., General, Cincinnati, O.

Bonner, S. P., Surgeon, Cincinnati, O.

Bain, Wm., Lieut., Chicago, Ill.

Buckhannan, R., Col., St. Louis.

Bruce, John, Colonel, Keokuk, Iowa.

Barrett, S. E., Major, Chicago, Ill.

Brinck, W. F., Major, St. Louis, Mo.

Brookman, J. B., Lieut., St. Louis, Mo.

Baily, G. W., Captain, St. Louis, Mo.

Brewster, W. B., Capt., St. Louis, Mo.

Blair, F. P., General, St. Louis, Mo.

Baggs, James, Surgeon, Ontario, O.

Black, W. P., Captain, Champaign, Ill.

Baily, W. N., Surgeon, Plymouth, Ind.

Bixby, A. S., Captain Iowa City, Iowa.

Barnes, J. W., Maj., Warsaw, Ill.

Blizzard, A. C., Lieut., Wilton, Iowa.

Bohn, A. V., Major, Dayton, O.

Blackburn, E. C., Captain, Chicago, Ill.

Benson, H. H., Captain, Muscatine, Iowa.

Borland, J. J., Lieut., Chicago, Ill.

Barber, J., Adjutant, Cleveland, Ohio.

Busey, S. T., General, Urbana, Ill.

Black, Charles, General, Champaign, Ill.

Boggis, Jas. H., Capt., Toledo, O.

Barnum, W. L., Col., Chicago, Ill.

Bracket, G. B., Captain, Denmark, Iowa.

Barto, A., Captain, Geneva, Kane Co., Ill.

Butler, E. G., Lieutenant.

Busse, G. A., Capt, Chicago, Ill.

Bennett, T. W., Gen., Richmond, Ind.

Barre, M. M., General, Quincy, Ill.

Bennett, S. J., Capt., Warrensburg, Mo.

Bigelow, H. E., Captain, Chicago, Ill.
Baker, S. R., Lieut.-Col., Peoria, Ill.
Benton, W. M., Lieut., Chicago, Ill.
Botkin, W. W., Lieut.-Col., Chicago, Ill.
Busse, F. C., Capt., Chicago, Ill.
Bird, H. P., Lieut., Mennekaunee, Wis.
Bryan, O. M., Surg., Sycamore, Ill.
Beath, C. L., Captain, McLean, Ill.
Barlow, W. H., Capt., Effingham, Ill.
Bloomfield, I. J., General, Bloomington, Ill.
Bell, J. B., Major.
Burton, Thomas, Lieutenant, Chicago, Ill.
Baker, John B., Captain, Dwight, Ill.
Blanden, L., General, Harvard, Ill.
Buchanan, R. W., Lieut., Ottawa, Ill.
Brush, C. H., Lieut.-Col., Ottawa, Ill.
Bowen, J. H., Capt., Cincinnati, O.
Bowen, S. M., General, N. Y. City.
Bruce, M., Colonel.
Barlow, A., Captain.
Boyden, A. H., Maj., Chicago, Ill.
Brown, H. S., Col., Chicago, Ill.
Campbell, S., Captain, Cincinnati, Ohio.
Coleman, D. C., Col., St. Louis, Mo.
Cadle, C., Jr., Col., Montgomery, Ala.
Cavender, J. S., Colonel, St. Louis, Mo.
Creamer, F. M., Colonel, Moulton, Ala.
Coates, J. H., Col., St. Louis, Mo.
Campbell, A. H., Bath, Ill.
Colcord, J. P., Lieut., St. Louis, Mo.
Carle, C., Major, Tamaroa, Ill.
Cooverdale, Robert, Captain, Circleville, O.
Castle, George E., Capt., Cairo, Ill.
Corse, J. M., Gen., Chicago, Ill.
Carper, L., Asst. Adj.-Gen., Burlington, Iowa.
Curtiss, J. S., Capt., Chicago, Ill.

Cunningham, C. H., Captain.
Coon, D. E., General, Selma, Ala.
Colby, Enoch, Lieut., Taylorsville, Ill.
Cole, F. W., Lieut., Springfield, Ill.
Cheeney, S. C., Lieut., Munroe, Wis.
Campbell, R. M., Captain, Monmouth, Ill.
Coates, J. H., Captain.
Carpenter, W. R., Maj., N. Y.
Cady, W. F., Surgeon, Lafayette, Ind.
Clarke, Geo. R., Lieut.-Col., Chicago, Ill.
Cook, John, General, Springfield, Ill.
Callahan, C. N., Maj. 3rd U. S. Artillery.
Callender, B. M., Capt., Chicago, Ill.
Christersen, Ch., Major, Oskosh, Wis.
Clark, W. A., Capt., West Liberty, Iowa.
Chadwick, C. C., Capt., Columbus, Ohio.
Cochran, M. B., Surgeon, Davenport, Iowa.
Carr, W. H., Captain, Quincy, Ill.
Case, Charles, Captain, Waukegan, Ill.
Craib, Wm. E., Lieut., Chicago, Ill.
Cooley, C. G., Capt., Chicago, Ill.
Clough, David, Lieutenant.
Cowles, H. R., Lieut.-Col., Washington, Iowa.
Cooper, E. H., Major, Joliet, Ill.
Crane, J. L., Chap., Springfield, Ill.
Cutler, John F., Adjutant, Cleveland, O.
Corning, A., Capt., Cairo, Ill.
Carskeidden, D., Colonel.
Callender, F. D., Gen., St. Louis, Mo.
Campbell, J. C., Captain.
Crowell, R. C., Major, Kansas City, Mo.
Colby, George W., Capt., Selma, Ala.
Douglas, J. C., Capt., Zanesville, Ohio.
Dunn, Wm., Capt., Washington, D. C.

Dawes, E. C., Maj., Cincinnati, O.
Dunn, Hugh, Capt., Zanesville, O.
Dodds, O. J., Lieut.-Col., Cincinnati, O.
Dayton, L. M., Lieut.-Colonel, St. Louis, Mo.
De Gress, Frank, Capt., City of Mexico, Mexico.
Duniling, F. C., Colonel, Virginia City, Mont.
Davis, H. M., Captain, Santa Fe, New Mex.
Dwight, H. O., Lieut., Northampton, Mass.
Dickerson, Joseph, Capt., Cadiz, O.
Doyle, M. A., Lieut., St. Louis, Mo.
Dickey, F. L., Col., Springfield, Ill.
De Gress, J. C., Captain, U. S. A.
Durham, J. B., Capt., Kankakee, Ill.
Derrickson, R. P., Capt., Chicago, Ill.
Duncan, L. A., Major, Niles, Mich.
Dean, H. H., Col., Rockford, Ill.
Dement, H. D., Capt., Dixon, Ill.
Dunn, Jr., W. H., Capt., Washington, D. C.
Dyer, D. P., Col., Louisiana, Mo.
Dodge, G. M., General, Council Bluffs, Iowa.
Duncan, E. A., Surg., Vicksburg, Miss.
Eaton, C. G., General, Clyde, O.
Edwards, A. W., Maj., Carlinville, Ill.
Evans, R. N., Major, Bloomington, Ill.
Ewing, Charles, General, Washington, D. C.
Everest, J. G., Capt., Chicago, Ill.
Elliott, I. H., Gen., Princeton, Ill.
Erskine, A. E., Gen., Chicago. Ill.
Everts, L. H., Maj., Geneva, Kane Co., Ill.
Everts, J., Lieut., Yorkville, Ill.
Eggleston, E. L., Lieut., Litchfield, Mich.
Ewing, H. A., Lieutenant.
Essrager, B., Captain.
Emmerson, G. W., Col., Chicago, Ill.
Eddy, N., Col., South Bend, Ind.
Emery, C. F., Captain.
Eldridge, H. N., General, Chicago, Ill.
Engert, S., Lieutenant.
Edwards, S. R., Lieutenant.

Everett, E., Surgeon, Quincy, Ill.
Fry, J. C., Colonel, Sidney, O.
Fairchild, Cassius, Gen., Milwaukee, Wis.
Ford, Geo. E., Col., Philadelphia, Penn.
Force, M. F., Gen., Cincinnati, O.
Franklin, E. C., Maj., St. Louis, Mo.
Flad, H. C., Col., St. Louis, Mo.
Fisher, C. W., Colonel, Ottumwa, Iowa.
Fox, F. W., Capt., St. Louis, Mo.
Forbis, Wm., Col., St. Louis, Mo.
Flint, M. R., Capt., Shipman, Ill.
Fitch, J. A., Maj., Chicago, Ill.
Fletcher, T. C., Col., St. Louis, Mo.
Foote, W. E., Surg., Cincinnati, O.
Farey, R. B., Capt., Lamoille, Ill.
Fiffe, J. R., Lieut., Magnolia. Ill.
Ferry, Jr., Wm. M., Col., Grand Haven, Mich.
Frowe, S. S., Capt., Springfield, Ill.
Fisher, F. P., Lieut., Chicago, Ill.
Fearing, B. D., Gen., Cincinnati, Ohio.
Fabrique, A. H., Maj., St. Louis, Mo.
Fuller, J. W., Gen., Toledo, O.
Fox, J. H. C., Captain.
Ferrier, T. E., Lieutenant.
Foster, J. T., Col., Chicago, Ill.
Frick, C. A.. Capt., Keithsburg, Ill.
Fisk, C. B., Gen., St. Louis, Mo.
Foster, J. S., Capt., Amelia, O.
Ford, M., Captain.
Foster, J. W., Col., Evansville, Ind.
Foot, G. L., Lieut.-Col., Lacon, Ill.
Funke, Otto, Col., Peoria, Ill.
Felton, Chas. H., Lieut., Chicago, Ill.
Fallows, Samuel, Gen., Milwaukee, Wis.
Fry, T. W., Col., Lafayette, Ind.
Fry, J. C., Col., Sidney, O.
Flansburg, N., Lieutenant, Galena, Henry Co., Ill.
Foster, Lyonel, Surgeon.
Furguson. D., Lieutenant.
Gile, D. H., Capt., Louisville, Ky.
Griffin, C. E., Lieut., Hamilton, O.
Goodwin, Geo. J., Capt., St. Louis, Mo.
Gilmore, F. H., Capt., St. Louis, Mo.

Graves, W. H., Col., Toledo, O.
Grier, D. P., Gen., Peoria, Ill.
Goodbrake, C., Surg., Clinton, Ill.
Glading, C., Lieut., Chicago, Ill.
Grave, P., Lieut.-Col., Albion, Mich.
Gere, W. B., Colonel.
Godfrey. H. W., Lieut., Quincy, Ill.
Graves, S. E., Capt., Adrian, Mich.
Garber, M. C., Col., Madison, Ind.
Guthrie, J. W., Assist.-Surgeon.
Grey, H. L., Lieutenant.
Gresham, W. Q., Gen., New Albany, Ind.
Gooding, E. L., Capt., Lockport, Ill.
Gregg, Jno. W., Capt., Chicago, Ill.
Hill, E. S., Surgeon, Oxford, O.
Hunt, F. B., Col., Cincinnati, O.
Highway, A. E., Surg., Cincinnati, Ohio.
Henry, C. D., Captain.
Hoover, J. S., Col., Middleton, Ind.
Hartshorne, D. W., Major, Cincinnati. O.
Henerich, John S., Lieut., Cincinnati, O.
Harper, T. L., Maj., Cincinnati, O.
Hughes, J. H., Lieut., Cincinnati, Ohio.
Heath, T. T., Gen., Cincinnati, O.
Hodges, W. R., Capt., St. Louis, Mo.
Harding, Chester, Gen., St. Louis, Mo.
Hawkins, W. J., Maj., St. Louis, Mo.
Holtzinger, L. M., Lieut., St. Louis, Mo.
Hequembourg, W. A., Lieut.-Col., St. Louis, Mo.
Haverly, C. R., Capt., St. Louis, Mo.
Hedley, F. Y., Capt., Bunker Hill, Ill.
Hunter. G. H., Capt., Ottawa, Ill.
How, J. F., Lieut.-Col., St. Louis, Mo.
Hicks, S. J., Col., Salem, Ill.
High, Frank, Lieut., St. Louis, Mo.
Herbert, J. T., Lieut.-Col., Liverpool, O.
Heath, W. H., Lieut., St. Louis, Mo.
Henry, W. C., Maj., Freestown, O.
Hitt, J. E., Capt., Oregon, Ill.

Hammond, J. H., General, Chillicothe, Mo.
Hill, W. W., Lieut.-Col., Cincinnati, O.
Hickenlooper, A., Gen., Cincinnati, Ohio.
Hitt, J. W., Lieut., Mt. Morris, Ill.
Holman, J. H., Gen., St. Louis, Mo.
Hildt, Geo. H., Lieut.-Col., Canal Dover, O.
Hendrick, J. M., Col., Ottumwa, Iowa.
Hopkins, M., Assist.-Surgeon.
Hall, John P., Col., Morganfield, Union Co., Ky.
Hamilton, C. S., Gen., Fond du Lac, Wis.
Hunt, Wm., Lieut., Springfield. O.
Harts, D. H., Capt., Chicago, Ill.
Higgens, A. D., Lieutenant.
Hoyt, H. W. B., Captain.
High, F., Captain.
Hill. J. M., Captain.
Healford, G. H., Lieut., Chicago, Ill.
Hatch, R. B., Lieut.-Col., Chicago, Ill.
Hart, L. W., Capt., Cleveland, O.
Hitchcock, P. M., Lieut., Cleveland, O.
Hawthorn, John, Lieutenant.
Hensey, G. E., Capt., Keosanqua, Iowa.
Hamilton, J. D., Captain.
Hawke, A. J., Lieut.-Col., New Albany, Ind.
Hale. G. W., Adj., Chicago, Ill.
Hurlbut, S. A., Gen., Belvidere, Ill.
Hosmer, H P., Capt., Chicago, Ill.
Hunt, J. S., Surg., Chicago, Ill.
Hoover, H., Captain, Muscatine, Iowa.
Hugunin, Jas. R., Gen., Chicago, Ill.
Howe, Jas. H., Col., Chicago, Ill.
Hotaling, J. R., Maj., Rochelle, Ill.
Hunting, C. H., Lieut., Chicago, Ill.
Hamill, W. B., Lieut., Cedar Falls, Iowa.
Hamilton, J. C., Maj., Owatonna, Minn
Hoge, Geo. B., Col., Ft. Duncan, Texas.
Hurry, W. C., Major.
Hazen, W. B., Gen., Ft. Harker, Kansas.

Irwin, B. J. D., Surgeon, Detroit, Mich.

Jacobs, W. C., Major, Akron, O.

Jenney, W. L. B., Major, Chicago, Ill.

Judd, Wm. H., Captain, Jefferson City, Mo.

Johnson, W. A., Captain, Grand Lake, Ark.

Johnson, E. S., Maj., Springfield, Illinois.

Joel, E. M., Lieut.-Col., St. Louis, Missouri.

Jonas, E., Captain, Quincy, Ill.

Janes, II. W., Captain, Fortress Monroe, Va.

Jones, Theodore, Gen., Columbus, Ohio.

Jacobs, W. C., Surg., Akron, O.

Johnston, N., Lieut.

Kersey, II. E., Lieut., Bethalti, Madison Co., Ill.

Kellogg, C. C., Col., Oberlin, O.

Klink, J. G., Col., Rochester, N. Y.

King, S. Noble, Lieut., Blooming-ton, Ill.

Keppler, C. W., Capt., Newark, O.

Kniffner, Wm. C., Gen., Belleville, Illinois.

Ketteler, C. H., Capt., Waterloo, Illinois.

Keer, Daniel, Lieut., Edwardsville, Illinois.

Kinsman, O. D., Lieut.-Col., Clinton, Iowa.

Knox, Kilburn, Col., Philadelphia, Pennsylvania.

Keeler, Wm. B., Col., Muscatine, Iowa.

Keables, B. F., Maj., Pella, Ia.

Kenyon, N. C., Lieut.-Col., Chatsworth. Ill.

Knox, Wm. A., Surgeon, Chicago, Illinois.

Kennard, G. W., Major, Champaign, Ill.

Knipe, J. F., Gen., Harrisburg, Pennsylvania.

Krughoff, Louis, Major, Nashville, Illinois.

Kalb, J. C., Surg., Columbus, O.

Kemper, A , Capt., St. Louis, Mo.

Knispel, C. P., Captain, Belleville, Illinois.

Kinney, T. J., Gen., Vermont, Ill.

Kleckner, G. S., Captain.

Klein, Otto.

Keeler, M. E., Lieut., Belvidere, Illinois.

Kinslow, A. S., Lieut., Ottawa, Ill.

Kittoe, E. D., Surg., Galena, Ill.

Landrum, W. J., Col., Lancaster, Kentucky.

Leggett, M. D., Maj.-Gen., Zanesville, O.

Laniman, J., Lieut., Napoleon, O.

Lain, S. M., Captain.

Lewis, J. V., Capt., St. Louis, Mo.

Landeman, O. C., Capt., St. Louis, Missouri.

Loomis, John Mason, Col., Chicago, Ill.

Logan, John A., Gen., Washington, D. C.

Logan, John, Col., Carlinsville, Ill.

Lippincott, Charles E., General, Chandlerville, Ill.

Lowe, S. A., Capt., Chicago, Ill.

Logan, Thomas, Lieut.-Col., Carthage, Ill.

Leuke, J. B., Lieut.-Col., Davenport, Ia.

Lewis, J. C., Capt., Buchanan, Ill.

Lutz, N. L., Capt., Chicago. Ill.

Leib, II., Gen., Springfield, Ill.

Lucas, E. W., Lieut.-Col., Iowa City, Iowa.

Lacey, M. M., Major, Richmond, Indiana.

Lariner, James R., Capt., Bloomington, Ill.

Ledyard, G. C., Captain, Chicago, Illinois.

Lanstrum, C., Captain, Galesburg, Illinois.

Lovejoy, F. E., Adj., Litchfield, Michigan.

Lawrence, E. C., Lieut., Chicago, Illinois.

Loop, C. B., Major, Belvidere, Ill.

Lynch, W. F., Col., Elgin, Ill.

LaMotle, R. S., Major.

Murphy, D. A., Lieut., St. Louis, Missouri.

Mason, R. II., Capt., Chicago, Ill.

Murphy, P. II., Colonel, St. Louis, Missouri.

Miles, Joseph, Lieut., Louisville, Kentucky.

Moss, J. Thomson, Lieut., Cincinnati, O.

Munson, G. D., Lieut.-Col., Zanesville, O.

Mueller, A.

Meumann, Theodore, Col., East St. Louis, Ill.
Miller, P., Major, Liverpool, O.
Miller, M., Gen., Galena, Ill.
Martin, A., Lieut.
Mitman, William, Capt.
Moffat, T. S., Capt., Chicago, Ill.
Mead, W. G., Lieut., Chicago, Ill.
Mahon, Samuel, Major, Ottumwa, Iowa.
Merrill, N. II., Capt., Buchanan, Michigan.
Mather, T. S., Col., Springfield, Illinois.
Marsh, J. R., Dr., Chicago, Ill.
Madgeburg, F. II., Capt., Milwaukee, Wis.
Martin, James, Gen., Salem, Ill.
Morton, ——, Col., St. Louis, Mo.
Mitchell, S. M., Gen., Columbus, Ohio.
Merril, W. T., Captain.
Mason, W. B., Capt., Bloomington, Illinois.
Matz, O. II., Col., Ass't Engineer, Chicago, Ill.
Maguire, G. A., Capt., St. Louis, Missouri.
Moore, J. A., Chaplain.
Marshal, Wm. R., Gen., St. Paul, Minnesota.
Markland, A. II., Col., Washington, D. C.
Merrill, S., Gen., DesMoines, Ia.
Manville, C. P., Lieutenant.
Munroe, J. II., Major, Muscatine, Iowa.
Mayer, D. W., General.
Moore, J. T., Lieut.-Col., Lima, Ohio.
Moore, John, Col., Parkersburg, West Virginia.
Mower, J. A., Gen., New Orleans, Louisiana.
May, Dwight, Gen., Kalamazoo, Michigan.
Martin, O., Lieutenant.
Moore, L. W., Capt., Edwardsville, Illinois.
Mason, George, Major, Chicago, Illinois.
Martin, Edward, Lieut., Chicago, Illinois.
McDowell, M., Major, Cincinnati, Ohio.
McClernand, J. A., Gen., Springfield, Ill.

Mac Feeley, R., Col., Chicago, Ill.
McCook, Ed., Gen., Springfield, Illinois.
McGrew, J. S., Lieut.-Col., Cincinnati, O.
McDonald, Jon., Lieut.-Col., Saint Louis, Mo.
McLean, Capt., St. Louis, Mo.
McGruth, John, Major.
McArthur, John, Gen., Chicago, Illinois.
McCoy, J. C., Lieut.-Col., Peatville, Ill.
McFall, Gen., St. Louis, Mo.
McKinney, Capt., Peoria, Ill.
McClayberry, R. W., Major.
McAulery, J. T., Capt., Chicago, Illinois.
McIntosh, A., Capt., Joliet, Ill.
McDermott, R., Lieut.-Col., Dayton, O.
McCartney, J. A., Lieut., Chicago, Illinois.
McCauley, P. II., Major, Milwaukee, Wis.
McGrath, P., Capt., Chicago, Ill.
McNeil, II. C., Lieut., Davenport, Iowa.
McMillan, Charles, Surgeon, N. Y. City.
McArthur, II. C., Major, Memphis, Missouri.
McGinnis, G. S., Gen., Indianapolis, Ind.
McKindly, S. J., Captain.
McCaleb, II. A., Col., Ottawa, Ill.
Nichols, F. C., Major, St. Joseph, Wisconsin.
Noble, J. W., Gen., St. Louis, Mo.
Newsham, T. J., Major, Edwardsville, Ill.
Neely, J. C., Capt., Chicago, Ill.
Nichols, E. A., Capt., Chicago, Ill.
Noleman, R. D., Capt., Centralia, Illinois.
Newton, D. C., Captain, Batavia, Kane Co., Ill.
Nesh, J., Captain.
Nichols, R., Surgeon, Bloomington, Ill.
Norton, J. B., Major, Earlville, Ill.
Noble, II. T., Col., Dixon, Ill.
Neil, J. B., Major, Columbus, O.
Nutt, E. E., Captain.
Noyes, E. F., Gen., Cincinnati, O.
Nichols, A. N., Major.
Nelson, William, Major U. S. A.

O'Connell, John, Capt., St. Louis, Missouri.
Oglesby, R. J., Gen., Decatur, Ill.
Owsley, W. T., Surgeon, Paducah, Kentucky.
Oliver, II.
O'Kane, J., Lieut.-Colonel.
Oliver, J. M., Gen., Little Rock, Arkansas.
Patier, Charles O., Captain, Cairo, Illinois.
Parker, Eli, General, Washington, D. C.
Peckham, James, Col., St. Louis, Missouri.
Phillips, Julius, Capt., Hillsboro, Illinois.
Parrott, J. C., General, Keokuk, Iowa.
Porter, F. G., Surgeon, St. Louis, Missouri.
Putnam, C. N., Captain.
Padon, William, Major, Troy, Ill.
Pitzman, Julius, Capt., St. Louis, Missouri.
Phillips, J. J., Lieut.-Col., Hillsboro, Ill.
Pope, A. J., Major, Sigourney, Ia.
Pike, R. W., Lieut., Chicago, Ill.
Parker, W. B., Lieut., Chicago, Ill.
Parker, W. B., Lieut., Douglas, Ia.
Puterbaugh, G., Capt., Peoria, Ill.
Perkins, John L., Major, Burlington, Ia.
Pitman, W. G., Captain, Madison, Kentucky.
Pressel, D. W., Lieut., Keokuk, Ia.
Pullen, J. O., Capt., Bloomington, Illinois.
Putnam, W. H., Capt., DesMoines, Iowa.
Peters, M. H., Captain.
Pope, John, Gen., Detroit, Mich.
Perry, J. J., Captain.
Page, E. E., Lieut., Naperville, Ill.
Plummer, S. E., Surgeon, Rock Island, Ill.
Pierce, G. T., Colonel, Valparaiso, Indiana.
Pike, E. W., Lieut., Chicago, Ill.
Poke, D. W., Lieut., Warrensburg, Missouri.
Proutz, Ira, Captain, Dayton, O.
Pearson, R. N., Gen., Springfield, Illinois.
Polk, William, Captain, Freeport, Illinois.

Peek, W. G., Major, Ironton, Mo.
Pummill, John, Lieut.-Col., Cincinnati, Ohio.
Potter, J. B., Surgeon, Columbus, Ohio.
Paddock, G. L., Major, Chicago, Illinois.
Pierson, G. L., Lieutenant.
Pride, G. G., Col., New York City.
Perry, A. C., Major, Michigan City, Ind.
Peirounette, C. A., Capt., Arlington, Ill.
Powell, E., Maj., Chicago, Ill.
Peterson, R. H., Lieut.-Col., Philadelphia, Pa.
Potts, B. F., Gen., Columbus, O.
Quinby, S. J., Surgeon, Memphis, Tennessee.
Rawlins, J. A., Gen., Washington, D. C.
Romer, Francis, Col., St. Louis, Missouri.
Ravold, Wm., Lieut., St. Louis, Missouri.
Randolph, M., Capt., Cincinnati, Ohio.
Reynolds, Thos., Col., Madison, Wisconsin.
Rowett, R., Gen., Carlinville, Ill.
Reed, H. T., Gen., Keokuk, Iowa.
Ryan, A. H., Col., Fort Smith, Arkansas.
Ross, E. C., Major, Washington City.
Reed, John, Capt., St. Louis, Mo.
Roots, L. H., Lieut.-Col., DeValls Bluff, Ark.
Reid, David O., Captain, Rock Island, Ill.
Ruff, W. A., Capt., Chicago, Ill.
Reese, Theodore, Captain, Evanston, Ill.
Rowley, W. R., Gen., Galena, Ill.
Ross, L. F., Gen., Avon, Ill.
Ruggles, J. M., Gen., Havana, Ill.
Richmond, J. F., Capt., St. Charles, Ill.
Ribsame, Chris., Captain, Decatur, Ill.
Reynolds, J. S., Gen., Chicago, Ill.
Reid, J. M., Lieut.-Col., Keokuk, Iowa.
Rogers, J., Lieut., Chicago, Ill.
Ransom, J P., Lieutenant.
Rogers, Geo. C., Gen., Chicago, Ill.

Roberts, A. J., Lieutenant.
Rumsey, J. W., Capt., Chicago, Ill.
Rumsey, I. P., Capt., Chicago, Ill.
Routh, John L., Capt., Blooming-
ton, Ill.
Rossett, L., Lieut., Springfield, Ill.
Reid, R. M., Adj., Rock Island, Ill.
Rosenbaum, H., Capt., Toledo, O.
Rutger, F., Lieut., Belvidere, Ill.
Randall, J. R., Capt., Wilmington,
Ill.
Rice, E. W., Maj.-Gen., Oskaloo-
sa, Iowa.
Rose. L. M., Capt., Cincinnati, O.
Riggin, John, Gen., St. Louis, Mo.
Reiley, W. N., Captain.
Rittenouer, E., Lieut., Chicago, Ill.
Rusk, J. M., Gen., Madison, Wis.
Rose, F. M., Maj., Winona, Minn.
Smith, John E., Maj.-Gen., Galena,
Ill.
Silversparre, A., Captain, Chicago,
Ill.
Sullivan, P. J., Col., Cincinnati, O.
Smith, Giles A., Maj.-Gen., Bloom-
ington, Ill.
Swayne, Wager, Gen., Columbus,
Ohio.
Spooner, B., Gen., Lawrenceburgh,
Ind.
Spear, E., Capt., Warren, O.
Simpson, P. J., Lieut.-Col., Green-
ville, O.
Schuster, George, St. Louis, Mo.
Sanborn, J. B., General, St. Paul,
Minn.
Sheldon, C. S., St. Louis, Mo.
Sanford, W. W., Gen., St. Louis,
Mo.
Simpson, Samuel P., Lieut.-Col.,
Jefferson City, Mo.
Short, R. W., Capt., Brighton, Ill.
Steckle, J. H., Lieut., St. Louis,
Mo.
Seymour, W. B., Captain.
Spring, E. S., Lieut., Macon, Mo.
Simmons, T. H., Lieutenant.
Strong, W. E., Gen., Chicago, Ill.
Stebbins, F. G., Lieutenant.
Smith, A. J., Gen., St. Louis, Mo.
Sabine, A., Major, Jeffersonville,
Ind.
Safeley, J. J., Maj., Ottumwa, Iowa.
Schofield, H., Col., Washington,
Ind.
Semple, Jas., Lieut., Keokuk, Iowa.
Sears, D. B., Lieut., Moline, Ill.

Sotterfield, T. R., Chaplain.
Smith, H. B., Captain.
Sherburne, E. A., Captain.
Stewart, Owen, Col., Chicago, Ill.
Smith, M. L., Gen., St. Louis, Mo.
Stafford, E. F., Capt., Batavia, Ill.
Silva, C. P., Lieut., Chicago, Ill.
Swarthout, W., Lieut.-Col., Quin-
cy, Ill.
Scheel, T. E., Lieut., E. St. Louis,
Mo.
Scates, W. B., Gen., Chicago, Ill.
Starring, F. A., Gen., Chicago, Ill.
Smith, R. A., Captain.
Shane, John, Col., Vinton, Iowa.
Scribner, W. S., Lieut., Helena,
Montana.
Sturges, H., Capt., Lincoln, Ill.
Shedd, Warren, General, Warrens-
burg, Mo.
Smith, A. J., Capt., Chillicothe, O.
Still, Rob. A., Capt., Chicago, Ill.
Simpson, John E., Maj., Indianap-
olis, Ind.
Smith, Miles, Col., Keokuk, Iowa.
Scammon, Charles T., Maj., Chi-
cago, Ill.
Stewart, W. H., Capt., Ottumwa,
Iowa.
Smith, H. H., Champaign, Ill.
Smith, J. M., Capt., Chicago, Ill.
Stone, J. C., Colonel, Burlington,
Iowa.
Smith, J. A., Capt., Mattoon, Ill.
Smith, W. S., Gen., Chicago, Ill.
Scott, John, Col., Nevada, Iowa.
Sanders, A. H., Gen., Davenport,
Iowa.
Stockdale, S. H., Maj., New Or-
leans, La. .
Stockton, Joseph, Gen., Chicago,
Ill.
Sprague, J. W., General, Winona,
Minn.
Stewart, A. S., Capt., Woodstock,
Ill.
Skinner, H. Lieut.-Col., Winona,
Minn.
Strong, W. A., Capt., Chicago, Ill.
Taylor, Ezra, Gen., Chicago, Ill.
Tytler, S. S., Lieutenant.
Towne, R. R., Lieut.-Colonel, Du
Quoin, Ill.
Towne, H. M., Lieutenant.
Tompkins, Logan, Maj., St. Louis,
Mo.
Townsend, C. D., Maj., Chicago, Ill.

Teed, D., Captain, Evanston, Ill.
Tyner, N. N., Captain, Davenport, Iowa.
Tullis, Jas., Lieut.-Col., Lafayette, Ind.
Tillson, John, Gen., Quincy, Ill.
Thomas, D. C., General.
Toby, E. P., Lieut., Chicago, Ill.
Thomson, T. H., Capt., Geneva, Ill.
Terry, U. J., Lieutenant.
Taggart, C.. Capt., Freeport, Ill.
True, J. M., Gen., Mattoon, Ill.
Taylor, F. M., Lieut., Chicago, Ill.
True, J. W., Maj., Mattoon, Ill.
Titcomb, J. S., Captain.
Towner, H. N., Maj., Chicago, Ill.
Thompson, J. N., Maj., St. Joseph, Mo.
Taggart, Sam'l L., Dubuque, Iowa.
Underwood, N. C., Lieut., Chicago, Ill.
Underwood, B. W., Lieut., Chicago, Ill.
Van Seller, H., Lieut.-Col., Paris, Ill.
Van Blessing, L., Col., Toledo, O.
Voges, Theo., Capt., Cleveland, O.
Vanhoff, Henry D., Lieut., Springfield, Ill.
Vogelson, W. M., Lieut.-Col., Columbus, O.
Van Duzen, D., Col., Litchfield, Ill.
Wright, W. R., Col., Canton, Ill.
Winslow, C. S., Gen., Cincinnati, Ohio.
Wilson, H., Col., Sidney, O.
Woods, C. R., Maj.-Gen., Newark, Ohio.
Wyne, Wm. M., Lieut., Columbus, Ohio.
Walsh, P. J., Maj., Cincinnati, O.
Waterhouse, N. C., Col., Hannibal, Mo.
Walcutt, C. C., Gen., Columbus, Ohio.
Woods, W. B., Gen., Newark, O.
Wilson, T. P., General, St. Paul, Minn.
Ward, Durbin, Gen., Lebanon, O.
Welch, D. N., Capt., New Haven, Conn.
Walker, J. B., Capt., Cincinnati, O.
Woodhull, Max., Gen., N. Y. City.
Wanglein, H., Gen., Belleville, Ill.
Webber, D., Col., Cincinnati, O.
Ware, W. E., Maj., St. Louis, Mo.

Webster, D. H., Capt., LaCrosse, Wis.
Wright, H., Capt., Franklin, Ill.
Williams, M. H., Col., Dixon, Ill.
Willard, L. S., Major, Litchfield, Ill.
Wagner, Louis, Lieutenant.
Wilheims, J. H., Captain.
Wright, W. W., General, Leavenworth, Kan.
Woodworth, J. M., Surg., Chicago, Ill.
Wallace, Wm. L., Gen., Ashland, Ohio.
Wilson, T. P., Capt., Cambridge, Ohio.
Whittenhall, D. S., Captain.
Webber, C., Col., Springfield, Ill.
Wilson, F. C., Lieut., Chicago, Ill.
Woodward, F. J., Capt., South Pass, Union Co., Ill.
Wetmore, S. R., Col., St. Louis, Mo.
Webster, J. D., Gen., Chicago, Ill.
Wickliffe, J H., Lieutenant.
Whittlesey, L. H., Col., Chicago, Ill.
Webber, J. C., Gen., Springfield, Ill.
White, J. G., Captain.
Welker, F.. Capt., Mt. Vernon, O.
White, J. W., Col., Aurora, Ill.
Wood, E. J., Lieut.-Col., Goshen, Ind.
Wilson, F. H., Maj., Newark, O.
Warner, Jno., Lieut.-Col., Clinton, Ill.
Wilcox, J. S., Gen., Elgin, Ill.
White, M. H., Maj., Cincinnati, O.
Welles, G. E., Gen., Toledo, O.
Winans, J. L., Lieut., Benton Harbor, Mich.
Waid, H. A., Lieutenant.
Warner, V., Capt., Clinton, Ill.
Williams, C. C., Capt., Boonsborough, Iowa.
Williams, G. C., Lieutenant.
Woodbury, H. H., Adj., Chicago, Ill.
Webber, A. B., Captain.
Wallace, Thomas, Capt., Chicago, Ill.
Walker, W. B., Lieut., Harvard, Ill.
Warrens, C. H., Lieutenant.
Whiting, ——, Lieutenant.
Weaver, C. R., Col., Ft. Madison, Iowa.

Wilson, J. H., Maj.-Gen., Keokuk, Iowa.

Wilson, O. M., Maj., Indianapolis, Ind.

Williams, D. H., Lieut.-Colonel, Rochester, Minn.

Woods, P. N., Surgeon, Fairfield, Iowa.

Wood, John, Col., Quincy, Ill.

Worden, A., Maj., Oskosh, Wis.

Wood, W. W., Lieut., Belvidere, Ill.

York, L. E., Gen., Cincinnati, O.

Young, Wm., Capt., Freeport, Ill.

Zickerick, Wm., Capt., Fond du Lac, Wis.

Zearing, J. R., Maj., Dover, Ill.

LIST OF MEMBERS OF THE SOCIETY OF THE ARMY OF THE OHIO.

[*Furnished by the Secretary of the Society.*]

J. M. Schofield, U. S. A., Maj.-Gen. Army of Ohio.

J. D. Cox, Major-Gen. 23rd A. C., Cincinnati, O.

Alfred H. Terry, Major-Gen. U. S. A., 10th A. C.

Jas. H. Ledlie, Brig.-Gen. 9th A. C., Chicago, Ill.

J. S. Casement, Brig.-Gen., Painesville, O., 23rd A. C.

I. N. Stiles, Brig.-Gen. 23rd A. C. Army Ohio, Chicago, Ill.

Wm. M. Wherry, Brev. Col. U. S. A., A. D. C. Army Ohio.

J. A. Campbell, Lieut.-Col. U. S. A., A. D. C. Army Ohio.

G. W. Schofield, Brevet Col. U. S. A., A. D. C. Army Ohio.

Wm. Ennis, Brev. Capt. U. S. A., 4th A. C.

C. J. True, Col. 23rd A. C., Lexington, Ky.

Jno. Mason Brown, Col. 23rd A. C., Frankfort, Ky.

Julius White, Brig. and Brev. Major-Gen. 23rd and 9th Corps, Chicago, Ill.

H. J. Hayden, Brevet Maj. 9th C., Boston, Mass.

Horace Capron, Col. and Brevet Brig.-Gen. 23rd A. C. U. S. A., Washington, D. C.

George Stoneman, Brig. and Maj.-Gen. Dist. No. 1, Richmond, Va.

Walter S. Babcock, Lieut.-Col. 12th U. S. C. H. A. 23rd C., Chicago, Illinois.

Horace Dexter, Capt. 17th Mass. 23rd C., Chicago, Ill.

E. H. Hobson, Brig.-Gen. 23rd A. C., Greensburg, Ky.

Emory S. Bond, Lieut.-Col. 112th Ill. Inf., Chicago, Ill.

S. M. Letcher, Brevet Col. Chief Cm. Gen. Schofield's Staff, Lexington, Ky.

C. Fitz Simons, Brevet Brig.-Gen. 9th C., Chicago, Ill.

C. D. Rhodes, Captain A. A. G. Vols., Chicago, Ill.

W. M. Dunn, Brevet Brig.-Gen. U. S. A.

A. C. Loomis, Lieut. 23rd A. C., Chicago, Ill.

R. A. Remick, Lieut. 23rd A. C., Chicago, Ill.

E. W. Seymour, Lieut. Res. Arty. Brig., Chicago, Ill.

D. C. Bradley, Capt. 23rd A. C., Chicago, Ill.

C. H. Maple, Capt. and C. S. 23rd Chicago, Ill.

J. W. Brockway, Capt. Elgin Bat. 23rd A. C., Chicago, Ill.

A. M. Wood, Capt. 23rd A. C., Chicago, Ill.

D. G. Rush, Major U. S. V., Chicago, Ill.

W. W. Wheeler, Col. 28th Mich., Chicago, Ill.

Wm. E. Clarke, Major Army Ohio, Chicago, Ill.

Thos. H. McBride, Capt. 100th P. V. 9th A. C.

Henry C. Brennan, Capt. 20th Ky. Vol. Inf., Lexington, Ky.

R. W. Smith, Brevet Brig.-Gen. 16th Ill. Cav. 9th A. C., Chicago, Illinois.

George Howison, 1st Lieut. 79th N. Y. Highlanders, Chicago, Ill.

J. P. Tanner, Jr., 104th O. V. I., Chicago, Ill.

Geo. L. Hartsuff, Brevet Maj.-Gen. Ass't Adj.-Gen. U. S. A.

J. W. Wallace, Capt. 16th Ky. Vet. Vol. Chicago, Ill.

E. W. Whitaker, Brevet Brig.-Gen. U. S. V. Cav. Hartford, Conn.

O. E. Babcock, Brevet Brig.-Gen. Gen. Grant's Staff, U. S. A., Washington, D. C.

Albert B. Capron, Capt. 14th Ill.
Cav., Kenosha, Wis.
Henry Curtis, Jr., Brevet Lieut.-
Col. Vol. and A. A. G. 23rd C.,
Rock Island, Ill.
Isaac R. Sherwood, B. B. General
111th O. V. I., Bryda, O
Jas. G. Hatchitt, 23rd A. C., Frank-
fort, Ky.
M. G. Ransom, Lieut. Bat. D 1st
Ohio Art., Cleveland, O.
G. S. Wormer, B. B. Gen. 1st Brig.
4th Div. 23rd A. C., Detroit,
Michigan.
W. E. Hobson, Col. 13th Ky. V. I.
23rd A. C., Bowling Green, Ky.
J. Stearns Smith, Adj. 6th N. H.
V. Vol. 9th A. C., Chicago, Ill.
Levi T. Schofield, Capt. 103rd O.
V. I., Cleveland, O.
Elisha Mix, B. B. Gen., Allegan,
Mich.
R. S. Montgomery, Capt. 23rd A.
C., Rock Island, Ill.
L. S. Trowbridge, Col. and Brevet
Maj.-Gen. 10th Mich. Cav. 23rd
A. C., Detroit, Mich.
W. H. Bailhache, Capt. A. Q. M.
2nd Div. 23rd A. C., Quincy, Ill.
Jno. C. Joss, 1st Lieut. 3rd Div.
9th A. C., Centreville, Mich.
Jno. Mehringer, Brig.-Gen. 2nd
Div. 23rd A. C., Louisville, Ky.
H. M. Bacon, Chaplain 63rd Ind.
Vol., Toledo, O.
C. A. Zollinger, Col. 129th Mich.,
New Haven, Mich.
J. H. Wells, Capt. 29th Mich. 23rd
A. C., Kalamazoo, Mich.
Geo. S. Neuman, 1st Lieut. 17th
Mich. Inf. 9th A. C., Chicago,
Illinois.
Adam Waite, Maj. 100th and 189th
Ohio, Toledo, O.
Andrew Young, Capt. 65th Ill. Inf.,
Chicago, Ill.
C. E. Sargeant, Capt. 103rd Ohio,
Racine, Wis.
W. H. Harris, Lieut.-Col. Headq'rs
Army of Ohio, Indianapolis, Ind.
Wm. O. Watts, Capt. 37th Ky.
N. Daniels, Capt. Sig. Office, May-
ville, Wis.
H. Tindall, Lieut.-Col.
B. O. Carr, Col. and A. Q. M.,
formerly of General Schofield's
Staff.

H. H. French, Major Headq'rs A.
of Ohio, Chicago, Ill.
H. S. Pickards, Major 103rd O. V.
I., Cleveland, O.
J. H. Colvin, Capt. Colvin's Bat.
Ill. Light Art., Chicago, Ill.
J. J. Ruby, Lieut. 14th Ill. Cav.,
Chicago. Ill.
R. M. J. Miller, Captain 65th Ind.
Vol. Inf., Princeton, Ind.
S. G. Remington. Private 19th O.
Bat., Adrian, Mich.
S. A. Whitfield, Capt 9th N. H. V.,
Cincinnati, O.
Jas. Daly, Captain, Chicago, Ill.
F. J. Joliat, Colonel 15th Mo. Vol.
Inf., Chicago, Ill.
O. B. Todd, Lieut. 120th Ind. Inf.,
Laporte, Ind.
W. S. Stewart, Col. 65th Ill. V. V.,
Chicago. Ill.
Geo. P. Lyon, 1st Lieut. 65th Ill.
V. Vol. Chief C. S. A. of O.,
Chicago, Ill.
R. B. Treat, Col., C. C. S. Army
of Ohio, New York.
C. P. Washburn, Capt. 118th O. V.
I., Little Rock, Ark.
H. H. Thomas, Capt. and A. A. G.
3rd Div. 23rd Corps, Nashville,
Tenn.
E. A. Scovill, Lieut.-Col. 128th O.
V. I., Cleveland, O.
O. L. Spaulding, Col. 23rd Mich.,
St. John's, Mich.
E. B. Whitman, Lieut.-Col. A. Q.
M., Capt. and A. Q. M. Army
Ohio, Louisville, Ky.
T. E. Milchrist, Captain 112th Ill.
Vol., Galva, Ill.
J. F. Bond, Brevet Brig.-Gen. A.
Q. M., Memphis, Tenn.
Milo S. Hascall, Brig.-Gen. 2nd
Div. 23rd A. C., Goshen, Ind.
E. L. Mottley, Lieut.-Col. 3rd Div.
1st Brig., Bowling Green, Ky.
T. J. Henderson, Brevet Brig.-Gen.
3rd Brig. 3rd Div. 23rd A. C.,
Princeton, Ill.
R. S. Baker, Captain 1st Brig. 1st
Div., 9th A. C., Port Huron,
Michigan.
Chris. Miller, Capt. 10th Ind. Vol.,
Chicago, Ill.
Theo. Crowl, 2nd Lieut. 178th C.
V. I., 23rd A. C., Darlington,
Pennsylvania.

E. A. Starling, Col. 35th Ky. Inf., Hopkinsville, Ky.

E. R. Kerstetter, Captain 2nd Div. 23rd A. C., Goshen, Ind.

L. J. Croxton, Capt. and A. Q. M., Goshen, Ind.

M. D. Manson, Brig.-Gen. 23rd A. C., Crawfordsville, Ind.

M. B. Hascall, Lieut.-Col. Army Ohio, Goshen, Ind.

N. S. Barnes, Lieut.-Col. Surg. U. S. V., Chicago, Ill.

J. E. Mullaly, Maj. 17th Miss. Vol. 23rd A. C., Chicago, Ill.

H. C. Babcock, 1st Lieut. 23rd A. C., Waupun, Wis.

Rufus Cheney, Paymaster.

N. M. Curtis, Brig. and Brev. Maj.-Gen., Ogdensburg, N. Y.

A. Pearson, 1st Lieut. 4th Div. 23rd A. C., Ot awa, Ill.

O. W. Steel, Col. 23rd A. C., New York.

N. H. Church, Capt. 124th U. S. C. T. and Adj. G. D. of K., Potska, Indiana.

J. W. Ames, Brevet Brig.-Gen. 3rd Brig. 3rd Div. 10th Corps, Burlington. Iowa.

A. A. Dewey, Capt. 112th Ill. 23rd A. C., Chicago, Ill.

S. C. Burham, Colonel and C. S., formerly of General Schofield's Staff.

J. S. McClelland, 1st. Lieut. 5th U. S. T. of 129th Ind., Galesburg, Illinois.

Sol. DeLong. Lieut.-Col. 23rd A. C., Fort Wayne, Ind.

Capt. C. McKinney 10th Ill., Dallas City. Ill.

Thos. L. Young, Brevet Brig.-Gen. 118th Ohio Vol. Inf., Cincinnati, Ohio.

H. G. Griffin, 1st Lieut. 112th Ill. Inf., Cambridge, Ill.

R. F. Steele, 2nd Lieut. 112th Ill. Inf., Genesco, Ill.

J. C. Phillips, Captain 23rd A. C., Chicago, Ill.

B. F. Toof, 1st Lieut. 83rd Ill., Dallas City, Ill.

R. H. Lomax, 1st Lieut. 83rd Ill., Dallas City, Ill.

W. A. Gibson, Private 124th Ind. Vol., Cincinnati, O.

E. H. Bacon, Captain, New York.

D. Kuckman, Private 29th N. Y. Vol. 11th A. C., Eton, Ohio.

S. D. Burchard. Captain and A. Q. M., Beaver Dam. Wis.

Sam. W. Kroff, Private 9th A. C., Chicago, Ill.

Chas. Waite, Brig.-Gen. 9th A. C., Sycamore, Ill.

A. J. Hiller, Private 180th O. Vol., Dayton, O.

R. R. Griffith, Capt. 9th Wis. Bat. 23rd A. C.

Edwin Waite, Capt. 9th A. C., Sycamore, Ill.

R. S. Botsford, Capt. 10th A. C., Waukegan, Ill.

Jasper Packard, Brevet Brig.-Gen. 23rd A. C., Laporte, Ind.

Frank Wilson, Capt. 19th O. Bat. 23rd A. C., Cleveland, O.

Wm. L. Thomas, Sergt. 23rd A. C., Flowerfield, Mich.

C. F. Knapp, Capt. 39th Ill., Chicago, Illinois.

Wm. M. Luff, Brevet Major 12th Ill. Cav., Chicago, Ill.

Jos. E. Lockwood, Brevet Major Chief Com. of Musters, Chicago, Illinois.

Chas. H. Graves, Capt. and Brev. Lieut.-Col. 34th Inf. 10th A. C., Gen. Terry's Staff.

H. K. Milward, Col. 18th Ky. Inf., Lexington, Ky.

Geo. O. Williams, Captain 6th Ky. Cav., Omaha, Neb.

L. P. Wann, Capt. 9th A. C.

J. F. Bradley, Major 9th A. C., Chicago, Ill.

Fred. Clemons, Brevet Lieut.-Col. 23rd A. C., Palmyra, N. Y.

N. J. Frink, Maj. 28th Mich., Marshall, Mich.

Geo. B. Green, Adj. 23rd Mich., Detroit, Mich.

Wm. Hartsuff, Brevet Brig.-Gen.

Jas. A. Kenly, Lieut. 3rd Pa. Reg., Johnstown, Pa.

Benj. B. Smith, Major 23rd A. C., New Mexico.

M. W. Toole, Captain 65th Ill., Austin, Texas.

T. H. Fisher, Capt. 5th Ind. Cav., Chicago, Ill.

Jno. W. McKinney, 2nd Lieut. 189th O. V. I., Chicago, Ill.

B. McVickar, Major, Chicago, Ill.

N. H. Merrill, 2nd Lieut. 35th Mich. Inf., Buchanan, Mich.

John R. Reno, 2nd Lieut. 25th Ky. Vol., Granville, Ky.

John C. Crawford, Capt. 1st Minnesota, Winona, Minn.

J. E. Flagg, B. Capt., 150th Ill.

J. F. Huffer, Brevet Major 23rd A. C., Louisville, Ky.

H. N. Davis, Brevet Major and C. S., Beloit, Wis.

Jno. B. Handy, Capt. 25th Mich. Inf., 23rd A. C., Three Rivers, Michigan.

H. W. Wells, Major Chief of Art. 23rd A. C., Peoria, Ill.

Charles W. Clarke, Capt. 69th U. S. C. Inf., Jackson, Miss.

Henry Palmer, Brevet Lieut.-Col. Surg. U. S. V., Janesville, Wis.

Wm. W. H. Beadle, Brevet Brig.-Gen. 1st Mich. S. S., Boscobel, Wisconsin.

D. D. Thorpe, 2nd Lieut. 25th Mich. Inf., Three Rivers, Mich.

Geo. Taylor, Chaplain 8th Mich. Inf., Ann Arbor, Mich.

Sam. Chadwick, Captain, Three Rivers, Mich.

D. M. Doty, Capt. 118th O. V. I., Elkhart, Ind.

Wm. W. Burden, Capt. 140th Ind. Vol., Chicago, Ill.

Lewis Wolfley, Maj. 3rd Ky. Cav., New Orleans, La.

Wm. H. Backus, Captain 1st Colorado Cav., Oberlin, Ohio.

W. H. B. Ramsey, Lieut. 51st P. V., Indianapolis, Ind.

A. H. Markland, Col. Mail Dep't, P. O. D., Washington, D. C.

A. Willich, Brig.-Gen. 4th Corps, Cincinnati, O.

Henry C. Pike, Capt. 23rd Corps, Chicago, Ill.

LIST OF MEMBERS OF THE SOCIETY OF THE ARMY OF GEORGIA.

Allen, M. V., Capt. 195th Ill., Shabona Grove, Ill.

Anderson, E. G., Private 74th Ind., Ft. Wayne, Ind.

Anderson, E. L., Capt. 52nd Ohio, Cincinnati, O.

Allen, H. I., Capt. 156th Ill., Rockton, Ill.

Arnold, S. V., 1st Lieut. 104th Ill., Lockport, Ill.

Barnum, H. A., Brev. Maj.-Gen., Syracuse, N. Y.

Burst, J. W., 1st Lieut. 105th Ill., Ill.

Butler, D. J., Private 22nd Wis., Chicago.

Buck, H., Maj., 52nd O. V. I., Cincinnati.

Blood, Capt. 32nd Ill., Chicago.

Brown, R. B., Capt. 2nd Mass., St. Louis, Mo.

Boltz, Ferd. F., Capt. 88th Ind., Ft. Wayne, Ind.

Buttrick, E. K., A. A. G. 1st Div. 20th Corps, Milwaukee, Wis.

Burdick, J. D., Captain 31st Wis., Chicago, Ill.

Breman, Jno., 2nd Lieut., Chicago, Ill.

Booth, Wilber C., Sergeant 113th O. V. I., Columbus, O.

Bows, Wm., Captain 22nd Wis., Cresco, Iowa.

Barnes, S. S., Capt. 9th Mich., Chicago.

Culocu, C. G., Captain 105th Ill., Sandwich, Ill.

Clark, H. S., 1st Lieut. 73rd Ill., Mattoon, Ill.

Clay. H. H., Maj. 102nd Ill., Galesburg, Ill.

Cogswell, Wm., Brev. Brig.-Gen., Salem, Mass.

Cole, Geo. E., Private 10th Mich., Chicago.

Crawford, F. C., Brevet Major, Terre Haute, Ind.

Coe, A. L., Capt. 51st Ill., Chicago.

Chadrick, S., Captain 28th Mich., Mich.

Chrebro, O. B., Private 20th Army Corps, Chicago.

Crane, A. B., Lieut.-Col. 85th Ind., New York.

Dyer, R. F., Sergeant 104th Ill., Ill.

Deardoff, D. P., Capt. 74th Ind., Goshen, Ind.

Deane, Charles H., Brev. Lieut.-Col., Peoria, Ill.

Dodge, ——, Asst.-Surg. 74th Ind., Elkhart, Ind.

Daniels, S. T., Capt. 105th Ill., Wheaton, Ill.

Detzler, E. H., 2nd Lieut. 105th Ill., Ill.

Deihl, Charles, Captain 23rd Ill., Chicago.

Donelson, Augustus, 1st Ill. Art.

Deyden, W. A., 14th Corps, Monmouth, Ill.

Dutton, E. F., Brev. Brig.-Gen., Sycamore, Ill.

Day, W. H., Brev. Major 10th O. Cav., Dubuque, Iowa.

Dustin, Daniel, Brev. Brig.-Gen., 105th Ill., Sycamore, Ill.

Dysart, A. P., Col. 34th Ill., Ill.

Evans, D., Sergeant 31st Wis., St. Paul.

Emmit, J. H., Lieutenant 34th Ill., Franklin, Ill.

Elliott, Frank, Battery M 1st N. Y. Art., Medina, N. Y.

Ellis, Milo D., Capt. 87th Ind. Peru, Ind.

Flint, C. C., 1st Lieut. 13th Mich., St. Louis, Mo.

Fraser, Geo. N. C., Capt. 5th Ohio, Cincinnati.

Farrington, Geo. E., 1st Lieut. 85th Ind., Terre Haute, Ind.

Green, George, Major 78th Ill., Chicago.
Greenhut, J., Captain 82nd Ill., Chicago.
Grouty, Y., Brev. Brig.-Gen., Cincinnati.
Grisher, A., Capt. 16th Ill. Cav., Chicago.
Hatchard, Thomas, Surgeon 22nd Wis., Milwaukee, Wis.
Hinkley, W., Capt. 3rd Wis., Monroe, Wis.,
Hill, H. R., Lieut.-Col. 115th O. V. I., East Liverpool, O.
Hicks, B. M., Capt. — Mich., —, Mich.
Hartley, C. S., Capt. 28th Penn. Vol., Chicago.
Howe, Charles, Lieut. 1st Ill. Art., Henry, Ill.
Hanson, James, Capt. 33rd Mich., Chicago.
Herrick Charles K., Private 82nd Ill.. Chicago.
Hinkley, L. D., 1st Lieutenant 10th Wis., —, Wis.
Heath, Geo. B., Capt. 105th Ill., —, Ill
Hammerid, J. P., Chicago.
Hansel, H. N., Lieut. 21st Wis., Toledo, O.
Jordan, T. M., Surgeon 78th Ill., Chicago.
Klein, Jacob, Captain 25th Inf., Washington, D. C.
Kenode, M. A., Lieut. 11th Mo., Centralia, Ill.
Halb, J. C., 1st Sergeant, 42nd O. V. I., Columbus, O.
Knipe, Joseph F., Brig.-Gen., 20th Corps.
Lee, Alfred E., Capt. 82nd O. V. I., Delaware, O.
Leete, James M., Lieut.-Col., St. Louis, Mo.
Langley, G. W., Col. 125th Ill., Champaign, Ill.
Lippert, P. H., 1st Lieut. 24th Ill., Chicago,
Lucas, A. F., — 84th Ind., Monmouth, Ill.
Lewis, Geo. F., 1st Lieut. 31st Wis., Elgin, Ill.
Lewis, A. T., —, 31st Wis., Elgin, Ill.
Long, H. C., Capt. 78th Ind., Rochester, Ind.

Lacy, H. A., Capt. —, Detroit Mich.
Mindil, Geo. W., Brev. Maj.-Gen. Philadelphia, Penn.
Miller, —, Col. 33rd Ind., Williamsport, Ind.
May, D. R., Capt. 22nd Wis., Racine, Wis.
McClurg, A. C., Brev. Brig.-Gen., Chicago, Ill.
McWilliam, John, Lieut. 128th Ill., Odell, Ill.
Newman, C. E., Capt. 2nd Mich., Chicago, Ill.
Pease, Gramal, Private 83rd Ill., Victoria, Ill.
Peters, M. H., Major 74th Ohio, Watseka, Ill.
Peasle, L. L., 1st Lieut. 105th Ill., Naperville, Ill.
Robinson, I. S., Brev. Maj.-Gen., Kenton, O.
Ramsey, A. B., Assist.-Surg., Three Rivers, Mich.
Reynolds, G. W., Capt. 83rd Ill., —, Ill.
Rogers, T. S., Captain 105th Ill., —, Ill.
Rockefeller, F., Cleveland, O.
Slocum, Henry W., Major-General, Brooklyn, N. Y.
Smith, F. C., Brev. Brig.-General, Oneida, Ill.
Stephens, E. B., Brev. Maj. 137th N. Y., —, N. Y.
Smith, John D., Lieut. 92nd O. V. I., Alton, Ill.
Scroggs, George, Lieut. 125th Ill., Champaign, Ill.
Salomon, E. S., Brev. Brig.-Gen., Chicago.
Smith, A. A., Brev. Brig.-General, Galesburg, Ill.
Sears, P. C., Captain 33rd Mass., Chicago.
Smith, Melvin, 1st Lieut. 105th Ill., Wheaton, Ill.
Sexton, W. H., 1st Lieut. 83rd Ill., Monmouth, Ill.
Speed, John, Lieut. and A. A. A. G., Louisville, Ky.
Slocum, John G., — 102nd Ill., Oneida, —.
Taylor, David, Jr., Capt. 113th O. V. I., Taylor's Station, O.
Tuttle, R. M., Capt. 20th Corps, Hornelsville, N. Y.

Vliet, John B., Capt. 31st Wis., Lawrence, Kan.

Vallette, H. F., Lieut.-Col. 105th Ill., Wheaton, Ill.

Thomas, W. R., Capt., ——, Sycamore, Ill.

Talbott, J. B., Private 83rd Ill., Galesburg, Ill.

Scott, W., Jr., 1st Lieut. 105th Ill., Maysville, Ill.

Vanderver, Wm., Brev. Maj.-Gen., Dubuque, Iowa.

Whittelsey, Henry M., Brev. Brig.-Gen., Washington, D. C.

Waterman, Alf., Surg., 105th Ill., Wheaton, Ill.

Matteson, A. B., Capt. 102nd Ill., Oneida, Ill.

Wade, A. B., Col., 73rd Ind., South Bend, Ind.

Widner, John H., Major 26th Wis. Vol., Milwaukee, Wis.

Warner, Wm., Capt. 82nd Ill., Chicago.

Willard, H. H., D. C.

Wells, George H., 1st Surg. 123rd N. Y., Chicago.

Whitemire, H. C., Capt. 2nd Ill Art., Sycamore, Ill.

Wilward, H. K., Col. 18th Ky. V V. I., Lexington, Ky.

Wilcox, R. H., Orderly Sergeant 123rd N. Y., ——, N. Y.

Wolfley, Lewis, Maj. 3rd Ky. Cav., New Orleans, La.

The above is a true list of names of members of the Society Army of Georgia, so near as I am able to copy from their autographs.

DAVID TAYLOR, JR.,
Recording Sec. Army of Georgia.

www.ingramcontent.com/pod-product-compliance
Lightning Source LLC
Chambersburg PA
CBHW021121270326
41929CB00009B/994